COMPROMISE IN ETHICS, LAW, AND POLITICS

NOMOS

XXI

NOMOS

Lieber-Atherton, Publishers

New York University Press

NOMOS XXI

Yearbook of the American Society for Political and Legal Philosophy

COMPROMISE IN ETHICS, LAW, AND POLITICS

Edited by

J. Roland Pennock, *Swarthmore College*

and

John W. Chapman, *University of Pittsburgh*

New York: New York University Press • 1979

Compromise in Ethics, Law, and Politics: Nomos XXI
edited by J. Roland Pennock and John W. Chapman

Library of Congress Cataloging in Publication Data
Main entry under title:

Compromise in ethics, law, and politics.
 (Nomos ; 21)
 Includes bibliographical references
  1.   Political ethics — Addresses, essays, lectures.
2.   Compromise (Ethics — Addresses, essays, lectures.
3.   Compromise (Law) — Addresses, essays, lectures.
I.   Pennock, James Roland.   II.   Chapman, John William,
1923-   III.   Series.
JA79.C65   320'.01   79-63469
ISBN   0-8147-6574-2

Printed in the United States of America

PREFACE

The membership of the American Society for Political and Legal Philosophy chose "compromise" as the topic of their meetings held in conjunction with the American Association of Law Teachers in Houston, in December 1976. Whether they did so with the thought that lawmen were especially good at compromising, averse to it, interested in it, or simply conversant with it is not known. Perhaps none of these things. Possibly their feeling was that we are living at a time when interests tend to be denigrated and rights are sprouting from every tree, whether or not it has standing. The end of ideology itself having come to an end, it may well be time to reconsider the concept and practice of compromise.

Tensions are present, both internal and external. The former have to do with the moral and immoral aspects of compromise; these are dealt with in several papers. The external tensions have already been implicitly adverted to. Today more and more our social institutions, indeed life itself, are being politicized. No doubt, politics is "the art of compromise." But aggressive and competitive assertions of "rights" render compromise more difficult, even as it becomes more necessary. As the claims of groups and individuals multiply our sense of justice is strained, and our hold on the common good weakens.

These problems are nowhere directly taken up in the ensuing pages, at least not in these terms. Yet much that is said here is directly relevant to the amelioration of our malaise. And it may be hoped that the analyses and reflections of our authors will prove useful for the coming volumes on "Private Property and Its Contemporary Significance" and "Human Rights."

The first part of this volume comprises three chapters in which the nature of compromise is discussed. Martin Golding opens up many vistas in what he calls a "Preliminary Inquiry." Despite his deliberately tentative approach, he does manage—not surprisingly, considering the concept in question—to take positions with which other contributors disagree. Golding also makes points that illuminate types of situations that he does not himself consider. This is particularly true of his insistence that each party to a compromise must recognize some moral legitimacy in the other's case and that a measure of mutual trust is essential. The emergence in the West of religious toleration and the acceptance of religious freedom made possible the Western practice of politics as compromise. Today one need think only of the Sinai and SALT to appreciate the force of Golding's analysis.

Distinguishing between compromising interests and compromising principles, Theodore Benditt nonetheless discusses possibilities and grounds for compromising both. Accepting the challenge that compromise is sometimes thought of as good and sometimes as bad, Arthur Kuflik argues that this fact does not imply that the concept is either incoherent or paradoxical. He concludes by suggesting that justice itself may be a sort of compromise, not between the strong and the weak, as some may think; rather, justice as compromise takes its place among people whose interests conflict, but "who hold one another in equal regard as persons" (p. 00).

At this point we break for a historical interlude. David Resnick opens it with an analysis of Aristotle's use of compromise in the search for institutions that would receive general support and that would also be just. The next two authors, George Armstrong Kelly and Paul Thomas, deal with Hegel and Marxism, respectively. In inviting these contributions the editors naively supposed that probably these scholars would be concerned with relations between compromise and the "dialectic." But our authors were more imaginative. Kelly, noting that "Compromise" is a word that sits askew in the Hegelian vocabulary" (p. 00), still finds that Hegel makes room for it in his vision of civil society. Work is left, of course, for the state to do. Here the rational element, the element of absolute reason, should penetrate life in the shape of impartial justice. In large measure, Hegel expected, this infusion of justice would be accomplished automatically. But not entirely so. As to what happens beyond the scope of rational automaticity, however, Hegel's "owl of Minerva" does not seem to see clearly. Does the state compromise conflicting interests and ideas or subject them to rational rule; or is it left to chance or at least to "the cunning of reason"? Kelly's analysis reveals fundamental ambiguity in the Hegelian theory of the state.

Paul Thomas approaches Marx from the vantage point of the "historical compromise" promoted by "Eurocommunism." Working back through Antonio Gramsci and others, he arrives at the "early" Marx and there finds, contrary to Leninist thinking and developments, support for the proclaimed "historical compromise." Thomas shows Marx to have been rather less uncompromising than the "orthodox" Marxist-Leninists would have him.

Two chapters deal with compromise and politics. Joseph Carens ponders various aspects of this subject, and he concludes with the notion, reminiscent of Richard Wollheim's "paradox of democracy," that sometimes we ought simply to do what is wrong. Hence the ambiguity of our attitudes toward compromise. Edgar Bodenheimer takes an even more positive attitude toward the practice of compromise. He sees it as essentially a synthesis among competing values, and he takes the resultant so produced to be superior to victory of any single value.

The final part is composed of three chapters concerned with compromise and the law. In the first of these, Martin Shapiro visualizes a continuum stretching from situations of pure consent, as in bargaining, to formal litigation, involving a solution imposed by the state. The practice of compromise occupies a midpoint along Shapiro's continuum. But even in litigation an element of compromise remains, and the whole system works because it offers adversaries a range of options, including that of compromise. Attacking doctrinaire legal theorists of either the rationalistic or the empiricist schools, Aleksander Peczenik, drawing upon practical examples, argues that "compromise and cumulation of different ideas, reasons, approaches, and so on, dominate legal practice, legal thinking, doctrinal study of law, and legal theory" (p. 00). Finally, John E. Coons develops an intriguing definition of compromise that differs from any of those that have preceded it in the volume. For him no moral tension and no paradox is involved in compromising. Rather, compromise is a matter of achieving what he calls "precise justice." And so he calls for the courts to abandon the "winner-take-all" view of civil disputes.

These, then, are but a few of the ideas and suggestions the reader will find in the following pages. It remains only to make acknowledgments and to express thanks: first, to our authors and to the chairman of the program committee, Robert S. Summers, who designed the panels that gave this volume its start and much of its substance. Benditt, Carens, Coons, Golding, and Shapiro all participated in the Houston meetings. The other six authors generously accepted invitations to make subsequent contributions. It is also our pleasure to note that *Nomos XXI*, like its two immediate predecessors in this series, has benefited from the financial support granted to the society by the John Dewey Foundation. More recently The Ritter Foundation has generously granted us a three-year subvention, which will enable the Society to enrich its programs. Finally, no acknowledgments would be complete without the name of our editorial assistant, Eleanor Greitzer, who does so much to foil those gremlins that torment editors.

J.R.P.
J.W.C.

CONTENTS

CONTRIBUTORS

THEODORE M. BENDITT
Philosophy, University of Alabama in Birmingham

EDGAR BODENHEIMER
Law, University of California, Davis

JOSEPH H. CARENS
Political Science, Lake Forest College

JOHN E. COONS
Law, University of California, Berkeley

MARTIN P. GOLDING
Philosophy, Duke University

GEORGE ARMSTRONG KELLY
Political Science

ARTHUR KUFLIK
Philosophy, University of Vermont

ALEKSANDER PECZENIK
Jurisprudence, University of Lund, Sweden

DAVID RESNICK
Political Science, University of Cincinnati

MARTIN SHAPIRO
Law, University of California, Berkeley

PAUL THOMAS
Political Science, University of California, Berkeley

PART I

THE NATURE OF
COMPROMISE

1

THE NATURE OF COMPROMISE:
A PRELIMINARY INQUIRY

MARTIN P. GOLDING

Twelve people were shipwrecked on a desert island: two Italian men and an Italian woman, two Frenchmen and a Frenchwoman, two Englishmen and an Englishwoman, and two Russians and a Russian woman. Plainly they had a serious problem, which they proceeded to deal with in the following manner. The Italians fought a battle to the death and the survivor took the woman for himself; the French settled down to a *ménage à trois;* the Englishmen killed the woman and settled down; and the Russians sent off a letter to Moscow asking for instructions. This story illustrates some of the ways of managing conflict; for instance, fighting, as in the case of the Italians (although a fight usually is taken as epitomizing conflict rather than a way of managing it); and removing the cause of rupture in relationships, as in the case of the English. The cases of the French and the Russians, respectively, illustrate the resolution of conflict through an amicable agreement and submission to a third party. These two cases come very close to the dictionary definition of "compromise," namely, "a settlement of differences by arbitration or by consent reached by mutual concessions.".[1]

In this paper I want to describe some of the layout of the field of those social activities that go under the heading of "compromise." The scope of the subject is vast and its importance can hardly be denied; it ought to be of great interest to ethics, social and political philosophy, and the philosophy of law. I should emphasize that what I am going to present is a preliminary inquiry; more programmatic than a finished piece of work. I have no startling theses to put forward, and I rather doubt that this is an area to which startling theses are appropriate. It is an area for patient research, and I should be pleased even if my only success is that of stimulating further inquiry by others.

Ideally, one supposes, an examination of compromise should result in a definition of "compromise" that formulates a set of necessary and sufficient conditions for the application of the term. Such an analysis would give us the "essence" of compromise, so to speak. The fact may be, however, that no single set of necessary and sufficient conditions covers all the cases; and, in any event, I shall not attempt to supply this kind of analysis. If I speak of myself as analyzing the concept of compromise, this should be understood in the looser sense of general characterization.

Before I turn directly to my task I want to make a number of introductory remarks. They are rather extensive, though hardly as extensive as the subject deserves. Plainly, an analysis of compromise ought to shed light on the problems engendered by this arena of social activities, and I want to use these introductory remarks as a way of formulating some of these problems. Fortunately the dictionary presents us with an "idoneous principle of tractation" (as Hobbes calls it), a fit starting point for stating the first problem, more because of the issue it poses than for the clarification it undoubtedly supplies.

Succinctly put, the problem is that the two mentioned modes of conflict resolution—mutual concessions and arbitration—seem to be so different that their inclusion under the same rubric is questionable. I do not know how literally the dictionary means us to take the word "arbitration." This term is used in a variety of ways in the literature, and evidently what "arbitration" refers to here is submission to a third party. But there are a variety of forms of third-party dispute settlement, and it is not clear that all of them should be viewed as coming under the head of "compromise." If the range could be narrowed down, we might be a long way toward bringing the third-party compromise techniques into a closer fit with mutual concessions, though signifiicant differences between them may still exist. I shall consider this issue later on.

My second preliminary remark may be introduced by mentioning stances that have been taken toward compromise. I think it is interesting that compromise is not so widely discussed by philosophers as one might expect. This relative absence of treatment perhaps reflects an attitude expressed in a statement attributed to George Santayana. "Compromise," says Santayana, "is odious to passionate natures because it seems a surrender; and to intellectual natures because it seems a confusion." I have not been able to trace the provenance of this quotation, so I do not know whether or not Santayana goes on to agree with it. The import, however, is clear. The compromiser is either weak-willed or hypocritical or irrational. Compromise, therefore, may be dismissed as lacking moral significance.

There are, on the other hand, numerous appreciations of compromise that disagree with this estimate. Lord Morley, for example, rejects the notion that compromise is necessarily identifiable with volitional or intellectual indifference, that compromise is "indolent acquiescence in error." But if I read Morley's *On Compromise* correctly, it seems that he accepts the "lawfulness" of compromise only insofar as it serves as a useful tactic in the battle of enlighted liberal reform against the dark forces of reaction. A less qualified, in fact an enthusiastic, endorsement of compromise comes from a seasoned diplomat, the late Edward Stettinius, who asserted: "Although it is sometimes alleged that there is something evil in compromise, actually, of course, compromise is necessary for progress as any sensible man knows. Compromise, when reached honorably and in a spirit of honesty by all concerned, is the only fair and rational way of reaching a reasonable agreement between two differing points of view."[2] Contrary, then, to the negative view taken in Santayana's statement, we find compromise lauded as the essence of good sense, prudence, and fairness.[3]

We have, here, a fundamental disagreement on the rationality and morality of compromise. These poles of opposition are in fact joined together in the paradoxical attitude that many people have toward politics, domestic and international. The politican or diplomat is, on the one hand, expected to make compromises and, on the other, is condemned for doing that very thing. Now, the problem of the place of rationality and morality in the sphere of compromise is many-faceted; and it is much more difficult than the problem I mentioned earlier, namely, the problem of how it is that seemingly different types of social activities can be grouped under the head of compromise. It would help us here, I think, if we distinguished the issue of the rationality and morality *of* compromise from the issue of the roles of rationality and morality *in* compromise. The second of these refers to the question of whether the compromise process requires adherence to certain intellectual and moral constraints as conditions for reaching a compromise, analogously to Lon Fuller's notion of the "internal morality of law" as a condition for lawmaking.[4] The former issue refers to the question of whether it is rational or moral to enter into the social activity of compromise in the first place, the question of the "lawfulness" of compromise as Morley calls it.

In my discussion I hope to shed light on a few aspects of rationality and morality *in* compromise, with no pretensions that my treatment is complete; I shall have almost nothing to say about the rationality and morality of compromise. It is of course a nice question as to whether there is an intimate connection between these two topics; whether, for instance, adherence to moral constraints in a social process makes it moral to engage in the process. On this matter, let me merely remark that much depends on what it is that is being compromised and what the compromise is. Furthermore, the denomination of a particular agreement as a compromise requires, in fact, that we know something about its context. It might be said that without knowing more about the context sending off a letter to Moscow should not necessarily be taken as representing a form of compromise, since it equally could be a device for postponing the issue, which is another way of dealing with conflict.

My third introductory remark is that if philosophers have tended to ignore our subject, the same cannot be said of game theorists, economists, and writers on industrial and international relations. I shall avail myself of some of their contributions, though more often indirectly than by explicit reference, especially in the case of game theory. The formal theory of games—which has virtually nothing to do with most everyday games—has made extremely valuable contributions to the understanding of conflict situations, particulary by exposing the logical structures they exhibit, and the theory also provides solutions or "optimal strategies" for many kinds of conflict. This approach, however, is basically restricted to the well-defined game: the conflict situation for which the rules governing the moves are explicit, where there are explicit rules of termination, and where the payoff matrix is known. But these features are hardly present in the usual circumstances in which compromises are achieved. For many conflicts, what counts as termination, for example, is unclear. To adapt the words of Thomas C. Schelling, if the phenomenon of compromise is fundamentally psychic, there can be no presumption that mathematical game theory is essential to the process by which it is reached.[5] This, of course, is no criticism of the formal theory, which, it may incidentally be noted, has provided the impetus of experimental studies of conflict, bargaining, and convergence of expectation.

My last introductory remark brings me closer to my task. It is plain that the scope of this inquiry has to be delimited and that one or the other avenue of approach has to be adopted in order to deal with it. The point, again, conveniently may be introduced with a quotation. I have in mind what is perhaps the most famous statement of all on compromise, from Edmund Burke's *Speech on Conciliation with America* (March 22, 1775); it is, says Burke, "a very great mistake to imagine that mankind follow up practically any speculative principle, either of government or of freedom, as far as it will go in argument or logical illation. . . . All government, indeed every human benefit and enjoyment, every virtue, and every prudent act, is founded on compromise and barter. We balance inconveniences, we give and take; we remit some rights, that we may enjoy others; and we choose rather to be happy citizens than subtle disputants." (Burke goes on to admit limits to compromise: no one would be unwilling to risk his life rather than fall under a purely arbitrary government; no one will barter away the "jewel of his soul.") This eulogistic statement virtually identifies compromise as a general mark of human relations. So understood, it is clearly too broad a topic for discussion here, to say the least. And we are no better off if we look at conflict, compromise's underside. Conflict, too, is a general mark of human relations. As Luce and Raiffa say in the first sentence of *Games and Decisions:* "In all of man's written record there has been a preoccupation with conflict of interest; possibly only the topics of God, love, and inner struggle have received comparable attention."[6] Conflict of interest (in the sense of conflict of interests, which is what Luce and Raiffa have in mind) is not the only kind of conflict that is relevant to our subject, though a conflict of interests may be at the base of all conflicts. I shall soon be more specific on the kinds of conflict situations I am concerned with.

As to avenues of approach, two are possible: end-state and process. The first looks to the result or outcome — the agreement or adjustment — and tries to see how it compares with the original situation for which it is alleged to be a compromise. The second looks to ways and means, the methods by which the result is reached, and it characterizes the result as a compromise in virtue of the process by which it is achieved. I suspect that adoption of the one or the other approach determines how one deals with the question of the fairness (and perhaps also the rationality) of a compromise. The end-state approach will tend to the view that a fair outcome is a unique point or set of points in the region of possible outcomes. Normative game theory seems to take this view. Given certain axioms or criteria of rationality or equity, the utilities of the possible outcomes, and the strategic possibilities available to the opponents, the desirable result may be deduced.[7] The process approach, on the other hand, has a laxer, shall we say, more compromising view of the matter. It will judge the fairness of the outcome in terms of the procedures followed in reaching it; for example, by whether it was reached "honorably and in a spirit of honesty by all concerned," to use Stettinius' words. Obviously, criteria of these notions are lacking. But then, in real- world conflicts the utilities are difficult to define and estimate, yet compromises are achieved. A process approach to the phenomenon of compromise requires that we go beyond mathematical game theory and into the disciplines of psychology, sociology, and moral philosophy.

In distinguishing these two kinds of approach I do not mean to suggest that there is a hard-and-fast separation between them. If the process of compromise requires concessions on the part of the disputants, it is trivially the case that certain possible outcomes are excluded. Moreover, if the process is to be described as "bargaining under constraints," the same will be true. In these respects a process approach does admit end-state considerations. Nevertheless, the distinction between these two approaches is significant and useful. It should be mentioned that, just as a judgment on the fairness of a compromise may depend on which approach is adopted, so also the designation of a result as a compromise (let alone a fair compromise) may also depend on which approach is adopted. This, however, should not surpise us, for the concept of compromise is rough-edged. An analysis of compromise, therefore, to some extent involves a reconstruction of the concept; and in consequence of the different approaches to the problem, the extensions of the term need not be identical.

I shall adopt the process approach and use it to examine two types of compromise: the *directly negotiated* compromise (i.e., where the parties to the compromise achieve it without outside assistance or intervention) and the *third-party* compromise. Less space will be devoted to the various forms of third-party dispute settlement. Let me begin with the directly negotiated compromise, which I am further going to restrict to the situation of *two*-person or two-party conflict. Possibly one of the few things that can be said with certainty about compromise is that it presupposes conflict; and conflict presupposes at least two discriminable units. Admittedly, a multiplicity of individuals may be parties in a conflict, but the complexity of such a circumstance makes it more resistant to analysis. Even for game theory, the N-person game has proved difficult because of the many ways of forming coalitions and of apportioning the payoffs.

In speaking of two-person or two-party conflict, I am using the terms "person" and "party" to cover human persons, nations, labor unions, and organized groups generally. Conflicts in which one or both of the parties is an unorganized group, or at least not a well-defined group, raise interesting questions, principally the question of who has the *authority* to negotiate a compromise for the group. The term "compromise" may apply in these situations only in an extended sense. This is a legitimate subject for analysis, especially for an understanding of politics, but I am not going to attempt such analysis here. The issue of authority also will arise later on, but in a rather different context.

It is no secret that two of the concepts involved in the notion of compromise are conflict and termination of conflict. Each of these, however, is in need of elucidation. Let us turn back, then, to conflict.

There is, of course, an enormous literature on the subject, which treats *(inter alia)* the sources of conflict, the effects of prior relationships of the parties, and so on.[8] Various taxonomies of conflict have been presented, too. For purposes of this inquiry, the fundamental division is between conflicts that can be terminated by means of a compromise (which I shall call "compromisable conflicts") and conflicts that cannot be so terminated. Most real-world conflicts presumably fall into the first class—a fortunate circumstance, for otherwise life would be much nastier than it is. Some real-world conflicts, however, do fall into the second class. Competitive games usually are of this kind, although some writers do not regard them as genuine social conflicts. Such games have a termination rule (e.g., the game ends after one hour of play), and when its conditions are fulfilled, the game is over and one side is declared the winner. The prize, even if it is just the title, is not subject to negotiation by the parties, however. If it were, the competitors would be playing something quite different from the standard form of the game. This is not to deny that competitive games require mutual cooperation between the opponents, for the players do cooperate at least to the extent that they join together to participate in the event. Cooperation and competition, in some form, are also present in the negotiation process that leads to a compromise, and my investigation is particularly concerned with eliciting the qualities that characterize cooperation and competition in this process.

Second, the compromisable conflict situation should be distinguished from the sort of cooperative behavior studied by the social psychologist Muzafer Sherif. Here, two groups are in conflict because they have mutually incompatible goals. Sherif has found that such groups can enter into effective cooperation when they share a "superordinate" goal, which is a goal that has a compelling appeal for the members of each group but that neither can achieve without the participation of the other.[9] This appears to be a noncontroversial solution, unless there are terms that have to be worked out as a basis for the cooperation. I might add that the *ménage à trois* of the shipwrecked French, mentioned at the beginning of this paper, would not represent a compromise agreement if it were the arrangement actually preferred by all parties, and hence noncontroversial.

To summarize our results to this point, the compromisable conflict situation is one in which there is a partial coincidence of interests and which, therefore, contains the seeds of competition and cooperation. Each side can assume that the other will try to get the best for itself, and each knows that the other knows this, so the situation is strategic. But, as I have suggested and shortly shall explain further, the situation is not purely strategic. We can say that the negotiation process is going to have to exhibit "cooperative rationality." Nevertheless, since a compromise is controversial, the parties' cooperativeness is different from other forms of cooperation.

This sketch of the conflict situation is still incomplete, however. One item has not yet been touched upon, namely, the *issue* that is being disputed. I earlier mentioned that there are many taxonomies of conflict, and some of the distinctions that are made can appropriately be brought up here. The types that are most relevant for this discussion are the following: conflicts of interests, conflicts of rights, and conflicts of principles; closely related to the last are ideological conflicts and structural conflicts, although these frequently also embody elements of conflicts of interests and of rights. It is important to acknowledge these distinctions because it can be argued that each type of conflict has its own special mode of resolution.[10] It is far from clear that conflicts that are rooted in differences of principle or ideology, for example, can be terminated either by a directly negotiated compromise or by submission to a third party. The best instances of structural conflicts come from the field of industrial disputes.[11] The negotiation of the collective bargaining agreement is not a market activity but a rule-making process in which, in effect, power is distributed between the parties. It is a compromise settlement of power conflicts.[12] To the extent that such disputes have overtones of conflicts of principle and ideology, they are difficult to settle. As has somewhere been remarked, the radical syndicalists can do everything but settle a strike, since they do not concede to the bosses the principle that management should do the managing. Although structural conflicts should not be lumped together with conflicts of principle and ideology, I shall postpone the little that I have to say about these three types of conflict to the end of my paper.

We are reduced, therefore, to conflicts of interests and conflicts of rights. The distinction between these two types of conflict is particularly significant in the context of third-party dispute settlement, for the "logic" involved is different for each type. It may seem that the distinction is not of much moment in the directly negotiated compromise, because parties that are willing to compromise over rights will tend to do so in terms of the interests these rights are seen as protecting. I think this is basically correct; it is certainly difficult to see how the opponents will come to a compromise if they insist upon standing on their rights. Still, it will pay to take a brief look at conflicts of rights, for there is a useful point that can be extracted from this kind of conflict.

A conflict of rights (i.e., a conflict in which the parties make incompatible rights claims) presupposes the existence of standards or principles on which the claims are based. Such a conflict has a number of forms: (1) one party alleges a violation by the other of a standard held in common by both parties; (2) the parties make conflicting claims against each other based upon conflicting interpretations of the meaning of a common standard or of its application to the given case; and (3) the parties make conflicting claims against each other, where each claim is based upon different (and possibly incompatible) standards. The first kind evidently involves a dispute over an issue of fact, and it may be dismissed from consideration here. The other kinds of conflicts of rights have a very interesting feature, if we assume that the two parties get together to settle their differences. As long as they stay within the realm of rights, their conflict will be not a game nor a fight but a debate, as Anatol Rapoport calls it. The aim

of each disputant will be to *convert* the other party to his own position.[13] This means that only a certain kind of rhetoric will be appropriate to the situation; each party will have to try to establish its
claim by appealing to norms or other value considerations held by
the other side. The process of resolution, the debate, is therefore subject to certain constraints; and these are moral and intellectual (rational) constraints, if only in a relative sense. This is the point I
wanted to extract from the conflict-of-rights situation. Now I want to
make another claim: something *like* this also holds for the process of
negotiating a compromise in the partial conflict-of-interests situation. It, too, is subject to moral and intellectual constraints. This is
what I had in mind when I earlier stated that the conflict situation is
not purely strategic.

When it is said that each party is "rational" in the sense that each
wants to minimize his losses, and that each is trying to achieve the
"best" from his own point of view, certain qualifications, in the case
of compromisable conflicts, need to be mentioned. Consider, again,
a situation of pure conflict, though perhaps not so neatly structured
as the formal theorists' zero-sum game. Suppose that the range of options allows for a loss-minimizing outcome. Will it always be the case
that this outcome will be selected by the choices the parties independently make? It is easily conceivable that one of the parties might ca-
pitulate unilaterally, so that the actual outcome is the worst one for
him and the best for the other. This could happen if the former party
were a selfless altruist. (And utter disaster could result if both parties
are altruists, as in O. Henry's story "The Gift of the Magi," which I
do not believe to be a fiction that is never actualized. In this story,
the wife cuts her long tresses in order to buy a chain for her husband's
watch, while the husband sells his watch in order to buy a comb for
his wife's hair!) Can we still say that each party is trying to do his best?
Is altruism "irrational"? The game theorist might be able to sidestep
this question by assigning a utility to altruism and by rewriting the
payoff matrix. It can still be assumed, then, that each party is trying
to do his best from his own point of view.

Fortunately, we do not need to resort to this expedient, because
the negotiated compromise situation does exclude *pure* altruism, for
otherwise there is nothing to negotiate. (The game theorist might
also argue that if one of the parties is a selfless altruist, the situation
does not pose a conflict issue but a "coordination" problem. A conflict situation would exist only if both were altruists, and each knew

this of the other, and each tried to outdo the other in being altruistic. We would then have a situation similar to that of the Indian tribe whose members tried to outdo one another in giving gifts.) We can say, therefore, that the parties to the conflict will try to do what is best from their own point of view. But, though the negotiated compromise situation excludes pure altruism, the parties must have a kind of cooperative attitude; otherwise negotiation will be impossible. And a cooperative attitude does put some constraint on one's pursuit of what is best for oneself.

This cooperative attitude derives, in part at least, from the nature of the compromisable conflict situation. Fot it involves a *partial coincidence of interests,* as in the "mixed-motive" game of the mathematical theorists. At a minimum, both parties have an interest in terminating their conflict, because, presumably, remaining in conflict leaves them both worse off than one or the other possible settlement. Moreover, and this is very important, they have an interest in terminating the conflict through negotiation, because the actions that they can unilaterally take to mitigate the conflict may not leave them as well off as they might otherwise be. Neither of the parties, however, can have the outcome that each ideally would want for himself. The issue therefore becomes: What will be the terms of their settlement? A compromise is, in this sense, always controversial. Each party, it may be assumed, will try to do the best for himself *in the circumstances,* and yet he must cooperate in the negotiating process if a compromise is going to be achieved. I think this implies that the compromise process is not one of pure bargaining or a purely strategic situation. More about this soon. The fact that there is a partial coincidence of interests in the compromisable conflict situation and that a failure to reach a settlement could leave both parties worse off than they might otherwise be has significant implications that need to be explored.

The fact that a compromise is always controversial means, of course, that the compromisable conflict situation is one for which there is no noncontroversial solution; or if there is such a solution, the parties are unable to locate it among the alternative outcomes (perhaps because of lack of intelligence or because of a lack of sufficient goodwill). It follows, I think, that it is a mistake to *identify* compromise and cooperation. Compromise does require cooperation, but not every form of cooperation involves compromise. Suppose you are driving down the road and your way is blocked by a fallen tree. You want the tree out of the road, and so does the farmer, who wants the tree moved so that he can do something with it. But neither of you can move it alone. You therefore get out of your car and help him move it out of the way. What you've both done is cooperate, but you haven't compromised in any respect. And much political "logrolling" is no more a form of compromise than this real logrolling. Logrolling involves cooperation; it may, but need not, involve compromise.

To develop this point, I shall at long last turn to the negotiating process itself. Of course, I have actually been talking about it all along, though in a somewhat surreptitious manner. If it was no secret that two of the concepts involved in the analysis of compromise are conflict and termination of conflict, it is also no secret that a third concept is also involved in it, namely, the concept of *concessions* or, more accurately, mutual concessions. This concept was contained in the dictionary definition of "compromise" mentioned at the beginning of this paper.

I must, with the reader's indulgence, turn back again to the compromisable conflict situation. As I have repeatedly emphasized, this is a situation in which there is a partial coincidence of interests. The parties, at the least, have an interest in terminating their conflict. But, if they each make unilateral moves in the hope of improving their positions, do the "best" for themselves, they may end up worse off than they might otherwise be, no matter how risk-minimizing these unilateral moves seem to be. Now, how can this impasse be broken? This question has been studied by the game theorists. The problem is, of course, to find some way of insuring that the parties do not independently make the "wrong" moves, the moves that would result in a less advantageous position than each might achieve; or, to put it the other way around, the problem is to find some of way of insuring that each party could be *trusted* to make the "right" move. (If I cannot trust you to make the right move, I will make what appears to me to be the risk-minimizing move, and so will you — with the consequence that neither gets a better outcome.) The game theorists point out that there are two ways out of the impasse: the first is to introduce *communication* between the parties so that a *bargaining* process is initiated that results in an enforceable agreement; the second is to introduce an *arbitrator* who knows the positions of both opponents, and who can in some way impose a settlement.

But what should the shape of the agreement or settlement be? This turns us to the normative side of game theory. Two kinds of "solutions" are offered: bargaining solutions and arbitration solutions, which depend on laying down certain axioms or conditions that an outcome has to satisfy. The basic difference between these kinds of solutions seems to be this. Bargaining solutions are based upon the relative "bargaining strength" of each opponent. Bargaining strength is essentially a measure of the *threats* that the parties can make against each other, and the interesting thing about a threat is that carrying it out involves a cost to oneself as well as to the other side. In arbitration solutions, on the other hand, it appears that some of the threat potentials are discounted, and an equity principle is introduced, which usually involves some way of comparing the utility scales of the parties. When the bargaining positions of the parties are symmetrical, bargaining solutions and arbitration solutions seem to come to pretty much the same conclusion, a symmetrical outcome, a 50-50 split of the net gain. As John Harsanyi has said: "Intuitively . . . a rational bargainer will not expect a rational opponent to grant him larger concessions than he would make himself under similar conditions."[14] This kind of 50-50 solution is endorsed by no less an authority on conflict than Abigail van Buren. I refer you to the syndicated "Dear Abby" column of December 8, 1976.[15]

Now, it seems to me that a negotiated compromise process combines some of the qualities of both bargaining and arbitration procedures. It involves strategic bargaining with threats, but some threats are excluded by something like an equity principle. That is, it involves bargaining under constraints, so that the result should not be a plain function of the relative bargaining strengths of the parties. This can be seen by considering what is entailed in the communication process. Before I turn to this, I want to follow up my usual roundabout method and very briefly discuss something else first. I want to look at "offensive bargaining" because it provides a good contrast to the compromise process.

In offensive bargaining the positions of the parties are almost as asymmetrical as can be. One side is powerful, the other weak; one side has a large threat potential, the other's is small. The powerful side puts forward its "offer," which is really a demand, and the weak side rejects it. The powerful side responds by upping the ante, that is, by making an offer that is even less attractive to the other side. The weak party can see where the process is going to lead: soon it will be made an "offer that it can't refuse." The weak side has its threat po-

tential, too, but should it use it? After all, carrying out the threat
would be costly to itself. So it must calculate whether it should accept
the current offer (demand) or whether to go for broke at some point,
for if it goes for broke it might be able to get the other side to make it
a more attractive offer. An instance of all this might be the positions
of the United States and Panama in renegotiating the Canal treaty if
the United States had not been constrained by international morality, if there be such an animal, and by the pressures of domestic and
international public opinion; and if Panama had not been constrained by the damage it could do to itself by making drastic threats.
A "degenerate case" of offensive bargaining is the Sibylline Books
legend, in which the weak party is hardly in a position to bargain at
all. The prophetess Sibyl of Cumae offered Tarquin the Proud, last
of the legendary kings of Rome, nine books containing prophecies.
Tarquin thought the price so high that he refused to buy. Sibyl then
burned three of the books and offered the remaining six at the same
price. When Tarquin refused again, she burned three more, and
Tarquin, fearing that she might destroy them all, bought the last
three books at the price originally asked for the nine. Fred Charles
Iklé, from whom I've taken this description of the legend, points out
that this kind of tactic was successfully used by Molotov against the
Finns in 1940.[16]

It is difficult to see why offensive bargaining should be excluded
from those strategic conflict situations for which it would be feasible.
The only factor that mitigates offensive bargaining is the bargaining
strength of the other side. Whether or not compromise is "the only
fair and rational way of reaching a reasonable agreement," as Stettinius says, I maintain that the negotiated compromise process excludes not only the Sibylline Books tactic but also offensive bargaining.

The compromise process involves, of course, communication between the parties. It is a process in which explicit proposals are put
forth with the aim of reaching an agreement where conflicting interests are present. It therefore presupposes a common language. But it
presupposes more than this: it presupposes a commonality or, more
exactly, a community. The compromise process is a conscious process
in which there is a degree of *moral acknowledgment* of the other
party. The other party is accorded some degree of *moral legitimacy*,
and so are some of his interests. This is the special quality that characterizes the cooperative attitude in the compromise process, of
which attitude I earlier spoke, and it contrasts with the kind of coop-

eration that characterizes the pure strategic bargaining process, which is more like the cooperation that is necessary in order to keep a competitive game going. The two parties who sit down together at the table to reach a settlement by compromise have rejected the prospect of reaching one by pure bargaining. I think this is at least part of what Stettinius might have had in mind in speaking of a compromise that is reached "honorably and in a spirit of honesty by all concerned."

I wish to emphasize, however, that in the compromise process *some* degree of moral legitimacy is accorded to the other side. It does not seem plausible to imagine that in a real-world conflict situation the parties will be willing entirely to abandon their threat potentials. The situation remains strategic to an extent, and the communication that conveys a concession can also be used to convey a demand or threat. But some of the threat potential is discounted (as in the arbitration solutions of the game theorists); and some equity principle, even if not explicitly formulated, is employed. Though a principle of *reciprocity* is present, it is never completely operative, except perhaps in an "ideal" form of the compromise situation. Where full reciprocity exists, the parties recognize each other as moral equals despite their relative bargaining strengths. In such a circumstance there will be a powerful tendency for rational compromisers to "split the difference," for as Harsanyi said, one party will not expect the other to grant him larger concessions than he himself would make under similar conditions. Their conditions are in a sense similar, for there is a powerful pull toward positional symmetry;[17] hence the symmetry of the outcome. The institution of a *degree* of moral legitimacy and reciprocity in the real-world situation does explain, however, why a party that has made a concession then expects the same of the other. This is one of the things that is meant by bargaining in "good faith," responding to a concession with a concession. And the fact that the compromise process is still also a bargaining process also explains why a party might find a demand or order to bargain in good faith a rather heavy demand to meet, which is often the case in labor-management disputes.[18]

The fact that the parties accord one another a degree of legitimacy has an important implication: it enhances the roles of rational argument and moral considerations in the compromise process. A party will have to attempt to *persuade*, rather than intimidate, the other side to accept its offers. It must do this by appealing to norms accepted by the other side. So the bargaining is conducted under intellectual and moral constraints, and it begins to take on the character-istics of a debate. To the extent that the parties approach the ideal of full reciprocity, a party will appeal to norms that are accepted not only by the other side but by itself as well. This means, it should be noticed, that the compromising of a conflict of interests has some of the features of a settlement of a conflict of rights. I should add, of course, that social and legal norms will also be operative in most real-life conflict situations, and these will serve as institutional constraints on the compromise process. An illegal offer cannot be made, and an illegal agreement cannot be entered into. To refer again to our ship-wrecked French friends, the *ménage à trois* might have been ruled out as a possible outcome from the start.

Another important implication of moral legitimacy is *trust*. A party can be trusted to mean what he says and to mean it sincerely— one must tell the truth and sincerely intend to do what one says one intends to do—but perhaps only to the degree that the legitimacy of the other is recognized. It is often said, on the question of the applicability of formal game theory to real-world conflicts, that the concept of trust falls outside the province of mathematics. If the aim of the bargaining process is reaching an enforceable agreement, what guarantees that a party will stick to his side of the bargain? Must he mean what he says? Can he be trusted? Obviously, bluffing and deception are recognized tactics in bargaining, and the theoreticians take this into account. Of course, even the "compleat strategist" cannot be a complete bluffer, for this would be self-defeating. Still, the problem of trust remains. The cooperative attitude implied in the compromise process, however, does introduce trust into the situation. It is an aspect of the honesty and honorableness of which Stettinius speaks, and it derives from the moral legitimation of the other. Here it would be possible to elaborate a Kantian kind of argument in favor of truth-telling and sincerity, especially for the "ideal" form of compromise process (where there is full reciprocity and moral respect for the other), but I shall refrain from doing so. As I have stressed, legitimacy probably is never fully accorded. I suspect, however, that even in the usual bargaining process a tinge of mutual moral legitimation is present, expressed in the parties' willingness to sit down together at the bargaining table in the first place. The implication of moral legitimacy may account for the current difficulties in getting Israel and the PLO to compromise or even to bargain. (Notice that the term "a right to exist" plays a role in the rhetoric of both sides.)

There may be times when it is not moral to accord moral legitimacy, but this question belongs to the topic of the morality *of* compromise, which I am not considering here.

The introduction of trust, and trustworthiness too, helps to explain the possibility of accommodation, for a convergence of expectation is required to terminate the conflict. Achieving this goal will be easier when each side knows that the other is trying to get the best for itself, but not to the point of wringing out the last drop of gain that it can. The termination of conflict, as I earlier stated, is one of the main concepts entering into the analysis of compromise. It is, in fact, the most difficult of all to elucidate, just as it is harder to terminate a conflict than to begin one. Some conflicts may have a natural termination, for example, when one of the sides dies. In our case, it is the parties themselves who must provide the rules of termination.[19] One of the problems for analysis here is what we mean by the word "agreement." This is not so difficult a matter when the parties have to agree on a single event, the one-shot division of a piece of cake, for example; but trouble starts when they have to commit themselves to a series of future events.

I am not going to go into this issue, nor shall I discuss what a fair compromise is. If I were to do so, I would go on to combine my discussion of the moral legitimation of the other with a discussion of the utility scales of the parties, taking into account the fact that utility is very difficult to measure in the real-world situation. Instead, I'm going to turn to the other half of the definition of "compromise," submission to a third party, which is the second part of my program. It seems easier to begin a paper on conflict than to terminate one, but I promise to be brief. Only two of our three concepts need attention: mutual concessions (which are the heart of the compromise process) and termination of conflict. I shall touch on a few of their highlights. (Strictly speaking, some third-party processes may involve analogues to mutual concessions rather than mutual concessions as such.)

It will be useful to begin at the end, that is, with termination of conflict. From whence does the third party derive its *authority* to terminate a conflict? To ask this is to commit the fallacy of multiple questions, for there may be forms of third-party dispute settlement in which the third party has no authority to terminate the conflict. But how, then, does he get into the picture? Perhaps the question of authority (of one kind or another) cannot be escaped.

It is necessary to distinguish, as I have done elsewhere, three main types of the sort of third-party dispute settlement that are relevant to our purpose: adjudication, conciliation, and therapeutic integration.[20] These terms are used in many ways in the literature, and examples might help in explaining what I understand by them. Under adjudication I include civil and criminal litigation, grievance arbitration, and commercial arbitration; labor mediation and certain kinds of marriage counseling (intensive family therapy) are, respectively, examples of conciliation and therapeutic integration. What ties these three forms of conflict resolution together is the fact that in all of them the third party is expected to be neutral or impartial; and it is a nice question whether the standards of fair procedure, which derive from this expectation of impartiality, are the same for all three forms. We can put this aside, and we can also exclude discussion of therapeutic integration, which is a mystery anyway. I might add, though, that we don't know which form of third-party dispute settlement the shipwrecked Russians were submitting to when they sent their letter to Moscow.

The aim of adjudication is to terminate a conflict by rendering a *final decision* in the given case. In other words, the third party decides the outcome. There appear to be two conditions that have to be satisfied in order for this to be possible. The first condition of "finality" is political, and it concerns the authority of the third party. Often this will be no problem, for the third party may derive his authority from his official status in the public legal system, which grants him jurisdiction, or from a legally enforceable agreement between the parties. The second condition of "finality" is logical. In order for the third party to be able to decide the parties' conflict, it must be given a certain form. It has to be framed in a proposition (or set of propositions) that is asserted by one side and that is contradicted by the other. Unless issue is joined in this fashion, the third party cannot render a final decision in their dispute, for what he does is decide which one of these mutually incompatible claims is correct or right. (Notice that the third party settles with finality the particular dispute that is put in this logical form. In so doing he does not necessarily resolve the original conflict between the parties. This conflict, in all its ramifications, might be resolvable only by a psychotherapist.)

Now, how can compromise enter into adjudication? In two ways, apparently. The first concerns the selection of the third party, especially when the legal system does not grant someone jurisdiction in the given dispute, so that the authority of the adjudicator will have to derive from an agreement between the parties. The fact that they might agree on this, however, does not necessarily entail that they have compromised on the matter, for compromise presupposes that they initially disagreed on who should adjudicate their dispute. In any case, the only interesting question arises when they finally do agree on who the third party should be and yet the decision of the third party is in no way legally enforceable. How will his decision terminate the conflict? Why should a party abide by his decision? If the parties do not provide for this by exchanging hostages or by some such other method that makes it in the interest of each to abide by his decision, they are simply going to have to *trust* one another to do so. Since the conditions of trust in this kind of adjudication are pretty much the same as in conciliation, I shall postpone the topic for a moment. Other sorts of points about trust were mentioned in my discussion of the bilaterally negotiated compromise.

The other way in which compromise can enter into adjudication relates to the decision, the outcome. "Compromise," here, might mean two things. It might mean, first, that the decision is based upon the third party's sense of fairness or sense of where the balance of the equities falls in the particular case, rather than being based upon explicit standards common to the disputants. But I do not think this is what we usually mean. Second, "compromise" might here mean that the adjudicator splits the difference (of gains or losses) between the parties. This, I think, is the more usual connotation of the term in this kind of context. Now, there may be sound reasons of policy and justice for doing this sort of thing, imposing an outcome, especially if the law and the facts in the case are unclear.[21] And the parties might feel all the happier if this were done. But notice what happens: the conflict is terminated, in some sense, but the *parties'* case is not decided, for the third party will not really be adjudicating *their* dispute! That is, the third party hasn't decided whose claims were right. This procedure troubles me, therefore; but I also must confess that it troubles me that it troubles me.[22]

I turn finally to conciliation, and I shall be very brief, although the subject deserves a good deal more. Fortunately, I shall be able to rely on some things I have already said. If compromise has a home in third-party dispute settlement, it is surely here.

A conciliator typically enters the picture when the parties to a conflict are unable to settle it between themselves. They need his *help* in order to reach an agreement, but this kind of third party does not terminate the conflict. The conflict will come to an end when the parties' expectations converge and if they can trust each other to stick by their agreement. Since the conciliator does not terminate the conflict, the question of authority in any strict sense does not arise, but some justification of his presence is required. And this justification resides in the trust that they both have in him. What they trust is his intelligence, his ability to understand their positions and their interests; they trust his probity and his ability to keep a confidence. They need him to clear the air, to diffuse a tense situation, to introduce an air of calm and objectivity. These points are well discussed in the literature on labor mediation. Additionally, there are discussions of bringing the parties together, setting up an agenda, laying out procedures, and so on. All this is well known, and I need not deal with it.

What interests me most is the fact that the third party, the conciliator, is accorded moral legitimacy by the disputants because of this objectivity, neutrality, and impartiality; and that these factors (or better yet, factor—because they come down to the same thing) in turn imply a corresponding accordation of moral legitimacy to the parties from him. These factors also imply *equal* treatment of the parties in the conciliation process. There is, therefore, a pressure toward regarding the conflict as a symmetrical one, despite the differences in the bargaining strengths of the opponents. The third party will tend to view the conflict as a conflict between similar individuals who ought to be perceived as similar. This does not mean that bargaining strength can be ignored, of course. But it is easy to see how powerful the tendency will be to achieve a symmetrical outcome, a 50-50 split. This notion, however, is not always very precise in real-life conflicts; it is difficult to measure power, for example, and the question of how power should be distributed between the parties might be the major issue in a conflict. Still, resolution depends on getting expectations to converge, and we can think of this point of convergence as residing midway between the initial stances of the parties. In other words, the conciliator has (what Schelling and Iklé call) a "focal point" toward which he can attempt to bring the parties. It would be interesting to compare the role of focal points in conciliation, especially in circumstances where the quantitative considerations are essentially loose and metaphorical, with the role of focal points in the "arbitration solutions" of the mathematical game theorists.

The need for objectivity and impartiality obviously imposes intellectual and moral constraints upon the third party that will be exhibited in his dealings with the opponents. The role of appeals to rational and moral considerations that are accepted by the opponents, which was noted in the discussion of the bilateral compromise process, is doubly enhanced here. Because the conciliator will tend to view the parties as similars, if not equals, these considerations will tend to apply to both sides in common. A compromise that is reached on the basis of mutually accepted considerations probably will be one that the parties can trust each other to carry out. At any rate, the importance of appeals to rational and moral considerations that a party individually accepts is especially evident when the negotiators are agents of groups that are in conflict. After reaching their agreement the negotiators must go back to their principals for an endorsement of it. They are in a better position to do this if they can attribute the agreement to an impartial conciliator who has commended the outcome to them on the basis of considerations that they mutually find compelling. The function of the conciliator, it has been said, is to make everybody happy with a solution that nobody wants; and this achieved by persuading them that it is something they ought to want. By way of very brief summary of this section, let me say that the link between the third-party compromise process and the bilateral compromise process is the idea of moral legitimation.

These points all deserve to be elaborated upon, but I cannot do this here. Two additional items of special interest concern the conciliator's responsibility for the result, and the significance of the fact that the third party in conciliation exercises substantial control over the communication process. Unfortunately, these cannot be discussed either, now.

Let me conclude by redeeming my pledge to say a few words about conflicts of principle or ideology and structural conflicts. My previous topic, conciliation, would be a natural lead into this subject because a conciliator has to keep the parties' attention on bread-and-butter issues and away from conflicts of principle. Conflicts of principle, perhaps, cannot be resolved as such. But conflicts between parties who differ over matters of principle can be sidestepped if they can agree on superordinate goals or can agree on structures for dispute resolution. The resolution of structural conflicts has an analogous form; the parties may agree on the creation of structures or pro-. cedures for resolving structural conflicts. In a way, this is what a democratic society is all about: agreement on democratic structures for resolving conflict. It might be noted that the Russians who were shipwrecked on the desert island at least agreed to send a letter to Moscow asking for instructions on how to resolve their conflict. It would be interesting to know what answer they got back. But had the story told us this it would have spoiled a good joke.

Notes

1. Webster's New Collegiate Dictionary, 7th ed. (Springfield, Mass.: G. & C. Merriam, 1973).

2. Cited in Fred Charles Iklé, *How Nations Negotiate* (New York: Praeger, 1967), p. 206.

3. See R. B. Braithwaite, *The Theory.of Games as a Tool for the Moral Philosopher* (Cambridge: At the University Press, 1955), pp. 6 and 52.

4. Lon Fuller, *The Morality of Law*, rev. ed. (New Haven: Yale University Press, 1969), chap. 2.

5. Thomas C. Schelling, *The Strategy of Conflict* (Cambridge: Harvard University Press, 1960), p. 114.

6. R. Duncan Luce and Howard Raiffa, *Games and Deicisions* (New York: John Wiley, 1958), p. 1.

7. See, however, Anatol Rapoport, "Game Theory and Human Conflict," in Elton B. McNeil, ed., *The Nature of Human Conflict* (Englewood Cliffs, N.J.: Prentice-Hall, 1965), pp. 198ff.; Schelling, *Strategy of Conflict*, pp. 280ff.

8. For a survey, see R.W. Mack and R.C. Snyder, "The Analysis of Social Conflict— Toward an Overview and Synthesis," in Clagett G. Smith, ed., *Conflict Resolution: Contributions of the Behavioral Sciences* (Notre Dame, Ind.: University of Notre Dame Press, 1971), pp. 3-35.

9. Muzafer Sherif, *In Common Predicament* (Boston: Houghton Mifflin, 1966), pp. 89ff.

10. See, generally, Georg Simmel, *Conflict,* trans. K. Wolff (Glencoe, Ill.: The Free Press, 1955).

11. The term "structural conflicts" is taken from Anatol Rapoport, *Conflict in Man-Made Environment* (Baltimore: Penguin Books, 1974), chap. 16, "A Taxonomy of Conflicts."

12. See A. Flanders, "The Nature of Collective Bargaining," in A. Flanders, ed., *Collective Bargaining* (Harmondsowrth: Penguin Books, 1969), pp. 11-41.

13. See Rapoport, *Conflict in Man-Made Environment*, p. 185; A. Rapoport, *Fights, Games, and Debates* (Ann Arbor, Mich.: The University of Michigan Press, 1960).

14. Cited in Schelling, *Strategy of Conflict*, p. 279. Appendix B of Schelling's book is a critique of symmetry in game theory.

15. Dear Abby: I hope you will take time to give me your opinion on a problem that involves two partners in a small business. Partner A bought a $100 ticket to a charity ball with company funds, a normal procedure. The day of the ball, partner A asked partner B if he would like to use the ticket. Partner A offered it to others. No takers. At the last minute partner A decided to go himself.

    The ticket was the winning number. It won $4,000! Partner A insists the money is his. Partner B thinks it should be split 50-50. What do you think? P.R.

    Dear P.R.: If partner A, with the knowledge and consent of partner B, invested company funds in an oil well, and it brought in a million-dollar gusher, wouldn't partner B be entitled to half the proceeds? The same principle applies.

16. Iklé, *How Nations Negotiate,* p. 211.

17. On "symmetric conflicts" (the parties are similar and perceive themselves as such), see Rapoport, *Conflict in Man-Made Environment,* p. 176.

18. I earlier remarked that a result that is regarded as a compromise on the basis of using one of the approaches to compromise may not be regarded as a compromise from the point of view of some other approach. The above discussion illustrates this point. From an end-state perspective, many outcomes of a bargaining process will be called compromises that will not be compromises according to a process approach. The latter, but not the former, requires that the parties recognize each other's moral legitimacy. When two hunters in a Hobbesian state of nature agree to split a piece of game, the result is not a compromise from a process perspective, as I have analyzed it, though it might be regarded as such from an end-state point of view. I believe that the analysis I am presenting here does have significant application to very many social and political situations.

19. See Lewis A. Coser, "The Termination of Conflict," in Smith, ed., *Conflict Resolution,* n. 6, pp. 486-91.

20. See Martin P. Golding *Philosophy of Law* (Englewood Cliffs, N.J.: Prentice-Hall, 1975), chap. 6.

21. See the symposium, "Approaches to Court Imposed Compromise—The Uses of Doubt and Reason," *Northwestern Univ. Law Rev.,* 58 (1964), 731; and especially the contribution by John E. Coons.

22. One important point omitted in the foregoing discussion of adjudication is that adjudication seems more appropriate to conflicts of rights than to conflicts of interests (unless these are framed in terms of rights, which is often done).

2

COMPROMISING INTERESTS
AND PRINCIPLES
THEODORE M. BENDITT

The aims of these remarks are to help illuminate the notion of compromise and to contrast compromise in conflicts-of-interests cases with those involving conflicts of principles. The difference, as I see it, has to do with the bases of compromise in the two cases, and this in turn has implications for the character of the compromise process in each case.

Sometimes when we talk of a compromise we are referring to the outcome of a certain sort of interaction between or among people. This outcome might be the policy, a piece of legislation, or whatever that has been agreed upon. At other times when we talk of compromise we are referring to a process by which agreements are reached. In this article we will be considering the latter.

Compromise implies conflict: either an open rupture or a difference that could lead to an open rupture must be resolved. Compromise involves both parties (I will limit the discussion to bilateral cases) altering their claims or positions in order to reach an accommodation. If only one party alters his position, the action constitutes not compromise but capitulation, and though this might merely be due to one person's having come to agree with the other (his opponent, or so I shall call him), in other cases it might constitute appeasement.

So far, compromise has not been distinguished from bargain, for in bargaining, too, there is mutual inducement—each party agreeing to give up something in order to get the other to give up something. Indeed, compromise involves aspects of bargaining, for at each stage of the process someone proposes a resolution and pushes (argues, cajoles, etc.) for it. But nevertheless compromising and (mere) bargaining differ, though the difference seems to be only a matter of the attitude of the parties. In compromise a person has a certain sort of respect for his opponent, because of which he is willing to agree to an accommodation rather than make the best deal for himself that he can. The clearest case exhibitng the distinction is one of unequal power. If A is able to impose on B a solution that is favorable to A and uses his power to do so, he is not compromising but bargaining, and perhaps driving a hard bargain. On the other hand, that the outcome is equally favorable to both does not show that there was a compromise, for what is really mere bargaining can look like compromise if there is equal bargaining power. In the end it is often very difficult to tell whether an accommodation-seeking process is a case of bargaining or compromising, for hard bargaining can often be conducted in what appears to be the spirit of compromise.

Compromise is possible with respect to both conflicts of interests and conflicts of principle, though, as we shall see, the latter is the more difficult case, both conceptually and practically. However, we should note as a preliminary that, strictly speaking, it is not interests or principles that are compromised but claims that have been put forward or policies that are favored. A person can agree to less than he wants or is entitled to, but his interests are not thereby reduced. Thus, compromising a conflict of interests does not mean that one's interests are realized or fulfilled; rather, it means that one has (often quite rationally) agreed to accept less than it is in his interest to get. [1] Similar points apply for conflicts of principles.

Conflicts of interests and of principle can be present in the same case. For example, in labor-management disputes there may be, in addition to the obvious conflicts of interests, issues of principle such as who is responsible for, and entitled to, a greater share of corporate profitability, or who ought to make production and investment decisions. In the attempt to make the settlements of disputes easier the parties may, expressly or by tacit understanding, ignore one or another of these sorts of conflicts. Usually it is the conflict of principle that is avoided in favor of bread-and-butter issues. To quote Robert Paul Wolff:

> It is much easier to accept a compromise between competing interests—particularly when they are expressible in terms of a nu-

merical scale like money—than between opposed principles
which purport to be objectively valid. The genius of American
politics is its ability to treat even matters of principle as though
they are conflicts of interest. (It has been remarked that the genius of French politics is its ability to treat even conflicts of interest as matters of principle.)[2]

CONFLICTS OF INTERESTS

According to Professor Golding, compromises of conflicts of interests range between pure (offensive) bargaining and the ideal of full
reciprocity, in which "the parties recognize each other as moral
equals despite their relative bargaining strengths." (p. 17) Compromise is more than pure bargaining because it involves some degree of
moral acknowledgement of the opponent. But it seldom attains the
ideal of full reciprocity because "legitimacy probably is never fully
accorded," (p. 18) so that it is in part a bargaining situation in
which each party wants the best for himself. (And it is a strategic bargaining situation because each party knows this of the other.)

While this may be descriptive of many resolution-seeking processes
that are (perhaps euphemistically) called compromises, it is difficult
to give sense to the idea of only partially recognizing the moral legitimacy of an opponent's interests. One possibility is that party A regards the kinds of interests B is claiming as morally defective and
thus not as worthy as his own of being promoted. This would explain
only a limited class of cases, however, for in most conflict-of-interest
situations the kinds of interests being claimed on each side are the
same. So to grant only partial recognition to the opponent's interests
in such a case is to regard the opponent himself as less morally worthy
than oneself. But since, in the usual case at any rate, there is no
moral justification for this, it is morally impossible to regard as desirable compromises in which less than full moral legitimacy is granted.
This argument will not work, of course, for the previously mentioned
case in which it is the opponent's interests, and not the opponent
himself, that are regarded as morally defective, for it might be true
that some interests are morally worthier than others. This will be discussed later on.

Another problem area in Golding's characterization of compromise concerns the compatibility of partial recognition of the moral
legitimacy of the opponent with some of our ideas about compromising conflicts of interests. Suppose A has greater bargaining power
than B and that among possible resolutions of their conflict A could

impose a range of outcomes 0_1 . . . 0_6 on B, 0_6 being the hardest on B. Suppose finally that A refrains from imposing 0_6, settling instead for 0_5. (We will suppose that even 0_5 is not a fair outcome, one that an impartial arbitrator would choose.) Now while A might regard 0_5 as a compromise solution in that he has made a concession in order to get B's agreement, B is hardly likely to regard it as a compromise, though he might call it a compromise to avoid offending A. For B to regard it as a compromise he would have to have the sense that due consideration of his interests had been taken and that A and B together had sought a resolution both could agree on because they thought it fair. After all, the reason the weaker party in a dispute often wants an impartial third party to propose a compromise is that he doubts his opponent will really seek one.

Though compromising conflicts of interests is similar in some respects to bargaining in that it involves proposal, attempt to secure agreement, and mutual concession, it differs in that it involves giving due consideration to the interests of the opponent and attempting to find a fair accommodation. Actual occurrences of face-to-face negotiation, however, can contain elements of both. The parties may move from one to the other as they gain or lose confidence in the attitude of their opponent, and the enterprise may degenerate into the attempt of each to cut his losses, if it does not break down entirely.

It might seem that these remarks apply to the ideal case of compromise but not to many actual cases. The claim might be made that recognition of the moral legitimacy of the opponent or of his interests is not essential to compromise. A person can, after all, act *as if* he recognized the moral legitimacy of his opponent. One can enter imaginatively into the spirit of what his opponent wants and try to find a fair accommodation — or rather, what would be a fair accommodation if the interests involved were all legitimate — and yet one's opponent might be the devil. This line of thought is, however, mistaken. If one is according trumped-up weight to his opponent's interests, one is according less than full weight in the situation to his own; he is treating his own interests as not being fully legitimate; he is taking an "as-if" attitude toward them similar to the attitude this objection imagines him taking toward his opponent. To do this is to fail to treat oneself as a moral equal; but one is not engaged in a process of compromise if he does not treat himself as a moral equal. Hence to take an "as-if" attitude toward the opponent's interests is to fail to be seeking a genuine compromise between oneself and one's opponent. Presumably a person would do this only if he were acting under some coercive constraint; but to seek an accommodation in a situation in which the alternative is to be forced into a still worse situation is not to compromise. Strictly speaking, a compromise can not be forced on a person: if a thief breaks into my house and claims that the satisfaction of his interests requires a division of my goods and that we must work out an accommodation that takes both of our interests into account, I can hardly be said to have entered into a compromise if I comply.

The question I want to raise now is how compromise is possible. What are its presuppositions—especially its moral presuppositions? This is, to be sure, not a very precise question, but hopefully it will become clearer as it is answered.

A conflict-of-interests problem is often a resource-allocation problem, where resources are understood in a wide sense and include anything that is distributable. Money, tangible goods, power, and prerogative are distributable, and they are also compromisable. Even where the conflict concerns an indivisible good—for example, custody of a child—there can still be an allocation of resources and hence a compromise. For, as the sociologist Georg Simmel points out in his book *Conflict*, indivisible goods can be "represented"—that is, one of the parties can be offered a substitute of sufficient value to induce him to yield. Simmel regards this as "one of mankind's greatest inventions." Uncivilized men and children, he says, find only the objects of immediate desire valuable; civilized economy depends on being able to give up a·particular object of desire for something regarded as equally valuable. "Renunciation of the valued object, because one receives the value quantum contained in it in some other form, is the means, truly miraculous in its simplicity, of accommodating opposite interests without fight."[3]

Insofar as conflicts of interests are resource-allocation problems, they are problems of justice, and the morality of compromise is a matter of whom we are dealing with and which of their interests count (and to what degree, for not all interests are of equal weight). If one has no ground for assuming that a person with whom one comes into conflict is morally inferior, then compromise is morally possible in any conflict situation; it will always be required to regard one's opponent as morally legitimate. And if the opponent's interests are similar to one's own, one has no ground for not recognizing the moral legitimacy of his interests. But if the opponent's interests are different in kind from one's own, compromise is possible only if one recognizes a plurality of interests or some principle of tolerance. A fanatic does not recognize a plurality of interests or a principle of toleration, and a fanatic will not compromise (though he may make deals). Clearly, then, compromise is related to recognizing a plurality of interests or a principle of toleration. It is worth noting that an idealist, though not necessarily rejecting the possibility of a plurality of interests, regards some claimed interests (or merely actual wants) as illegitimate, and is to that extent unable to compromise.

To sum up this part of the discussion: to enter into negotiation in the proper spirit (the so-called spirit of compromise) is to be prepared to give due consideration to the legitimate interests of an opponent regarded as morally equal, and in some cases the possibility of doing this depends on value pluralism or on toleration. This implies that if the opponent's interests are not legitimate, one is not negotiating a compromise but doing something else instead, and it also implies that what one is doing may be morally questionable.

CONFLICTS OF PRINCIPLES

Ordinarily it is considerably more difficult to achieve compromises when principles rather than interests are in conflict, or where the conflict is seen as one of principles rather than interests. First, insofar as the opposed principles purport to be objectively valid, as Wolff puts it, and each party thinks of himself as right (and thus as in the right), neither will think of his opponent as having a legitimate claim that must be taken into account and satisfied to some degree. This is in sharp contrast to the situation involving conflicts of interests. My opponent may be morally equal and his interests morally legitimate, but why should I make concessions merely because he is willing to do likewise when to do so, as I see it, is to agree to what is mistaken?

Second, our principles often define us, at least in part. We expect people to stand for something, and we think less of a person who is not willing to espouse any principles, and even worse of one who vacillates, particularly when it appears that the principles he espouses serve his own interests. So to compromise on matters of principle is to risk a loss of esteem, not only on the part of others, but even on one's own part. Third, and another cause of loss of esteem, is what many regard as a duty of conscientiousness—a duty to act in accordance with one's own sincerely held beliefs rather than with beliefs one does not accept.

Finally, "the parties' consciousness of being mere representatives of supra-individual claims, of fighting not for themselves but only for a cause, can give the conflict a radicalism and mercilessness which find their analogy in the general behavior of certain very selfless and very idealistically inclined persons."[4] Perhaps Simmel overstates this point somewhat in distinguishing so sharply between principles and ideals on the one hand and interests on the other. But however we make the distinction between ideals and interests, there is undoubtedly a difference in the character of the conflict when priniciples and ideals are explicitly involved as opposed to when the parties see the conflict as between interests. There are at least two reasons for this. First, people do not wish to be seen by others or even, very often, by themselves, as entirely self-interested; second, where principles and ideals are involved there is an investment of personality, often owing to one's having made sacrifices on behalf of the principle or ideal, that makes one more intransigent.

Can one legitimately (i.e., rationally and morally) compromise where principles are involved? Ayn Rand says no: "It is only in regard to concretes or particulars, implementing a mutually accepted basic principle, that one may compromise. . . . There can be no compromise on basic principles or on fundamental issues."[5] Others, however, have thought compromise of principles acceptable, indeed necessary, though not an unmixed good. T. V. Smith, for example, in *The Ethics of Compromise*, says: "Compromise is the process . . . whereby each party to a conflict gives up something dear, but not invaluable, in order to get something which is truly invaluable. In the very nature of the case, therefore, compromise is a sacrifice exacted particularly of 'good' men, a sacrifice which their very goodness requires but renders odious."[6]

There are two cases of compromise of principle to consider: (1) face-to-face negotiation on a particular conflict of principles, and (2) agreeing to structures such as democratic institutions to resolve disputes of principle. We will take up the second case first—only very briefly, though, as it requires a great deal more discussion than can be given here.

The possibility of instituting democratic procedures as a means of resolving conflicts of principles raises two questions. First, how can one agree to such institutions? Second, how can one go along with a democratically reached result that is contrary to one's own principles? One answer to the first question is that instituting such procedures is necessary to avoid war and achieve peace without coercion.

Another, and quite interesting, answer is that the outcomes of procedures such as majority rule are more likely to be right than any given individual's principles—as long, at any rate, as people vote for the policies they think ought to be adopted as opposed to those that are more in their own interests. This was Rousseau's view, and though it may seem dubious, there is a theorem of Condorcet in 1785 that is sometimes cited in support of it. What it says is that if every voter has a better than even chance of getting the right answer to a question, then in the long run the majority will get the right result substantially more often than any individual. It is not clear how much this proves unless we have reason to accept the assumption that each voter has a slightly better than average chance of getting the correct result. Nevertheless, it does seem reasonable to think that many persons, particulary when they discuss a problem together in an attempt to solve it, are more likely to arrive at the correct conclusion than any one of them alone. This seems reasonable because such community effort operates to increase the information available, to augment the stock of arguments considered, and to act as a check on the possible partiality of some individuals.[7]

The question of how one can go along with a democratically reached result that is contrary to one's own principles has recently been discussed as the so-called paradox of democracy. The paradox is that a person might think that a certain policy ought to be implemented but, being a democrat, be committed to thinking also that a different policy ought to be implemented if that is what the majority prefers. Thus, he thinks that two incompatible policies each ought to be implemented. An analogous problem can be constructed for directly negotiated compromises of conflicts of principles. Resolving the paradox requires denying that one believes of each of the incompatible policies that it ought to be implemented, and showing instead exactly what judgments are being made and that they are consistent. This will not be undertaken here.[8]

Compromise of principles can also, as previously indicated, take place in a framework of face-to-face negotiation where structures for resolution of the dispute are lacking. In such cases a person must either give way, hold his ground (with whatever consequences might follow), or find an accommodation to which he must assent but which deviates from his principle. How can one do this?

Compromise, as we saw earlier, involves acknowledging the moral legitimacy of one's opponent. For conflicts of interests this means giv-

ing the opponent's interests due consideration in attempting to find a
fair division of resources. But where principles are in conflict we cannot think in terms of giving due consideration to the opponent's principle as well as one's own, for at least one of them is mistaken and
hence entitled to no consideration. So the question is: what possible
basis of respect for one's opponent can provide a basis for an accommodation with what one takes to be error?

As a preliminary to considering this question, though, it will be
helpful to bring out some points concerning the character of a conflict of principles. First, in a typical case the conflict is not immediately over the principles but over some policy or program whose implementation is in question. Each party has taken a position as to
what the policy or program should be, which he takes to be sup-
ported or required by principles he regards as correct or appropriate.
Second, since no policy or program is merely the denial (simple negation) or another, policies or programs alternative to A's and B's are
possible; in particular, it is possible that positions *between* A's and
B's can be forumlated—or at least, since that is a vague notion, positions the parties would recognize as in-between positions can be formulated. Thus, when principles conflict, there may be *room* for
compromise. Finally, the principles themselves might be general
moral-political-social considerations (e.g., that effort is to be re-
warded and that democratic institutions are to be strengthened) that
have a dimension of weight or importance and can be outweighed on
some occasions without being abandoned,[9] or they might be more
narrowly rulelike (e.g., that nothing may be allowed to infringe civil
liberties), in which case they are not regarded as subject to balancing
with other considerations. A conflict is a conflict of principles when
competing policies or programs are backed up by conflicting principles or by different weights being given to similar principles.

Now, why might a person agree to an accommodation where the
dispute is grounded in principles? Often, of course, pragmatic considerations make it necessary to seek an accord. The party who walks
out of a meeting rather than compromise his principles risks being
stuck with a worse outcome than he could have had. ("Conscience either compromises or gets compromised."[10]) And in extreme cases the
risks are even greater—compromise may be essential to peace. But
sometimes the distribution of power is such that A can impose his position on B. Is there any ground for compromise of principle in such
a case?

It seems to me that there are two possible grounds of compromise in such a case: (1) that one recognizes the force of the opponent's argument and, though not agreeing with the opponent's position, is not absolutely certain of his own; (2) that one responds to the sincerity and earnestness of one's opponent, though disagreeing with him. Care must be taken with respect to (1), which subdivides into two cases, only one of which is of interest to us. First, A might agree to an accommodation in the sense that he modifies his position, having recognized the force of the argument for B's position and against his own. This is not the case intended in (1). We are interested instead in the case in which A does not find the arguments for B's position sufficiently convincing to lead him to modify his position, but recognizes the strength of those arguments and allows that he (A) might be mistaken.

Perhaps there could be disagreements of principle in which a person need give no thought to the possibility that he is mistaken, but in most conflicts of principle that arise among people it would be sheer arrogance to insist, in the face of the acknowledged force of the opponent's argument, that it is certain that the opponent is mistaken and that no additional considerations could lead one to alter his position. This is not to say a person cannot be quite reasonable in believing himself right and his opponent wrong; it is only to concede that though one thinks himself right, he might be wrong.

Suppose A were to believe, with appropriate humility, that it is possible he is mistaken. This of course does not mean he must think that if he is wrong, B is right, for other possibilities exist — in particular, possibilities between A's and B's positions. Now, if A is wrong, it is probably because he has given improper weight to the considerations favoring his position, so that (as it would appear to him) if he gave them their proper weight, one of the positions between A's and B's would likely be the correct one. Thus, if A is to act on the possibility that he is mistaken, he has reason to go along with some alternative between his and B's.

But does A have reason to act on the possibility that he is mistaken? An attitude of humility together with a recognition of one's opponent as a sincere and intelligent, though mistaken, surveyor of the moral landscape, seem to me to give one good ground for compromising a conflict of principles. Nevertheless, though it would be a good thing to compromise in such circumstances, it would hardly seem to be required of a person that he do so. Here, then, is a difference between compromising conflicts of interests and conflicts of principles. A further difference is that whereas with conflicts of interests one must give due consideration to the opponent's interests, there is no analogous requirement to give the opponent's principles as much weight as one's own in proposing compromises, so that when principles conflict straightforward bargaining would not be wrong.

One final point must be made on the appropriateness of compromising conflicts of principles. There is a strategic problem — whether one's opponent really subscribes to the position he claims to prefer and the principle he appeals to in defending it, or has instead taken a public stance in favor of that position in the hope that a compromise will produce a result close to what he really favors. Clearly, inasmuch as the good of compromising conflicts of principles is connected with one's responding to the sincerity and earnestness of one's opponent, it would not be a morally good thing to compromise in this case. Obviously, then, compromising principles beomes yet more difficult when one doubts the opponent's sincerity.

So far we have seen that grounds for compromising some conflicts of principles do exist. Can these grounds be extended to all such conflicts, or are there limits to such compromises? T. V. Smith takes the view that there are modest limits to compromise. He holds that compromise is desirable only when necessary; it is an alternative to war and aims at promoting peace, and thus has no place where those ends cannot be attained. So, he says, to compromise with those who are intolerant or in cases where the only prospect is continued sacrifice is pointless. Finally, he holds that compromise is desirable only when it is dynamic and progressive rather than stagnating, and by this he apparently has in mind the progress of science, the betterment of the human condition, and the perfectibility of people. But if these conditions are satisfied, according to Smith, there is no limit to what is compromisable: "the limit of compromise is not fixed beyond all doubt, by an appeal to conscience."[11] Though Smith makes these remarks in talking about forced "compromises" — those made necessary by pragmatic considerations — he would presumably hold the same view for unforced compromises.

It is difficult to go along with Smith's contention that what is compromisable is without limits. Granted that the limit of compromise is not fixed beyond doubt in the sense that we cannot formulate a standard accurately telling us in advance what the limit is, it would seem nevertheless that there are limits. For example, however earnest someone is about the propriety of genocide as a means of solving pressing social and economic problems, no one should accept an un-forced compromise that merely waters down the genocidal policy. Unfortunately, knowing that compromise has limits, but not knowing what they are, can sometimes leave us in a quandary, with no generalizable resolutions.

NOTES

1. I have discussed the distinction between conflicting interests and conflicting claims in more detail in "Law and the Balancing of Interests," *Social Theory and Practice*, 3 (Spring 1975), 325-28.

2. Robert Paul Wolff, "Beyond Tolerance," in Robert Wolff; Barrington Moore, Jr.; and Herbert Marcuse, eds., *A Critique of Pure Tolerance* (Boston: Beacon Press, 1965), p. 21.

3. Georg Simmel, *Conflict* and *The Web of Group-Affiliations* (New York: The Free Press, 1955), p. 116.

4. Ibid., p. 39. See also Lewis A. Coser, *The Functions of Social Conflict* (London: Routledge & Kegan Paul, 1956), pp. 111ff (commenting on Simmel).

5. Ayn Rand, "Doesn't Life Require Compromise?" in *The Virtue of Selfishness* (New York: New American Library, 1964), pp. 85-86.

6. T. V. Smith, *The Ethics of Compromise* (Boston: Starr King Press, 1956), p. 45.

7. See Brian Barry, "The Public Interest," *Proceedings of the Aristotelian Society* (Supp.), 38 (1964), 12-13; and John Rawls, *A Theory of Justice* (Cambridge: Harvard University Press, 1971), pp. 358-59.

8. A useful summary of various attempts to do this is provided by Ted Honderich, "A Difficulty with Democracy," *Philosophy and Public Affairs*, 3 (Winter 1974). Honderich's own resolution of the paradox is plausible and can be adapted to directly negotiated compromises.

9. See Ronald Dworkin, "The Model of Rules, " *Univ. of Chicago Law Rev.*, 35 (Autumn 1967), 22-29; reprinted under the title "The Model of Rules I," in Ronald Dworkin, *Taking Rights Seriously* (Cambridge: Harvard University Press, 1977), pp. 22-28.

10. Smith, *Ethics of Compromise,* p. 55.

11. Ibid., p. 54; see also pp. 64ff.

3

MORALITY AND COMPROMISE
ARTHUR KUFLIK

There is at least an air of paradox surrounding the connection between morality and compromise. As we want to say that the person of goodwill is a person of firm principle, we are often inclined to suppose that the willingness to compromise is a sad but sure sign of moral turpitude. Yet we also want to picture the morally decent person as a person who is striving to be concessive and accommodating with fellow humanity, and so we are sometimes moved to regard the willingness to compromise as a profound expression of moral goodwill.

Are we here betraying our susceptibility to two irreconcilable conceptions of how persons ought to live? Or are we giving voice to a single, traditional conception—although a conception that is less than fully coherent? I shall argue that we need not accept either interpretation. We may reject the supposition that there is anything truly paradoxical about our disposition to speak of compromise in both favorable and unfavorable terms.

Offhand, it would seem that we could resolve the paradox simply by noting that "compromise is as compromise does; some compromises are desirable; some necessary; others are dishonorable."[1] But, of course, this maneuver leaves unanswered many important questions—about the nature of morality and the nature of compromise. Our problem is to understand *how it is possible* for persons to be compromising toward each other without thereby compromising their own moral integrity in the bargain. I suggest that the relationship between morality and compromise can be clarified if we consider the following claims:

(1) Principles of right and wrong limit what may be legitimately compromised; from a moral standpoint, some claims are nonnegotiable.

(2) The role of morality in relation to compromise is not merely limitative: subject to the relevant restrictions, compromise is often to be regarded as not just tolerable but as positively desirable.

(3) In addition to limiting what may be compromised, and within those limits, frequently commending compromise to us, moral considerations can play a still more constructive role; for they sometimes guide us in the selection of an appropriate procedure for resolving our conflicts and help us to work out the substance of an actual compromise agreement.

In what follows these points are amplified. First, though, certain problems in the theory and practice of democracy are discussed in order to confirm the plausibility of such reflections and to underscore the importance of finding some way to accommodate them within a single, coherent account of how persons ought to live. Finally, there is a brief examination of two traditions within which people have found it illuminating to represent the principles of right and wrong as though they were themselves the terms of a very special compromise agreement. Consideration is given to what can be learned from trying to picture morality itself as a compromise!

THE CONCEPT OF COMPROMISE

Before proceeding, perhaps a few words about how I shall here construe the concept of compromise are in order. In his paper, "The Concept of Compromise: A Preliminary Inquiry,"[2] Martin Golding calls our attention to two rather different ways of understanding what is meant by "compromise." On an "end-state" analysis, a resolution of conflict can be characterized as a compromise quite apart from *how* it was reached. According to the "process" analysis, however, a compromise just *is* a certain way of achieving conflict resolution, whatever the actual terms of settlement might be. Suggestively, Professor Golding notes that what has all the appearance of a compromise, when viewed from an "end-state" perspective, may fail to strike us as a compromise at all when we look at the matter from a "process" point of view.

That we do speak of "reaching a solution *through* compromise" suggests that compromise is not a destination, not an end result of a particular sort, but rather a special process for generating end results. Yet when we also speak, as we often do, of "imposing a compromise solution," the implication seems to be that compromises are outcomes that can be characterized without reference to the process by which they were achieved and that can be grafted, so to speak, onto situations in which there is conflict. Actually, upon further consideration, neither view seems to be wholly satisfactory. For it is often difficult to speak plausibly of compromise unless *both* procedural and end-state criteria have been met.

Consider a bargaining process in which concessions on one side are to be matched, on a one-to-one basis, by concessions on the other side. Typically the outcome of such a process will qualify as a compromise. But if at the end we find one side still enjoying significant advantages while the other side — having pressed fewer claims to begin with — has been forced, by the dynamics of the process itself, to concede away virtually every advantage, we will be reluctant to look upon the whole affair as a genuine case of compromise. By the same token, an outcome in which each side is afforded the satisfaction of *some*, though not all, of what it has claimed, would normally be regarded as a compromise. But that designation may be entirely inappropriate if what has happened has not been achieved either by arbitration or through a process of negotiation and mutual concession, but is rather the de facto result of a prolonged military struggle that has managed to exhaust all sides and produce a stalemate of indefinite duration. (Indeed, as history attests, military stalemates can be as stable as compromise agreements.)

These examples might suggest that we cannot speak of compromise at all unless there has been give-and-take by each (process), resulting in some gain and some loss for all (end state). I believe that even this claim is too strong. I suggest that in the central cases of what we call compromise we *will* find that both procedural and end-state elements do figure prominently; nevertheless, as with so many concepts, the concept of compromise is flexible enough to admit of "polar cases" in which one or the other of these criteria more or less drops out of the picture. Thus, at times, the mere fact that the contending parties have agreed to submit their dispute to the determination of a certain procedure will be sufficient to ascribe a compromise to them, however they fare in the end. On the other hand, if an uninvited third party should intervene in order to enforce a state of affairs in which each side is allowed some of what it claims, yet none is granted complete satisfaction, it may still be plausible to speak of a "compromise solution," although one that has been imposed; and this characterization has more to do with our perception of the end result than of the process.

DEMOCRACY AND COMPROMISE

At the outset it was suggested that morality commends compromise to us, but only within an appropriate framework of moral constraints. A brief discussion of democracy will lend support to this view.

Compromise pervades democratic politics. In a democratic society very little is accomplished that does not bear the marks of concession and accommodation. While it would be difficult to overlook the fact that democracy and compromise are somehow, perhaps intimately, related to one another, it is relatively easy to be puzzled about just what the connection is and whether it is admirable. Is there a justification in democratic theory for the widespread democratic practice of compromise?

One argument, at any rate, is this: the more difficult it is for citizens to exercise political power without first having to accommodate themselves to one another's claims, the more broadly based will be the support for whichever policies eventually do win acceptance, and hence, the more "popular" or "democratic" those policies will be. Indeed, one might go so far as to suggest that the primary purpose of truly democratic institutions is to inhibit the formation of policies that are not, in large measure, the product of accommodation on the widest possible scale. Here arises the suspicion that a true democrat is a person without any sense of the limits of legitimate compromise and that at the foundation of democratic theory is a morality of "pure compromise."[3]

Does democracy provide a counterexample to the thesis that compromise is acceptable only within certain bounds? I suggest not. An unqualified enthusiasm for the politics of compromise will come to grief at several turns.

Foremost perhaps is the possibility that *through* compromise a relatively stable majority coalition will form and effectively nullify the political influence of the remainder of the population. While *within* the ruling coalition mutual accommodation might well be the watchword, the legitimate grievances of citizens whose support is not required to maintain a controlling interest in the reins of power would go unredressed.

Here it may seem that the fault is with simple majority rule and

that to make the political process more truly "democratic" a more inclusive voting rule — rule by two-thirds or even unanimous rule —
would be appropriate. Such rules increase the likelihood that matters
will be decided by shifting coalitions of interest rather than by a per-
manently entrenched majority or by a fixed, majority coalition. On
this line of argument, as the proportion of votes required to carry a
proposal or elect a candidate is increased, the more likely it becomes
that beleaguered minority groups will hold the balance of power necessary to block violations of their equal rights and to promote the
equal consideration of their interests. The more broadly based support must be in order to enact a proposal or elect a candidate, the
wider the range of interests that must be taken into account in working out "compromise proposals" and in discovering viable "coalition
candidates." Following the argument to its conclusion, one might
suppose that unanimous rule is the democratic ideal.

But there is a serious drawback to this analysis. Under a more inclusive voting rule, individuals or interest groups that stand to lose
least if an unjust status quo is perpetuated are in a better bargaining
position to exact concessions to which they have no right, in return
for not blocking reform measures essential to the protection of the
rights and/or the vital interests of others. (Indeed, how often is it the
case in politics that adequate reform is not accomplished, but instead, new privileges are exchanged for old!) It is true that with a
more inclusive voting rule, there is more protection against the introduction of objectionable new schemes, but there is also less opportunity to secure relief from established injustices or from schemes
that may have been acceptable at one time but are no longer.

It is tempting to suppose that the democratic process will tend toward decisions that are more considerate of all alike if only the participants in the process are more "compromising at heart" — that is, if
they make it their business to work out compromises in which every
individual and/or interest group is represented in some degree.
Though the emphasis on the motivation of the participating parties
is well taken, one problem with this "solution," as it stands, is that it
is simply impossible to accommodate every interest. If certain interests are to be satisfied to any extent whatsoever, other interests will
have to be denied satisfaction altogether. But more significantly,
there are interests (and corresponding interest-groups) whose accommodation in any degree would be tantamount to the sacrifice of
other *persons* — not merely their present interests, but their very lives,

or if not their lives then their liberty to articulate interests, to make claims, and to enter into compromise arrangements.

The morality of "pure compromise" is incoherent. If universal mutual accommodation is to be possible, certain claims must be regarded as inadmissible from the outset. Moreover, persons must be supposed to have, or to be capable of forming, at least some interests or ends that are compatible with one another's status as coparticipants in the making of compromise agreements. I believe we can account for these restrictions on the range of permissible claims if we recognize that compromise is not a first principle. Underlying the ideal of mutual accommodation is the ideal of mutual respect.

The upshot of all this is that the politics of compromise must be viewed as operating within a larger framework of "constitutional constraints." It is of little consequence to our present discussion whether these constraints are officially inscribed in a particular place or formally adopted at a particular time (e.g., a constitutional convention). It is not to be supposed that written guarantees will literally constrain persons or groups who would otherwise be determined to seize power and to use it unjustly. The framework of "constitutional" guarantees is only as secure as the devotion of people to it. The point is rather that the democratic process has no special claim upon us to participate in it or to abide by its results unless there is prior assurance of some sort that certain matters are not subject to rule by democratic consensus. On the contrary, the very legitimacy of such rule is contingent upon whether persons are secure in the basic liberties of citizenship.

But there is wisdom in the view that democracy cannot function properly without citizens of a certain temperament, and this goes *beyond* the observation that citizens must respect one another's status as free and equal participants in the political process and then, in accordance with that, make it their business to work out compromise solutions in which everyone is represented. For when people wheel and deal their way to compromise solutions in which every interest group is allowed to exercise influence, each within its own special sphere, the end result is still likely to be, not justice for all, but injustice all around. (Consider in this connection Lowi's indictment of liberal democracy as "a universal ticket-fixing scheme.")[4]

So a further motivational adjustment is required. If the willingness to compromise is only a manifestation of the desire to advance one's own (individual or group) interests — albeit within the limitations imposed by constitutional democracy—then democratically enacted laws and policies will typically serve an amalgam of private interests at the long-term *expense* of the public interest. They will reflect what Rousseau called the aggregate will or the will of all *(volonté de tous)*, and not the General Will *(volonté général)*.[5] Unless mutual accommodation is the genuine expression of mutual respect, democracy is in danger of degenerating into a generalized "prisoner's dilemma"[6] — a state of affairs in which, though everyone seeks to promote self-interest (or special group-interest), the outcome is worse for each, and hence for all, than if everyone had been moved by consideration for the public interest instead. A host of contemporary difficulties concerning energy, environment, inflation, and so forth illustrate this point all too well.

And so we are led from a simple enthusiasm for "democracy as compromise" to a more complex vision of liberal constitutional democracy. There are claims that it is not permissible either to press or to accommodate. There are limits to what may be decided democratically. Within those limits mutual accommodation *is* commendable, but it must be inspired by mutual respect and a genuine concern to approximate to what is in the public interest, not merely by the desire to advance individual or special group-interest.

THE LIMITS OF LEGITIMATE COMPROMISE

As there are different conceptions of what is right, so it would seem there must be different views about which claims, if any, can be legitimately compromised. Indeed, it is tempting to suppose that on some views—notably utilitarianism, but presumably other teleological conceptions of right as well, no claims are beyond the limits of legitimate compromise, just as no rights are properly regarded as inalienable. For as the argument might go, it is always possible to conceive at least some circumstance in which the good that can be expected to result does warrant making a concession that on a more "absolutist" view of the matter would have to be condemned as unconditionally improper.

But it would be a mistake to conclude that opposing views on the question of whether there are any limits to legitimate compromise simply reflect the traditional controversy between teleological and deontological conceptions of right. Concerning the problem of how to deal with terrorist demands, for example, one of the most familiar arguments for a completely noncompromising posture can be presented in perfectly utilitarian terms: to make concessions is only to set an unfortunate precedent, inviting similar acts of intimidation later; in the long run, therefore, the best strategy—the course that minimizes the unhappy and destructive consequences of being at the mercy of terrorism—is to assume a rigid stance of refusal: refusal to release duly convicted perpetrators of previous acts of terrorism, refusal to surrender for special treatment individuals designated by the terrorists as objects of their wrath, and so forth.

Moreover, though pertinent, this example is not peculiar. Teleological justifications of seemingly "deontological" codes of conduct abound. Powerful considerations (e.g., the fundamental need for a sense of personal security, the importance of achieving social coordination on a large scale, etc.) militate in favor of the view that in general human well-being is best promoted not so much by a case- by-case appeal to the principle of utility itself as by acceptance of certain rather more specific and seemingly inflexible rules of conduct instead. (So Hume, Mill, and many others can be understood to have argued.)

In contrast with teleological arguments for setting limits to what may be compromised, deontological conceptions of right typically represent at least certain constraints on conduct as binding quite apart from the overall good that is to be achieved by their observance. However, there is reason to suspect that it will be possible to uncover such requirements only at a fairly high level of abstraction (e.g., "act only on maxims that you can at the same time will to be universal laws"; "treat like cases alike"; etc.). It is an interesting question, therefore, whether plausible deontological constraints can be formulated in terms that do translate, at the bargaining table, into a fixed list of concrete demands, properly labeled "nonnegotiable." In short, different views about the limits of legitimate compromise do not correspond in any very simple and straightforward way with the traditional division between teleologists and deontologists.

At this point it may appear that to decide just which claims, if any, ought to be regarded as noncompromisable, nothing short of a comprehensive and critical survey of competing normative conceptions is required. No doubt there is truth in this contention. Here I only wish to suggest that there may yet be a common denominator; a constraint on what may be legitimately compromised that would have to be acknowledged by rational exponents of otherwise radically divergent moral viewpoints. A plausible candidate for the honor of this position is the principle that persons cannot legitimately make concessions that are incompatible with their functioning as rationally self-accountable moral agents; or, more succinctly, that they cannot legitimately abdicate their moral autonomy. Moreover, from the ideal of moral autonomy, however abstract it may appear to be, it is at least arguable that other, more concrete and familiar restrictions derive—for example, freedom from complete and irrevocable enslavement, from unlimited censorship authority, from arbitrary interference as defined by the right to due process and the rule of law.

Now, it might be objected that a utilitarian, or anyone else who takes a fundamentally consequentialist approach, would reject this principle, for he could argue that even an agreement to be completely and irrevocably enslaved to another person would be perfectly legitimate, provided, of course, that the expected consequences were sufficiently attractive to offset the loss of whatever was traded away in the bargain.

Perhaps there is an absurdity in this supposition, even from a utilitarian standpoint. If one is not permitted—by the terms of a putatively legitimate agreement—to function as a critically reflective moral agent (if, for example, one has agreed to be a mere tool of another's will,) then one is henceforth without the legitimate means to "monitor" the arrangement, to assure that the other side is carrying through on its part of the bargain.

Suppose that to circumvent this difficulty one were to enter into an agreement binding the other side to a prior performance of some sort, a performance whose good significance would be complete and hence fully subject to one's own assessment by the time of the agreed-upon "abdication." Of course, it is possible to take issue with the notion of a "completed" good work (what good is done can usually be undone). But even waiving such doubts (as perhaps can be done in special cases), it must be said that in the event of an unforeseen "use" of oneself (or perhaps the cumulative effect of such uses), the evil of which would more than offset whatever good result one hand sought to obtain, one would be without the right to renounce the agreement—assuming, that is, that an "agreement" to become the mere tool of another's will were valid.

(Because our present topic is "compromise" I assume that some "concession" was made in *return* for autonomy abdication. But it is interesting to note that the agreement to become the mere tool of an-

other's will has been dismissed—for example, by Rousseau and by
Kant—precisely because it is, in their view, an essentially one-sided
arrangement. According to Rousseau, for example, there *can be no*
quid pro quo—no reasonable return—for this "concession".[7] In
terms that seem to echo Rousseau, Kant writes that "no one can
make an agreement or other legal transaction to the effect that he
has no rights but only duties." His argument, however, is that "By
such a contract he would deprive himself of [the right to] make a
contract and thus the contract would nullify itself."[8] In speaking explicitly of the condition of being "a mere instrument of another person," he uses the parallel argument that "No one can enter into such
a state of dependence and thus cease to be a person; for only as a person is he able to make a contract."[9])

None of this is to deny that under compulsion or duress a person
may be excused for acceding to demands that would not be worthy of
free, rational acceptance. But this is not to be confused with the
rather different claim that an agreement in which such demands are
accommodated is morally valid and binding. An implication of the
argument that autonomy abdication is not a legitimate concession is
that a person is not to be censured for subsequently renouncing an
"agreement" to abdicate autonomy once the threats that provided
the original impetus to accede are no longer potent. In truth, such an
"agreement" can be maintained only by sustained coercion.

There is another objection that misconstrues the point at issue.
Some may say that one *is* morally permitted to agree to an abdication
of autonomy, to become someone's total and permanent slave, for
example, because, in reality, one still retains the capacity to function
in a critically reflective manner whenever circumstances so warrant.
(The thought is that one *can*—i.e., is morally permitted to— "abdicate" autonomy precisely because, in another sense—i.e., psychologically—one *cannot*.) Since one continues to function as a thinking
being, one still retains the capacity to renege. But to say that one can
exercise the discretion to decide whether to continue observing the
agreement is to affirm the right to function autonomously, hence to
deny that the agreement was in any sense binding in the first place,
for that was an agreement to abdicate autonomy. In short, this response presupposes what it purports to deny: the illegitimacy of autonomy abdication.

Notice also that a person who is, legally speaking, the mere tool of
another's will *could* even be subjected to a frontal lobotomy or to

brainwashing and thus psychologically, not just legally, cease to function as a critically reflective or truly "thinking" being. Furthermore, if the agreement to abdicate autonomy were valid and binding, one would be without the *right* to complain about the prospect of a frontal lobotomy or of brainwashing. But even if such devices were not available, the fundamental issue would remain the same. The question is not whether it is psychologically possible to arrange matters with the intent of terminating all one's functioning as a critically reflective being. Rather, the issue is whether it is morally permissible to forfeit the right (or to abdicate the responsibility) to so function, and hence whether any agreement to do so would be valid and binding and legitimately enforceable.

Of course, the subject of inalienable rights is a study in itself. In a fuller treatment of this difficult matter it would be interesting to explore the extent to which, moving beyond the claims of rational self-accountability, different moral viewpoints support different accounts of what else (if anything) is nonnegotiable.

Fortunately it is unnecessary to attempt a task so formidable here; our present purpose is simply to understand how certain reflections about the relation between morality and compromise can be accommodated within a single coherent account, and in this connection, the thought that morality imposes limitations upon compromise (or indeed upon conduct generally) is hardly paradoxical. More puzzling is how, for persons of goodwill, operating within the bounds of moral propriety, it is possible for conflict to arise in the first place, and why, in the event of conflict, compromise is even tolerable, let alone commendable.

THE POSSIBILITY OF CONFLICT AND THE GOOD OF COMPROMISE

On some moral views, for example, there is simply no room either for conflict or for compromise among persons engaged in the legitimate pursuit of legitimate ends. Principles of right are said to define the boundaries within which each person must operate. As everyone is supposed to occupy his or her own fully protected region of "moral space," it follows that if conflict does arise, at least one of the contending parties is a "transgressor." Compromise makes moral sense only if there are illegitimate demands on all sides.

To be sure, many painful and destructive encounters would not occur if everyone were living well within the bounds of moral propriety. Conflict is often generated by the pursuit of interests that are altogether illegitimate, that are incompatible with the equal integrity of all. But conflict is not always the product of evil intent or the byproduct of moral thoughtlessness. For one thing, there are times when reasonable claims based on perfectly legitimate interests must also compete with one another. The cause of conflict is not animosity, greed, mania for power, or any other morally unsavory attitude on the part of those concerned, but simply scarcity. Thus, when persons of goodwill oppose one another and then negotiate in good faith they may discover, not that anyone has been pressing illegitimate claims, but that in the difficult nature of their circumstances not even all legitimate claims can be fully met. In addition, individuals must often base their respective moral judgments on a picture of their situation that is relevantly, but irremediably, incomplete. Their differences of opinion may have less to do with deficiencies of moral sensibility than with uncertainties that are inherent in the situation itself. Finally, even individuals who are adequately informed and acknowledge the same fundamental principles can find themselves in disagreement when an issue engages several morally relevant considerations at the same time. In such cases the sheer complexity of the matter enables reasonable persons to form somewhat different assessments.

Thus, conflict need not reflect either moral depravity or moral stupidity on anyone's part (any more than the absence of conflict proves that all have behaved properly; mistreated badly enough, persons have been known to lose the will to complain or even the consciousness of why they are entitled to do so.) Scarcity, uncertainty, complexity—these can also lead even conscientious individuals who share the same fundamental moral concerns to press competing claims. Now, when conflict does occur, for whatever reasons, there are a number of ways in which compromise can turn out to be not only tolerable but positively desirable.

For one thing, not every conflict is generated by conflicting moral opinion. Differences in taste, whim, fancy, or interests can also set people at odds. So long as competing aims and interests are compatible with basic rights and responsibilities, there is no moral obstacle to compromise. Indeed, mutual respect and a strong presumption in favor of peaceful settlement typically militate in favor of mutual accommodation. Thus, what is a compromise from the standpoint of competing interests need not be any compromise at all from the standpoint of morality, but may indeed be required.

Of course, persons of good will can and do oppose one another on moral grounds as well; however, if they carefully hear each other out and earnestly try to see matters from one another's perspective, people will often find themselves traveling some distance from their original positions and meeting each other partway. There are a number of ways to account for this phenomenon. Many factors—self-interest, unwitting bias in favor of those for whom we feel personal affection, a certain lack of imaginative identification with the predicament of persons who are not well-known to us—conspire to narrow our moral focus. Negotiations conducted in good faith can serve as a corrective. Each party to the dispute comes to recognize that some of its own claims are not legitimate and ought to be retracted, while certain claims made by the other side do have merit and ought to be accommodated. Even without such distortions of judgment as selfishness inflicts upon us, it is only reasonable to expect that different individuals—operating under the usual limitations of time, energy, and circumstance—will be sensitive to, and become increasingly preoccupied with, different aspects of the same, reasonably complicated moral problem. With respect to such issues, controversy is sometimes more to be welcomed than lamented, for it can become the occasion for persons to broaden their perspectives and enlarge their understanding. After exchanging reasons and arguments, each side may come to the realization that a solution must be found which somehow reflects, in due measure, the merit of all their claims. But a compromise solution that strikes a morally appropriate balance between valid concerns is not to be equated with a compromise of moral integrity.

Finally, there are times when even a long and arduous process of negotiation will at best mitigate, but not altogether eliminate moral disagreement. Nevertheless, persons of goodwill can, in perfectly good conscience, reach an accommodation with one another concerning a matter with respect to which they continue to hold opposing moral views. For one thing, each side may remain confident of its own position yet reach the considered judgment that a peaceful solution, lying somewhere within the parameters of their disagreement, is morally preferable either to settling the matter by force or to leaving it unsettled. (Of course, peace could also be achieved if either party were to submit completely to the other side's demands. But if out of respect for the other person one is willing to make concessions and thus bear a share of the burden of achieving a peaceful settlement, then out of *self*-respect, one may be unwilling to bear the *whole* burden.)

Alternatively, the disputants may come to the realization that the matter is so complex or so plagued by uncertainty that differences of opinion are within the realm of reason. All may have to concede that no side has been able to establish the superior wisdom of its position. In seeking a compromise, each acknowledges the reasonableness of the other side's view while insisting on comparable recognition for its own. Through mutual accommodation the parties express a sense of respect for one another's moral sincerity and goodwill in a difficult matter.

Once again, it would be a mistake to suppose that persons who compromise with one another in cases of this sort necessarily compromise their moral integrity. To see why, it is important to distinguish: (1) what one judges ought to be done about a matter that happens to be in dispute, leaving aside any consideration of the fact that there *is* a dispute; (2) what one judges ought to be done, *all things considered*. When an issue is in dispute there is more to be considered than the issue itself—for example, the importance of peace, the presumption against settling matters by force, the intrinsic good of participating in a process in which each side must hear the other side out and try to see matters from the other's point of view, the extent to which the matter does admit reasonable differences of opinion, the significance of a settlement in which each party feels assured of the other's respect for its own seriousness and sincerity in the matter.

Taking *all* this into account, a person of goodwill might well decide that compromise is the wisest course. But to judge, all things considered, that there ought to be compromise and to act accordingly, is hardly to compromise one's moral integrity. On the contrary, integrity is compromised, not when one acts, but when one elects *not* to act, on what one can clearly judge ought to be done, all things considered.

In these cases of morally acceptable compromise, what is it then that is compromised?

(1) Claims that reflect nonmoral "interest" rather than considered moral conviction.

or (2) Claims based on moral convictions that one can now perceive to have been mistaken.

· or (3) Legitimate claims that one has come to recognize must be

balanced against other legitimate claims in a more comprehensive view of the matter that is in dispute.

or   (4) Claims based on what one would judge ought to be done
about the matter in dispute if one were to abstract from
any consideration of the fact that there *is* a dispute, that
reasonable differences of opinion are possible, and that a
peaceful settlement achieved through a fair process that
fosters mutual understanding and respect is of great
moral significance in its own right.

What need *not* be compromised in any of these cases is moral integrity. Rather, as we have seen, a full moral assessment not only permits but often demands mutual accommodation.

Of course, to affirm that compromise is in many cases morally
commendable is *not* to deny that at times it is reprehensible. Obviously, much depends on the nature and extent of the conflict. There
are circumstances (Chamberlain at Munich?) in which even the cause
of peace is ill-served by accommodation. If this were not so, it would
be hard to explain how the term "compromise" has acquired a pejor-
ative as well as an honorific sense.

METHODS OF SETTLEMENT:
ARBITRATION VERSUS NEGOTIATION

According to one dictionary definition, "to compromise" is "to adjust and settle by mutual concessions."[10] But a compromise settlement can be reached in either of two rather different ways—"by arbitration or by consent."[11] Moreover, each method of settlement admits variations. A negotiated settlement will sometimes involve the
services of a mediator or conciliator—someone who has no binding
authority but who acts as a go-between, helping the contending parties to overcome some of their fear and suspicion of each other and
thus facilitating the discovery of a mutually agreeable solution. Arbitration may be undertaken either by a person who has been selected
by the contending parties themselves or by someone who acts under
some other authority; for example, the state. Should the parties to a
dispute resolve their differences by direct negotiation, or should a
third party be called upon to resolve the matter on their behalf?
What can be said for or against each of these methods of settlement?

In seeking a settlement by direct negotiation, an obvious pitfall is that the disputing parties will fail to reach any settlement at all. People cannot always work out their differences on their own. But even when negotiations fail to produce the terms of a settlement, the parties may come away convinced that a compromise solution is in order. For it is often easier to acknoweldge that what others have to say has some merit and even to concede that one's own view is not immune to reasonable criticism than to see just how competing claims ought to be adjusted. So although an agreement on the substance of the matter is not immediately forthcoming there may yet be a mutually agreeable third party whose informed, impartial, and sympathetic concern commands the respect of all sides.

(Suppose that in the light of a fair and impartial consideration of competing claims an arbiter concludes that it would be improper for one of the parties to the dispute to make any concessions at all. Yet the dictionary tells us that a compromise is a settlement "by arbitration or by consent." Why is arbitration to be regarded as a species of compromise at all? Perhaps an arbitrated settlement is to count as a case of compromise only if in the decision thus rendered mutual concessions are required. But there is another way to look at the matter, too. Even when the final settlement does not involve mutual adjustments, the agreement to submit the matter to the judgement of a disinterested third party could well constitute a significant compromise in its own right: first, the parties concede, in effect, that they are not the best judges of their own dispute; second, they affirm that they are prepared to make concessions to one another if, in the considered judgment of a competent judge, that is what they *ought* to do.)

It must also be said that in certain cases, even if the disputants should manage to reach a settlement on their own, there is some danger that it will be a settlement of the wrong sort. Although they can go through the motions of sitting down and talking things over, the parties to a dispute are sometimes simply too biased by their own involvement in the matter to be able to give each other a fair hearing. As they cannot achieve a disinterested appreciation of each other's position, they are liable to take one another's strengths and weaknesses more seriously than their reasons and arguments. What mutual adjustments they do make are more likely to be the product of mutual fear than of mutual understanding and respect. In such cases, one hopes that the balance of morally relevant considerations, and not the balance of force, will be more nearly reflected in the judgment of a disinterested third party. Suppose, however, that the arbiter is without the means to enforce a decision and that the contending parties are amenable only to considerations of interest and advantage. If it is thought to be the arbiter's prime responsibility to furnish a stable solution nonetheless, then in such circumstances the terms of an arbitrated settlement are not likely to be any more admirable than those of a negotiated settlement. Either way, the comparative merit of the competing claims will be secondary to the relative threat advantage of the claimants.

Moreover, in submitting to the terms of an externally devised solution, there is some danger that the parties will remain insufficiently *reconciled to one another.* Indeed, much can be said for the process of direct negotiation conducted in good faith, quite apart from its success or failure in producing a settlement. The willingness to look at matters from others' point of view—to hear them out and to respond directly to them with reasoned argument and with evidence, rather than with threats and deceptions—is a mark of respect, a measure of consideration in and of itself. Finally, if a settlement can be directly negotiated it is likely to be psychologically, if not morally, more binding. In general, the more thoroughly involved the parties have been in the decision process itself and the more directly responsible they are for the specific details of the settlement thus fashioned, the more deeply felt will be their sense of commitment.

So each method of settlement has advantages and disadvantages. Which is to be preferred? Here we might do well to distinguish (1) cases in which the disputants are associated with one another on a relatively transitory basis—the matter which is in dispute constituting perhaps the whole of their relationship—from (2) cases in which the parties stand, or ought to stand, in some more intimate and ongoing relationship. If it is unlikely that the disputants will have occasion to interact with one another again, then it may be reasonable to forego the rigors of a potentially protracted negotiation process (despite its obvious intrinsic merit) in favor of impartial arbitration. If, however, the parties must "live" with one another in any event, then it may be wiser for them to attempt a directly negotiated settlement first, with arbitration as the last resort.[12]

Obviously, the prospects for a genuine, long-term reconciliation are brightest when, having tried to address one another's fears and suspicions and understand one another's needs and interests, the parties can then proceed on the basis of a solution that they have worked out together.

Perhaps this will explain why, in respect to most domestic quarrels, for example, and in regard to many labor-management disputes, there is a strong, initial presumption in favor of a directly negotiated settlement, with arbitration as a last resort. Indeed, even when direct negotiations first reach an impasse, it is generally thought to be advisable for the parties to renew their efforts, aided by the presence of a conciliator, rather than to submit to arbitration.

Finally, of course, circumstances arise in which disputing parties can neither negotiate a settlement nor agree to the selection of an impartial arbiter. If, however, innocent third parties will be victimized by protracted conflict (for example, in the case of family conflicts, the children; in certain labor-management disputes in critical sectors of the economy, nearly everyone), then even compulsory and binding arbitration may be warranted.

MORALITY AS COMPROMISE

We have been looking at compromise from the standpoint of morality. To conclude our discussion it may be interesting to turn the subject inside out, so to speak, and to see whether the notion of compromise can illuminate the nature of morality—if not morality as a whole, then at least that complex of moral concerns for which the term "justice" has been reserved. The suggestion that the principles of right and/or of justice can be represented as the terms of a very special sort of compromise agreement has played a role in at least two traditions of moral thought.

Thus, in *The Republic* we find Glaucon conveying to Socrates what he calls "the common view" about "the nature and origin of justice" in this fashion:

They say that to do injustice is, by nature good; to suffer injustice, evil; but the evil is greater than the good. And so when men have both done and suffered injustice and have had experience of both, not being able to avoid the one and obtain the other they think that they had better agree among themselves to have neither; hence there arise laws and mutual covenants; and that which is ordained by law is termed by them lawful and just. This they affirm to be the origin and nature of justice; — it is a mean or compromise between the best of all, which is to do injustice and not be punished, and the worst of all, which is to suffer injustice without the power of retaliation; and justice, being at the middle point between the two, is tolerated not as a good, but as the lesser evil, and honoured by reason of the inability of men to do injustice.[13]

And in a similar vein Nietzsche contends:

Justice (fairness) originates among those who are approximately *equally powerful,* as Thucydides (in the terrible conversation between the Athenian and Melian ambassadors) comprehended correctly: where there is no clearly recognizable predominance and a fight would mean inconclusive mutual damage, there the idea originates that one might come to an understanding and negotiate one's claims; the intial character of justice is the character of a trade. Each satisfies the other inasmuch as each receives what he esteems more than the other does. One gives another what he wants, so that it becomes his, and in return one receives what one wants. Thus justice is repayment and exchange on the assumption of an approximately equal power position.[14]

In this tradition, the principles of justice are conceived to be the terms of a compromise agreement to which rationally self-interested persons, who are roughly equal in their ability to inflict harm upon one another and in their liability to suffer harm at one another's hands, would prudently agree. Of course, on this account it becomes a matter of some difficulty to explain why anyone should find the terms of that "agreement" binding when the opportunity to gain at others' expense, with impunity, is manifestly available. As the argument for justice turns on the assumption that persons enjoy roughly equal threat advantage, the implication seems to be that the less vulnerable we are, the less accommodating we ought to be. In circumstances of low visibility and limited vulnerability, justice would seem to lose much of its point. Well aware of this difficulty, Glaucon confronts Socrates with the case of the man who, possessing the mythical ring of Gyges, can become invisible at will. He beseeches him to dispel whatever misconceptions underlie the "common view" that persons who could perform all their dastardly deeds incognito, would have no reason to pass up the opportunity. It is to this problem that the remainder of *The Republic* is ostensibly addressed.

A less egoistic account of "justice as mutual accommodation" can be found in the "social-contract" tradition of Locke, Rousseau,

Kant, and most recently, Rawls. In the writings of these theorists, persons are conceived to enjoy a fundamental equality of status that is not contingent upon the de facto balance of power. Rather, what is decisive is that they are persons—that is, that they have lives to lead and the capacity to regulate their pursuits in accordance with mutually acceptable "terms of association."

This equality of status has been metaphorically conveyed in a number of different ways—through the imagery of a relatively benign state of nature (Locke, Rousseau), of a Kingdom of Ends (Kant), of an "original position of equal liberty" (Rawls). As persons pursuing their respective aims may find themselves in conflict (compare Kant, "pitched against one another through the antagonism of their freedom,"[15]) an accommodation must be worked out that adequately reflects the fundamental equality of their status as leaders of lives. The crucial question in the theory of justice becomes this: Are there any terms of association to which persons so conceived could and would unanimously agree? The principles of justice are said to be the solution to this very special bargaining problem. A just society represents an accommodation, not among those who are equal in strength and cunning, but among those who hold one another in equal regard as persons.

Now, the ideal of equal respect for persons is inspiring but problematically vague. And so it is at least suggestive to turn to the notion of a hypothetical bargaining situation in which persons who are symmetrically situated and equally represented as choosers and pursuers of ends are to "negotiate" the terms of their association with one another. It is merely a device for exploring what is implicit in the commitment to this ideal of equal respect and consideration for persons.

Two features of the idealized bargaining situation are especially worth noting here. Persons are not to propose principles that license claims they would not be prepared to accommodate when pressed by others. In effect, basic "concessions" must be mutual. At the very core of the theory of justice is the ideal of reciprocity. Equally significant is the requirement that agreement on terms of association be unanimous. Proposed principles must be acceptable to all, whatever their circumstances and points of view.

Here it is natural to object that whether or not this is the fundamental problem of social choice, it is a problem without a solution. There are no principles to which all persons, whatever their positions in life and whatever their points of view, could agree. One attempt to resolve this impasse in social-contract theory is John Rawls's by now famous resort to the "veil of ignorance."[16] The parties to the idealized contractual situation (which Rawls calls the Original Position) are not permitted to know (or less picturesquely, to take into account) their specific identities. They must deliberate in "ignorance" of their natural assets, their social standing, and even their respective conceptions of what is right and good (however these may evolve over the course of their lives). They do know that they are persons who have lives to lead, that is, that they have the capacity to form aims and aspirations and to direct their pursuits accordingly; moreover, as rational agents, they are said to be concerned about the conditions under which their ends will be formed and pursued. In thus restricting the knowledge and adjusting the motivation of the bargaining parties, the aim is to induce a unanimous agreement on terms of association. It is plausible to suppose that under these conditions the only principles to which they can be drawn to unanimous agreement are principles which secure and enhance each person's fundamental status as articulator and pursuer of ends.

A rather different solution has been furnished by J. L. Mackie, who writes:

> We must lower our sights a little and look not for principles which can be wholeheartedly endorsed from every point of view; but for ones which represent an acceptable compromise between the different actual points of view.[17]

In Rawls's theory, rational persons are said to have a higher-order interest in being able to determine their plans of life, and this is thought to provide a common ground of rational appeal that focuses their attention upon the primary goods and leads to the collective choice of the two principles of Rawlsian justice. On Mackie's view, however, the principles of right are not uniquely determined. As there is variation in the range of prevailing points of view, so there will be variation in the principles of right, for these principles must "represent an acceptable compromise" with respect to whatever points of view happen to be held at any given time. Thus, the ideal of equal respect for persons *is* significant (for it does call upon us to put ourselves in each and everyone's shoes before assenting to a principle), but it leaves the choice of fundamental principles somewhat open. So it is we who must "invent" and reinvent what is right and wrong in our quest to find a mutually acceptable accommodation.

Mackie is evidently (and with good reason) dubious about the possibility of finding principles that represent an acceptable compromise with respect to *every possible* point of view. But there is no reason to suppose that confining our attention to points of view that are presently held by someone will suffice to overcome the problem. For even "actual" points of view may be so profoundly opposed that there is simply no mutually acceptable mutual accommodation, no compromise that adherents to the views in question could accept. Perhaps Mackie means to define "acceptability" in some other way— not by reference to the viewpoints themselves but from some standpoint external to, and presumably "higher" than, whatever viewpoints are to be reconciled. But if so, what is right will not be quite so thoroughly a matter of invention as at first we were led to believe. In any event, we need to be told more about what is to count as an "acceptable" compromise.

In contrast with Mackie, Rawls views justice as (primarily) an accommodation among persons, not among points of view. A crucial feature of persons, however, is that they do have the capacity to form points of view about what is right and good and to direct their lives accordingly. The conditions under which the parties to the Original Position deliberate are meant to insure that all are equally represented as choosers and pursuers of ways of life. It is to persons conceived in *this* way that the principles of justice are said to be unanimously acceptable.

Critics have objected that unanimity is achieved at a price: the complaint is that in order to obtain a unanimous agreement on terms of association Rawls must introduce constraints on moral argumentation that are in need of as much or more supporting argument themselves.[18] Alternatively, some would say that the parties to the Original Position simply know too little to reach any agreement at all. Though I believe these objections can be met, it would take us too far astray to address them here. More pertinent to our present topic is the suggestion that with the advent of the veil of ignorance, Rawls's theory loses its "contractarian" character. All who deliberate under the constraints of the Original Position will reason in the same way to precisely the same conclusions. Since what is acceptable to any is acceptable to all, the parties cannot be said to "bargain" with one another in the usual sense, and so, it might be argued, the metaphor of justice as mutual accommodation fails. This is a misapprehension.

(1) In the first place, whether or not the parties to the Original Position can be said to "bargain" with one another, it remains

true to say that a just society is, as Rawls puts it, "a pact of reconciliation"[19] between the exponents of diverse moral and religious
beliefs. Justice represents a reasonable adjustment between one's
claim, as a free person, to be allowed to do as one chooses, and
others' claim upon oneself to be granted no less. Persons who in
real life are willing to simulate the deliberations of the hypothetical parties to Rawls's hypothetical situation show that they are
prepared to adjust their ends and restrict their pursuits in defer-
ence to one another's equal status as choosers and pursuers of ends.
It is for this reason one can say that to have a sense of justice is to
have an accommodating or concessive spirit. Even though the veil
of ignorance enables the parties to the Original Position to reach a
unanimous agreement, from the perspective of real persons in the
real world, the principles they agree to are "principles of accommodation."[20]

(2) As a matter of fact, however, "trade-off" arguments do figure
significantly in the reasoning which leads to the selection of the principles of justice and the principles that define the natural duties. A
few examples will clarify this point. Consider the rules of order in debate. Offhand, these rules might seem to constitute an unwarranted
restriction on the liberty to speak. But one must not forget that from
the perspective of the Original Position, to be at liberty to speak
whenever one pleases is to be subject to unregulated interruption by
others, for they would also have the liberty to speak when they please.
As H. L. A. Hart has put the point in expounding Rawls's doctrine
on this subject, "it is rational to trade off the liberty to speak when
you please for the more valuable benefit of being able to communi-
cate more or less effectively what you please."[21]

Next consider the argument for liberty of thought and conscience—a liberty that Rawls regards as perhaps the most fundamental of all, its recognition being a "fixed point" of our moral consciousness. Rawls is well aware that persons with strong convictions
may wish to suppress opposing views. But he maintains that the parties to the Original Position "cannot take chances" with their freedom to form their own convictions. In effect, this too is a trade-off.
The suggestion is that it is rational to forgo the opportunity to vie for
positions of authority to which the prerogatives of suppression are at-
tached in return for (in order to secure) the liberty to form one's convictions without such interference from others. According to Rawls,
the argument for liberty of thought and conscience can be extended

"to apply to other freedoms, although not always with the same force."[22] One might conjecture, therefore, that the entire list of basic liberties could be generated in the same manner: once it is recognized that from behind the veil of ignorance a liberty can only be secured at the "price" of its general and equal distribution, the parties will be led to renounce certain liberties (in return for the corresponding concession on the part of others) in order to secure other liberties more basic to their status as rational, self-directing agents.[23]

Comparable trade-off arguments are employed by Rawls in support of the natural duties of mutual respect and mutual aid. He writes:

> Their self-respect and their confidence in the value of their own system of ends cannot withstand the indifference much less the contempt of others. Everyone benefits then from living in a society where the duty of mutual respect is honored. The cost to self-interest is minor in comparison with the support for the sense of one's own worth.
>
> Similar reasoning supports the other natural duties. Consider, for example, the duty of mutual aid . . . while on particular occasions we are required to do things not in our own interests, we are likely to gain on balance at least over the longer run under normal circumstances . . . assuming that the chances of being the beneficiary are not much smaller than those of being the one who must give aid, the principle is clearly in our interest. But this is not the only argument for the duty of mutual aid or even the most important one . . . it makes little difference that we never, as things turn out, need this assistance and that occasionally we are called on to give it. The balance of gain, narrowly interpreted, may not matter. The primary value of the principle is not measured by the help we actually receive but rather by the sense of confidence and trust in other men's good intentions and the knowledge that they are there if we need them. Indeed, it is only necessary to imagine what a society would be like if it were publicly known that this duty was rejected.[24]

(3) Finally, as Rawls has more recently emphasized, it is still suggestive to think of the parties to the Original Position as agreeing to terms of association, and not merely selecting principles.[25] The principles of justice are to be as binding as though a firm mutual commit-

ment had been made to abide by them. Thus, when others are doing
their part as prescribed by just institutions we are not to make an ex-
ception of ourselves merely because no one else would notice. The
ring of Gyges does *not* alter the character of our moral responsiblities
toward one another. "Exceptions" to just rules are just only if they,
too, are licensed by principles to which it would have been reasonable for all to agree from a fair, initial situation.

Let me conclude by noting that the metaphor of justice as mutual
accommodation can serve to mark off one whole tradition of moral
thinking, not only from egoism, but from utilitarianism as well.
Speaking of the principles of right and of justice as though they were
the terms of a very fundamental compromise agreement is one way of
expressing the thought that at the very heart of morality is the
ideal—not of self-sacrifice for the general good nor of self-aggran-
dizement at the expense of others—but of mutual respect, and of
"cooperation among equals for mutual advantage."[26]

SUMMARY

In order to clarify the relation between morality and compromise,
I have addressed a number of topics. Perhaps it would be well to re-
call some of the conclusions reached along the way.

In a brief analysis of the "concept of compromise," I suggested
that in the standard cases of what we call compromise there is give-
and-take ("process") by each, eventuating in some gain and some loss
("end-state") for all; nevertheless, the concept of compromise is flexible enough to admit "polar cases" in which one or the other of these
features is absent. Against the view that the "true democrat" is a person without any sense of the limits of legitimate compromise, I argued that a morality of "pure compromise" is incoherent. If universal
mutual accommodation is to be possible, certain claims must be regarded as inadmissible from the outset. The politics of compromise
must be set within a larger framework of "constitutional" and motivational contraints. Underlying the principle of mutual accommodation is the ideal of mutual respect. I then tried to explain how a sense
of the limits of legitimate compromise could be grounded in either
teleological *or* deontological conceptions of right (as could the view
that there are no fixed limits at all). I also sketched a brief defense of
the suggestion that the right to function as a critically reflective

moral agent is "inalienable" and gives rise to certain "nonnegotiable" claims.

Turning to the central thesis of the first part of this paper, I contended that one *can* compromise with others without compromising one's moral integrity in the bargain. To make this point both more intelligible and more compelling, I first surveyed a number of ways in which conflict might arise and tried to identify in each case of morally acceptable (or indeed, commendable) compromise just what *is* compromised, if not moral integrity.

There followed an assessment of the different methods by which compromise might be achieved. I suggested that when the disputing parties stand in an ongoing relationship, there is often a presumption in favor of the directly negotiated settlement; if, however, the parties are less intimately related, or as is often the case, if they are simply too biased by their own involvement in the particular dispute to be able to attend to the merits of each other's claims, recourse to an impartial arbiter is likely to be preferable.

In the final section, I sought to explain what point there could be in thinking of the principles of justice as though they were themselves the terms of a fundamental compromise agreement. I contrasted two traditions within which this thought has played a signficant role. In one tradition, justice is the outcome of a prudent trade. Rationally self-interested persons are advised to renounce various means to the advancement of their ends in exchange for comparable concessions from others. The principles of justice are the terms of this compromise agreement. It is only because persons are fundamentally vulnerable to one another that fundamental concessions must be mutual. Thus, justice is reciprocity *on* "the assumption of an approximately equal power position." There is another tradition, however, in which persons are conceived to enjoy a fundamental equality of status that is not contingent upon the de facto balance of force. What is decisive is that they *are* persons, that they do have aims and aspirations and the capacity to regulate their pursuits in mutually acceptable ways. But persons pursuing their respective ends may yet find themselves in conflict, and so the problem is to find terms of association that adequately reflect their equal status as leaders of lives. The principles of justice are thought to be the solution to this problem. They represent a reasonable adjustment between one's claim, as a free person, to be allowed to do as one chooses, and others' claim upon oneself, to be granted no less. It is for this reason we can say that to have a sense of justice is to have an accommodating or concessive spirit. Justice is an accommodation, not among those who are roughly equal in strength and cunning, but among those who hold one another in equal regard as persons.

NOTES

1. Henry David Aiken, "Ideology—A Debate," *Commentary*, 38 (October 1964), 76. I am grateful to Lewis Lipsitz for bringing this article to my attention.

2. See p. 00-00 in this volume.

3. Aiken, in the piece cited above, attributes such a view to the sociologist Daniel Bell.

4. Theodore J. Lowi, *The End of Liberalism* (New York: W. W. Norton, 1969), p. 292.

5. Jean Jacques Rousseau, *The Social Contract*, book II, chap. 3 (Harmondsworth: Penguin Books, 1968), p. 72.

6. So named after an anecdote attributed to A. W. Tucker. See Luce and Raiffa, *Games and Decisions* (New York: John Wiley, 1967), pp. 94-102.

7. Rousseau, *Social Contract*, book I, chap. 4, pp. 54-55.

8. Immanuel Kant, *Theory and Practice* (Akademie Edition, p. 292). Here I follow the translation of Carl J. Friedrich (New York: Random House, 1949), p. 418.

9. *The Metaphysics of Morals* (Akademie Edition, p. 330). Here I follow the translation of H. B. Nisbet (New York: Cambridge University Press, 1970), p. 153.

10. *Webster's New International Dictionary*, 2nd edition (Springfield, Mass.: G. & C. Merriam Co., 1960).

11. Ibid.

12. To Martin Golding I am grateful for clarification on this matter. I am also indebted to Professor Golding for bringing to my attention a Talmudic discussion (Sanhedrin 7a) that is highly suggestive of the point developed here. Certain sages were of the opinion "that it is a meritorious act to ask the litigants whether they wish to resort to law or to a settlement"; indeed, some would "allow a settlement even when a case has been heard," though evidently not after the judge has rendered the decision.

13. Plato, *The Republic*, Book 2, in *The Dialogues of Plato* with an introduction by Raphael Demos and translated by Benjamin Jowett. (New York: Random House, 1937). pp. 622-23.

14. Friedrich Wilhelm Nietzsche, *Human, All-Too-Human*, Reprinted in *Basic Writings of Nietzsche*, Translated and Edited, with Commentaries

by Walter Kaufmann. (New York: Random House, 1968), Sec. 92, p. 148.

15. Kant, *Theory and Practice* (Akademie Edition, p. 306), trans. Carl J. Friedrich, pp. 428-29.

16. See John Rawls, *A Theory of Justice* (Cambridge Harvard University Press, Belknap Press, 1971), esp. chap 1, secs. 3-4; chap. 3; chap 9, sec. 82.

17. J. L. Mackie, *Ethics: Inventing Right and Wrong* (Harmondsworth: Penguin Books, 1977), p. 93.

18. Cf. Thomas Nagel, "Rawls on Justice," *Philosophical Review, 82 (April 1973), 226-29.*

19. Rawls, *A Theory of Justice,* p. 221.

20. Rawls, in "Fairness to Goodness" *(Philosophical Review,* 84 [October 1975], 539), remarks that "it is helpful to view the matter as follows: we want to work out principles of accommodation between different moralities much as a constitution insuring liberty of conscience and freedom of thought contains principles of accommodation between different religions."

21. H. L. A. Hart, "Rawls on Liberty and Its Priority," *Univ. of Chicago Law Rev., 40 (1973), 545.*

22. Rawls, *A Theory of Justice,* pp. 206-7.

23. But see Joel Feinberg, who doubts that there is a general solution to the problem of liberty trade-offs ("Justice, Fairness and Rationality," *Yale Law J,* 891 [April 1972], 1022-24); and see also H. L. A. Hart, who, in "Rawls on Liberty," calls into question the power of the veil of ignorance to induce a clear choice in all but a few of the liberty-related matters that are at issue here.

24. Rawls, *A Theory of Justice,* pp. 338-39.

25. Central to Rawls's original, programmatic discussion in "Justice as Fairness," *Philosophical Review,* 67 (April 1958), this point is developed again in his "Reply to Alexander and Musgrave," *Quarterly Journal of Economics,* 88 (November 1974), 650-53.

26. Rawls, *A Theory of Justice,* p. 14.

PART II

HISTORICAL INTERLUDE

4

JUSTICE, COMPROMISE, AND CONSTITUTIONAL RULES IN ARISTOTLE'S *POLITICS*

DAVID RESNICK

At first reflection it would seem that the concept of justice is antithetical to the practice of compromise. If politics is the art of the possible, then the practice of this art demands a tempering of the commitment to absolute principles of justice, and a recognition of necessity; the brute facts of the world impose themselves upon those who wish to act according to such principles. Justice presents absolute standards, while compromise is the typical device used by those who feel impelled to dilute this standard in the service of expediency or some notion of the greater good. We feel that to compromise is to give something up. To be sure, an acceptable compromise is one which both parties to dispute can live with, but to those committed to one side or another the terms hammered out in the process of arriving at a compromise can often appear slightly shabby.

A compromise can be a workable compromise, yet itself be unjust when compared with the standards of justice that apply to the subject matter at dispute. Especially where matters of principle are intertwined with self-interest, the process of compromise where it yields results also yields a sense of unease. Compromise presents a moral dilemma because, while the results may be better than those achieved by sheer intransigence, these results are open to severe moral condemnation from the point of view of those standing outside the concrete bargaining situation and yet committed to one side or the other. Pointing to the moral shortcomings of a compromise when compared with what ought to be the case presents fertile soil for those who wish to condemn without being, as it were, compromised themselves.

Yet to know whether or not a particular compromise is unjust we must be able to stand back and achieve the necessary distance that is provided by theoretical reflection. Rather than adopting the point of view of those disappointed advocates who are involved in the dispute, it is necessary firmly to grasp the arguments of both sides and the facts in the case. Justice often lies with neither disputant no matter how much each may passionately be convinced of the rightness of his case, and yet each may have grasped some crucial feature of the dispute that contributes to a more balanced understanding of the criteria that ought to govern such situations. The need to compromise may as often arise from the fact that justice lies with neither side as it does from the need of one or the other party to give up his principles in order to achieve a second-best solution.

The best possible strategy for constructing a compromise that would be acceptable to both parties is to show that the preferred compromise is in the self-interest of each party, arguing in effect that the strategy pursued by each only appears to be in their interest, whereas the new solution is actually in their true long-term interest as understood by each side; and furthermore that the solution is a more desirable one from the point of view of justice. The latter involves working out a theory of justice that is, ideally, acceptable to both sides and incorporates the features that seem to make each side's position just in its own light. The solution ought to calm the fears that a compromise means the sacrifice of some vital interest and still the moral qualms that are the inevitable accompaniment to disputes that raise issues of both morality and self-interest.

It is my belief that this is the strategy pursued by Aristotle in the *Politics* in which he presents a theory of political justice intended to settle the theoretical and practical disputes that surround one of the fundamental problems of politics: the distribution of political power in a society beset by continual class conflict. Rather than opting for a Marxist solution that looks toward the ending of class conflict by abolishing classes, or some sort of liberal democratic approach that seeks a neutral egalitarian solution by denying the fundamental presence of social class in politics, Aristotle confronts the issue of class conflict directly and attempts to work out a political theory that recognizes its inevitable presence. We need not be convinced of the success of his endeavor in order to appreciate his theoretical achievement.

In order to arrive at a theory of political compromise Aristotle poses the following hypothetical question:

> Let us suppose these rival claimants—for example, the good, the wealthy and well-born, and some sort of general body of citizens—all living together in a single state. Will they fall to disputing, which of them is to govern, or will they agree?. . . It is a question of determining who is to govern when the claims of different groups are simultaneously present.[1]

This sets the stage for the problem. Each group has some claim on holding political power; each claim is legitimate to some extent; yet all claims cannot simultaneously be satisifed. For Aristotle, these claims are not to be understood simply as attempts to monopolize political power in the crude self-interest of a distinct class; they represent different conceptions of distributive justice. While the general concept of distributive justice in theory ought to settle the dispute, it is characteristic of fundamental political arguments that each disputant possesses a different conception of distributive justice. That is to say, each class in the political community is thought to have a concept of distributive justice, and appeal to that concept as a way of presenting claims to desirable political goods. Yet, each class differs over a large number of controversial cases. This suggests that they possess a different theory of why standard cases are correct from the point of view of the concept of distributive justice. If we distinguish between the *concept* of distributive justice, which is the standard all disputants are thought to share, and the various *conceptions* of distributive justice that are peculiar to each social class, we can appreciate Aristotle's analysis of the various theories of justice set forth by social classes trying to justify their own monopoly of political power.

Aristotle is greatly concerned to explicate and account for these various *conceptions* of distributive justice, since they are at the heart of basic political struggles and can themselves be understood as partial or inadequate theories that find their place in a more comprehensive theory of political justice. Aristotle states:

> Both oligarchs and democrats have a hold on a sort of concep-
> tion of justice; but they both fail to carry it far enough, and nei-
> ther of them expresses the true conception of justice in the whole
> of its range. In democracies, for example, justice is considered
> to mean equality [in the distribution of office]. It does mean
> equality—but equality for those who are equal, and not for all.
> In oligarchies, again, inequality in the distribution of office is
> considered to be just; and indeed it is—but only for those who
> are unequal, and not for all. The advocates of oligarchy and de-
> mocracy both refuse to consider this factor—who are the per-
> sons to whom their principles properly apply—and they both
> make erroneous judgements.[2]

He then goes on to explain why they are making such mistakes and
offers two reasons. The first reason appeals to one of the familiar
maxims of what the English call natural justice. Men should not be
judges in their own case: "most men, as a rule, are bad judges where
their own interest are involved."[3] Aristotle is not content to cite a tru-
ism but goes on to show the particular theoretical mistake made by
each side. "They are misled by the fact that they are professing a sort
of conception of justice, and professing it up to a point, into thinking
that they profess one which is absolute and complete. The oligarchs
think that superiority in one point—in their case wealth—means superiority on all: the democrats believe that equality in one respect—
for instance, that of free birth—means equality all around."[4]

Aristotle's theoretical solution to the problem of distributive justice
is to consider the problem from the point of view of the purpose of
the political association itself. Each disputant is presenting his conception of distributive justice from the point of view of his particular
interests; the interest claims of rival parties are, in this instance, incompatible. Aristotle suggests a solution which involves analyzing the
reasons for the various distributive claims. That is to say, rather than
taking the interests of individuals as primary, Aristotle takes the good
of the whole. Each claim can be understood as just in a sense when
we come to understand the reasons for which such claims are assigned.

He sets forth the position that "the good in the sphere of politics is
justice; and justice consists in what tends to promote the common interest."[5] From this perspective particular political rights cannot be
primary; they must be deductions from the more general analysis of

what promotes the interest of the entire political community; the interests of the community ought not to be subordinated to the rights of individual groups or classes. Indeed, the very concept of "rights" is foreign to Aristotle's thought. In this sense, of course, Aristotle is at odds with much of modern liberal thought, which tends to see the priority of individual rights as a way of solving the problem of the distribution of political power.

Aristotle argues on the other hand that the various claims of right have, as it were, an empirical base in the makeup of a well-ordered polity. He says, "Claims to political rights must be based on the ground of contribution to the elements which constitute the being of the state. There is thus good ground for the claims to honour and office which are made by persons of good descent, free birth or wealth."[6] Since each social class is said to contribute one or another excellence to the state, its claim to deserve political power must be proportional to its contribution; no claim is absolute, and from the perspective of the participants what appears to be a compromise of basic principles such as the right of equality, is in reality to be thought of as a recognition of the complex nature of political society. As Aristotle says, "Not only is the polis composed of a number of men; it is also composed of different kinds of men, for similars cannot bring it into existence."[7] And furthermore, "the well-being of every polis depends on each of its elements rendering to the others an amount equivalent to what it receives from them."[8]

But Aristotle does not limit his critique of the different conceptions of political principles to undercutting the philosophical claims of various classes; he goes on to argue that a correct conception of political justice will yield not only a more just state but a more stable one. That is to say, injustice is not only a source of dispute but one of the principal causes of revolution. Men act upon their political principles whenever they get the opportunity, and thus differing conceptions of justice have significant political repercussions. Aristotle analyzes the causes of revolution in the following way:

We must first assume, as a basis of our argument, that the reason why there is a variety of different constitutions is the fact — already mentioned — that while men are all agreed on doing homage to justice, and to the principle of proportionate equality, they fail to achieve it in practice. Democracy arose in the strength of an opinion that those who were equal in any one re-

spect were equal absolutely, and in all respects. (Men are prone
to think that the fact of their all being equally free-born means
that they are all absolutely equal.) Oligarchy similarly arose
from an opinion that those who are unequal in some one respect
were altogether unequal. (Those who are superior in point of
wealth readily regard themselves as absolutely superior.) Acting
on such opinions, the democrats proceed to claim an equal
share in everything, on the ground that they are unequal—that
is to say, more than equal. Both democracy and oligarchy are
based on a sort of justice; but they both fall short of absolute justice. This is. the reason why either side turns to sedition if it does
not enjoy the share of constitutional rights which accords with
the conception of justice it happens to entertain.[9]

Aristotle criticizes constitutions based absolutely on one form of justice or another and advocates a mixed constitution.

But a constitutional system based absolutely, and on all points,
on either the oligarchical or the democratic conception of
equality is a poor sort of thing. The facts are evidence enough:
constitutions of this sort never endure. This reason is simple.
When one begins with an initial error, it is inevitable that one
should end badly.[10]

Thus, Aristotle's theory of political justice is held to be superior to
other, more narrow and partial theories because it leads to political
stability. Any account of justice that is constructed from the partial
position of a particular social class suffers from the defect that, if it
were acted upon to define the major social and political institutions
of a society, it would lead to revolution. Among the virtues of a theory of justice is that it be possible, not merely theoretically satisfying;
that it be connected to empirical reality in such a way as to serve as a
guide to action; and that it provide reasonable justification for believing that action guided by such a theory of justice would create a
society that would be enduring as well as just. Aristotle's theory of
justice is intended to move political actors from the understanding of
justice that is characteristic of their position in the social hierarchy
and raise them to the level of contemplating the good of society as a
whole. From this perspective he urges that each side to a dispute
about the distribution of political rights and power must reach a com-

promise that takes into account the legitimate claims of the other side.

In the *Politics* Aristotle is interested not only in constructing an adequate theory of political justice but in applying it to the conditions of Greek politics. The question he poses — how rival claimants to political power can settle their disputes, the question of who is to govern — can be answered only by a compromise. Once it is clear that no one claimant ought to rule, then it becomes a task of the analyst to suggest ways of compromising that will incorporate the legitimate claims of each, and thus construct a more stable and just polity. This is a problem of constitutional rule-making; and Aristotle offers a number of concrete suggestions on how to construct a political compromise that will be acceptable and result in a mixed constitution, a constitution that mixes both the relevant social classes and the relevant constitutional principles charactertisic of class constitutions.

It is important to note that general political principles, such as political equality, have to be translated into constitutional rules that provide the institutional mechanisms for the realization of such ideals. It is in the study of these rules that we see the concrete application of political principles; and an appreciation of the operation of such constitutional rules is vital for an understanding of how, in fact, powers and privileges are distributed in a society. While it is sometimes the case that formal constitutional rules are a mere facade and that excess formalistic analysis of the legalistic implication of rules misses the concrete realities of political power, we must not be misled by such cases into underestimating the political significance of constitutional rules for an extraordinarily wide range of issues.

Before discussing Aristotle's account of constitutional rules, I should like to point out that Aristotle did not naively believe that a constitution that papers over the differences between classes has much chance of succeeding without the underlying class basis to support the political institutions created by a compromise. A compromise for Aristotle is a mixture, a resultant that combines elements from each particular to yield a new compound having elements of both. The simplest and most familiar example is Aristotle's preference for the mean between extremes. As I shall show, his constitutional rule mixtures do not always rely, strictly speaking, on the mean between two extremes, yet the mean is a basic mode of Aristotelian argument. Aristotle offers a mixed regime as the best constitution for the majority of states and men, which is what I take to be the criterion for his theory of political justice, as distinct from his theory

of the ideal or best regime.[11] This polity has most chance of being realized if it is based upon a middle class.

Aristotle points out that, "In all states there may be distinguished
three parts, or classes of the citizen-body—the very rich; the very
poor; and the middle class which forms the mean. Now it is admitted, as a general principle, that moderation and the mean are
always the best." He then lists a litany of middle-class virtues.[12] The
middle class is devoid of the arrogance of the rich and the servility
and mean-spiritedness of the poor; the middle class is the class most
ready to listen to reason; and in general the middle class possesses the
temperament and capacities for political friendship and thus for constructing a just and stable society. Be this as it may, he concludes:

> It is clear from our argument, first, that the best form of politi-
> cal society is one where power is vested in the middle class, and
> secondly, that good government is attainable in those states
> where there is a large middle class—large enough, if possible, to
> be stronger than both of the other classes, but at any rate large
> enough to be stronger than either of them singly; for in that case
> its addition to either will suffice to turn the scale, and will pre-
> vent either of the opposing extremes from becoming dominant.[13]

Thus, when he analyzes the constitutional rules that lead to a mixed
regime as if they were a totally adequate device to reach a stable
compromise between the rich and the poor, between oligarchy and
democracy, these passages must be kept in mind. The stability of a
compromise depends upon the balance and composition of class
forces.

Aristotle lists three different methods of achieving a good mixture
of constitutions. The first is to combine rules from two different constitutions. As an illustration of how this type of mixture could be
achieved he cites rules for attending law courts. In oligarchies the
rich are fined if they do not attend, whereas in democracies the poor
are paid for attending. A combination of both rules would generate a
new rule that would pay the poor and fine the rich. A second method
of achieving a mixture is to take the mean between two different
rules. A constitution could have no property qualification or a very
low one for attendance, and another a very high property requirement. This type of combination is one in which we simply split the
difference. We do not combine the two rules in an additive way, as in

the first example, rather we achieve a mixture by taking the mean between two different rules. The third method is to combine elements from two different constitutional rules by selecting a part of one rule and combining it with a part of another rule. The example he offers is the rule for appointing magistrates. In a democracy they use a lot and no property qualifications; in an oligarchy they employ the vote and a property qualification. A mixture of the third type would be a new rule that would appoint magistrates by vote as in an oligarchy, but without a property qualification as in a democracy.[14]

Aristotle suggests an interesting criterion for a good constitutional compromise between oligarchy and democracy. When we examine such a regime it should appear as a true mixture and thus be able to be described as either a democracy or an oligarchy. He gives Sparta as an example. Because it contains a number of features characteristic of a democracy, some describe it as a democracy; but since it also contains oligarchical features, others list it among the oligarchies. He states that' "A properly constituted mixed 'polity' should look as if it contained both democratic and oligarchical elements—and as if it contained neither."[15] Thus, both an oligarch and a democrat could identify with such a mixed regime.

This approach to the classification and understanding of his three compromise or combination procedures depends upon different formal ways of combining rules to achieve a mixture. They are successful to the extent that they generate constitutional rules for a polity that make it appear that such a regime is neutral, favoring neither the rich nor the freeborn. The fact that a mixed regime could be called either a democracy or an oligarchy because it contains elements of both may help account for its stability—each element can identify with some features of the constitution—yet Aristotle is well aware of the fact that terminological ambiguity is no substitute for political analysis. To call it something else, a "polity", is also not satisfactory because a polity is a mixture, which does not really dissolve the class elements that compose it; in practice polities actually combine class elements in different proportions.

Alongside his three types of mixtures there is, as it were, another distinction that exists in common usage. Rather than distinguishing compromise regimes by technical constitutional rules, the Greeks referred to some regimes as polities and others as aristocracies. Aristotle objected to such terminology because strictly speaking we should reserve the term "aristocratic" to refer to regimes that mix three elements: free birth, wealth, and merit. Yet he does recognize the crucial distinction lying behind such usage. So-called aristocratic mixed regimes are distinguished from polities by the proportionate mix of only two elements. "Constitutions where the elements are so mixed that the tendency is more towards oligarchy are called aristocracies; those where the mixture is such that the tendency is more in favour of the masses are called 'polities.' "[16] By convention the rich are identified as "gentlemen," and thus mixed regimes containing a bias toward the rich are called aristocracies. The important point is not so much the correct terminology but the fact that any mixture contains more or less of each element; any polity is more oligarchical or more democratic. Not only may each type of constitution be combined according to a different combination procedure; each procedure can yield a result favorable to one side or another. Merely knowing that a mixture has been achieved according to one of Aristotle's combination procedures does not tell us whether the mixture is fair, or whether it will result in a stable compromise between different classes.

Constructing a just and stable polity requires not only a knowledge of how to combine different constitutional rules but also of how the rules themselves operate to favor one side or another; that is to say, why a certain rule is characteristic of an oligarchy and another of a democracy. For the most part, Aristotle simply lists political practices characteristic of each regime; but he often goes beyond mere description and attempts to analyze rules themselves. The most extensive analysis focuses on selection rules and appointment rules. The second and third combination procedures depend upon mixing such rules, while the first depends upon what may be called incentive rules.

Aristotle himself does not present an adequate theory of incentive rules, though the elements of such a theory are there and are embedded in Greek political practice. He is most sensitive to the way incentives operate to rig a constitution to the advantage of the rich in a polity. He knows that giving incentives to the rich to participate in political life while denying them to the poor will in fact increase the political power and influence of the oligarchs. Aristotle constantly reiterates the point that the better and more equitable a polity is from a class point of view, the greater its stability. The rich are warned against the attempt to tilt the polity in their direction, not only by usurping more power for themselves, but also by attempting to give illusory benefits to the people. Such benefits will never work in the long run.

In this context Aristotle lists five different devices adopted by the rich for "fobbing the masses off with sham rights." He distinguishes them in terms of the sphere of activity to which the rights relate: the assembly, the magistracies, the law courts, the possession of arms, and athletic practice. The primary way in which such rights are effectively denied the poor is by means of class legislation designed ostensibly to benefit the poor. Everyone is permitted to attend the assembly, but either only the rich are fined for nonattendance or they are fined much more than the poor. When it comes to holding the office of magistrate the rich are not allowed to decline, but the poor may plead an oath that their wealth or health do not permit them to serve, and so on with the other spheres of activity.

He is also careful to point out that democracies have their own way of rigging the rules in favor of the poor, though these rules do not seem to be solicitous of the welfare of the rich. "Democracies have their counter-devices: the poor receive payment for attendance at the assembly and the law courts; the rich are not fined if they fail to attend."[17] After noting that each constitution has its own form of class legislation, he repeats his suggestion of a fair compromise: "If we want to secure an equitable mixture of the two sides, we must combine elements drawn from both: in other words, we must both pay the poor for attendance and fine the rich for non-attendance. On this plan all would share in a common constitution; on the other, the constitution belongs to one side or other."[18]

On the face of it, it is not at all clear how this mixture will be equitable. To be sure, each party would share in the constitution, yet assuredly the rich would have a great deal to complain about. If the fines are high enough to turn out all the rich, and the payment sufficient to induce the poor to come, then in effect the entire citizen body would appear at the assembly. If there is some sort of majority rule for making decisions, then the rich will simply be swamped by the many. Thus, Aristotle's combination rule would seem to be a way for the poor to give sham rights to the rich. Aristotle is aware that there is some such problem when he discusses the ways in which democracies ought to move toward a more equitable class composition of the assembly. He states:

> It is also in the interest of a democracy that the parts of the state should be represented in the deliberative body by an equal number of members, either elected for the purpose or appointed by

the use of the lot. It is also in its interest, when the members of the populace largely exceed the notables who have political experience, that payment for attendance at the assembly should not be given to all the citizens, but only to so many as will balance the number of the notables or, alternatively, that the lot should be used to eliminate the excess of ordinary citizens over the notables.[19]

While he notes two methods of limiting attendance, paying only a few, or selecting only a few, he does not suggest simply paying the poor less so that fewer will attend. It seems that treating payment as an economic incentive that could be adjusted to achieve the desired level of turnout had not occurred to him.

Yet the practical effects of different levels of incentives had already been observed and noted. In the *Constitution of Athens* Aristotle records that Pericles instituted pay for the judges and that "some people blame him on this account and say that the courts deteriorated, since after that it was always the common men rather than the better men who were eager to participate in drawing the lot for duty in the law courts."[20] Furthermore, the consequence of increasing the incentives were not unnoticed, at least in the assembly. Again in the *Constitution of Athens* Aristotle observes that with the restoration of democracy at the end of the Peloponnesian War political leaders were acquainted with the incentive problem. "At first, they refused to allow payment for attendance at the Assembly of the People. But when the people did not come and the Prytanes had tried many things to induce the people to attend for the sake of ratification of proposals by their vote, Agyrrhius first introduced a fee of one obol; afterwards, Heracleides of Clazomenae, with the surname 'King,' a fee to two obols; and then again Agyrrhius a fee of three obols."[21] Assuming that the higher payments were not simply a form of public relief, or a way of bribing the poor, then we can account for higher payments as ways of inducing more people to attend.

Most of Aristotle's examples of incentive rules are class specific, applying to only one class and not to the entire citizen body. Yet to analyze the way in which incentives, and disincentives, work it is important to realize that it is the incidence of incentives that counts; whether or not the rule applies only to the rich or only to the poor is less important than its differential class impact. We might start by focusing on one very interesting constitutional rule that does not depend on wealth distinctions for its formal implementation. This rule is, on the face of it, indifferent to social class; but in practice it is designed to discriminate against the poor and to insure the domination of the rich. This rule is listed under the devices used by the rich to give the poor illusory rights. "In some states a different device is adopted in regard to attendance at the assembly and the law courts. All who have registered themselves may attend; those who fail to attend after registration are heavily fined. Here the intention is to stop men from registering, through fear of the fines they may incur, and ultimately to stop them from attending the courts and assembly as a result of their failure to register."[22] This type of rule is, in effect, a form of poll tax. If everyone is permitted to register but those who register are fined if they do not attend, we can analyze the rule in the following way. Assume that the fine is one hundred obols for missing a meeting, and there is a one in ten chance that anyone who registers may not be able to attend after he registers. Then, in effect, people are being taxed ten obols for the privilege of attending. That is to say, everyone who registers assumes the risk (whatever it happens to be) of not being able to attend; if the risk is the same for all (to simplify things), then everyone who registers, at the time of registering, is forced to pay the same probabilistic tax.

This rule is fundamentally different from one that simply excludes the poor from registering and attending. It is on the face of it universalistic; but because it is a flat tax it is a greater disincentive to the poor than to the rich and hence enhances the power of the latter. The fine could be set so that, in practice, it turns out that the rich always have a majority.

Within the system of formal equality and open offices, there are two broad classes of rules that can rig the actual distribution of political power. These may be called incentive rules and disincentive rules. An incentive rule is one that creates more participation than would otherwise be the case, an example would be a rule paying people to come to an assembly. A disincentive rule would be one taxing all for the privilege of participating. Each of these two different classes of rules may, in turn, employ two different devices for implementation, which I shall call positive and negative sanctions. An incentive rule designed to create greater participation can be written with positive sanctions or negative sanctions; an example of the former is one in which everybody is paid to vote (a positive sanction) and of the latter one in which everyone is fined for not voting (a neg-

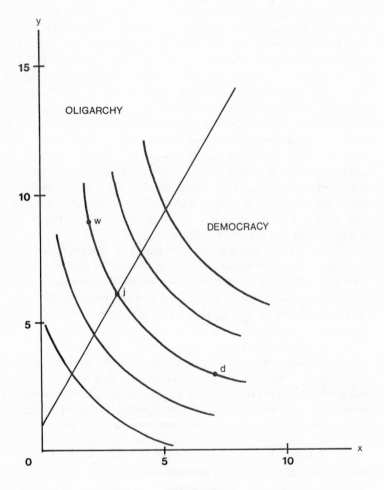

FIGURE 1

ative sanction). Finally, a rule may be uniform or class specific. That same incentive rule could also be written in a class-specific way, so that only the rich are fined or only the poor are paid.

Given this scheme, Artistole's compromise rule—"pay the poor and fine the rich"—is an example of a class-specific, incentive rule with positive sanctions for the poor and negative sanctions for the rich. If we were not concerned with turnout, with the amount of participation, but only with the proportional fairness of the mixture, we could write a disincentive rule: pay the poor for staying away and tax the rich for participating. The actual concrete compromise, the expected class composition of an assembly, for example, depends most crucially on the amount of incentives given to each class.

This can be seen by considering Figure 1 which models Aristotle's compromise rule. The X-axis represents increasing payments to the poor, the Y-axis increasing fines for the rich. The indifference curves are equal participation rates. The points d, j, and w are different combinations of fines and payments; d is a seven-obol payment to the poor and a three-obol fine for the rich, and so on. While the same number of people would turn out under the rule that paid the poor seven obols and fined the rich three obols (point d) as under the rule that paid the poor two obols and fined the rich nine obols (point w), the class makeup of the resultant assembly would be very different; under the first rule we would have a rather democratic assembly, and under the other a much more oligarchical one. What has to be negotiated in the compromise is not only the compromise rule but the values of the positive and negative sanctions. There may be a justice point, j, that would be thought equitable (say one that resulted in approximately equal class participation). In any case, Aristotle's equitable compromise rule needs to be supplemented in some way in order to allow us to determine the range of a just compromise; to put it another way, Aristotle's suggestion gives us the groundwork for a negotiated compromise, but it does not, by itself, provide a solution. Simply to combine rules from two opposing political systems is not sufficient to generate an equitable compromise; it is too formalistic unless we appreciate the underlying dynamics of the rules themselves. Once it is agreed that a compromise is desirable, then the terms must be hammered out.

Once we look at rules in this way we can see some interesting features that help explain the way rules are written. We have analyzed the registration and fine rule as a form of poll tax. This rule can be described as a universalistic disincentive rule with negative sanctions. All universalistic disincentive rules favor the rich whether they employ positive or negative sanctions; that is, it doesn't matter whether we tax everyone who votes or pay everyone to stay away; the effects on the distribution of political power are the same. Yet universalistic incentive rules have exactly the opposite effect, whether they employ positive or negative incentives. A rule that paid everyone the same amount to vote would favor the poor; a similar effect could be achieved by fining everyone who did not vote.

A poll tax is oligarchical and a poll fine is democratic, and this is not because one employs a fine and the other a tax or some such; it is because one is a universalistic disincentive rule and the other a universalistic incentive rule. The rules work this way simply because the poor are more responsive to sanctions, whether positive or negative, than are the rich. More poor people than rich people would change their behavior for one dollar or obol; to effect the same proportionate change in class behavior for the rich would require greater positive or negative sanctions. While this argument is illustrated by monetary sanctions, I believe it can be generalized to explain the differential effects on behavior of other forms of sanctions.

We can also understand why the rich would have a class-specific incentive rule that employed negative rather than positive sanctions. Assume that the rule is one that fines the rich ten obols for not attending the assembly and this turns out 70 percent of the rich. Since the poor are neither paid to attend nor fined for not attending, this is sufficient for the purpose of holding on to political power and making public policy decisions for the benefit of the rich. The poor are given their rights, but the rich retain their power. The same proportionate turnout of the rich could be achieved by making a rule that the rich would be paid, say, fifteen obols each for attending, and the poor would be paid nothing at all. Under this scheme the rich would still retain power, but the rule would seem grossly unfair. No one would be fooled by that rule.

The rule that fines the rich could be portrayed as one that manifests many political virtues; it recognizes the principle of equal voting and of equal political rights. Furthermore, it recognizes the moral duty of all to participate in the common decisions by introducing a fine for those who refuse to perform their civic duty; yet it is also fair and just to those who are too poor to pay the fine. A rational oligarch would, of course, recognize that the risk of paying a fine and the time spent in politics is more than compensated for by the goods that flow from the exercise of political power. A rule that pays the rich for participating and gives the poor nothing is so unfair on the face of it, so obviously a result of a rapacious oligarchical regime, that it would have very little to recommend it politically.

I hope that my remarks on incentive and disincentive rules show the usefulness of applying elementary techniques of microeconomic analysis to the problem of analyzing constitutional rules. This is intended as an extension and generalization of one part of Aristotle's theory of compromise. It is impossible in a short paper to explore all the complexities and subtleties of his treatment of appointment rules and selection rules. Yet, whatever the fascination of formal analysis, such analysis receives its true significance by placing the discussion in its proper setting. Aristotle demonstrates how constitutional rules are used to achieve various distributions of political power, but by embedding technical political science issues within the context of a general philosophical discussion of the nature of distributive justice he provides a perspective often lacking the modern political science.

Justice for Aristotle is not simply an abstract ideal but a practical political problem rooted in the reality of class conflict and competing political claims. Justice must promote the common interest, but the common interest requires that each class be willing to accept the fact that its own interests as well as the true concept of distributive justice requires compromise. He attempts to reconcile moral claims and arguments from self-interest by presenting an overall political theory that is intended as a guide for political practice. For Aristotle, compromise is not incompatible with the principles of justice, but rather true justice requires a principled compromise.

NOTES

1. Aristotle, *The Politics of Aristotle*, ed. and trans. Ernest Barker (New York: Oxford University Press, 1974), p. 133.
2. *Ibid.*, p. 117.
3. *Ibid.*
4. *Ibid.*, p. 118. See also p. 132 for a further account of the various claims to distribute political office.
5. *Ibid.*, p. 129.
6. *Ibid.*, p. 131.
7. *Ibid.*, p. 41.
8. *Ibid.*

9. *Ibid.*, p. 204.
10. *Ibid.*, p. 206.
11. *Ibid.*, p. 180.
12. *Ibid.*, pp. 180-81.
13. *Ibid.*, p. 182.
14. *Ibid.*, p. 177.
15. *Ibid.*, p. 178.
16. *Ibid.*, p. 222.
17. *Ibid.*, pp. 186-87.
18. *Ibid.*, p. 187.
19. *Ibid.*, p. 192.
20. Aristotle, *The Constitution of Athens,* trans. Kurt von Fritz and Ernest Kapp (New York: Hafner, 1964), p. 98.
21. *Ibid.*, p. 114.
22. Aristotle, *The Politics of Aristotle,* pp. 196-97.

5

MEDIATION VERSUS COMPROMISE IN HEGEL

GEORGE ARMSTRONG KELLY

"Compromise" is a word that sits askew in the Hegelian vocabulary. In the first place, Hegel was an *uncompromising* philosopher: his method deals with conflictual propositions, and his aim is to encompass them in a philosophical understanding that is unyielding in its claim to produce the truth of method and reason and no mere sum or balancing of subjective wills. As he writes of certain predecessors: "Unfortunately . . . as Fichte did later, [Rousseau] takes the will only in a determinate form as the invididual will, and he regards the individual will not as the absolutely rational element in the will, but only as the 'general will' which proceeds out of this individual will as out of a conscious will. The result is that he reduces the union of individuals in the state to a contract and therefore to something based on their arbitrary wills, their opinion, and their capriciously given consent . . ."[1] Whether or not Hegel imparts justice to Fichte and Rousseau in this passage, his aim is clear: to strike no bargains with transient or individual preferences, but to deal in the currency of reason's demands.

Nor is the Hegelian will placid or self-evident as it seeks its union with reality; it issues from an intensity of combat waged within as well as between willing subjects. In another striking passage he writes: "I am the struggle [i.e., as universal subject caught between the extremes of personal finitude and spiritual infinity], for this struggle is a conflict defined not by the indifference of the two sides in their distinction, but by their being bound together in one entity. I am not one of the fighters locked in battle, but both, and I am the struggle itself. I am fire and water."[2]

As Charles Taylor puts it, commenting on Hegel's intellectual position — his bridge between rationalism and Romanticism — "he stood out in his *uncompromising* [my italics] attempt to think through the requirements of [his] synthesis with surprising rigour and a quite impressive thoroughness."[3] These and numerous other texts and commentaries would suggest that Hegel is a most unlikely philosophical guide to the spirit of compromise in politics, given the undoubted fact that his practical philosophy is grounded in his total metaphysics and intended to "solve" and not "settle" political issues, to use Bertrand de Jouvenel's apt distinction.[4]

Yet, in the second place, there is a long line of interpretation beginning with Hegel's profligate pupils, the Young Hegelians, and extending into the present not only by way of their intellectual successors but also through a very distinct tradition of liberal and individualist thought — for example, Henri Michel's *L'Idée de l'état* (1890) and L. T. Hobhouse's *The Metaphysical Theory of the State* (1918) — which castigates Hegel as a consummate compromiser, a thinker grown old and fearful who, in his single-minded search for fixed moorings of totality, was willing to bargain away man's true freedom and self-transcendence for the value of political order and the supremacy of the powers that be. For both these traditions, Hegelian "compromise" (if it is permissible to use the term) is a dirty word. For the first, Hegel has emasculated his own dialectic (with its never ending power of criticism and negation) by virtue of his arrogant system, which halts at the Rubicon of ideology or partial truth. For the second, whose thinking runs not along the dialectic-system axis, but along the freedom-constraint axis, Hegel's truth is scarcely "partial" enough. He has simply ignored or suppressed acknowledgment of the virtuous powers of man to become his own master in combat against arbitrary political authority. In the one case, Hegel stands accused of a theological manipulation, swapping subject (men) with predicate (spirit). In the other, the "concrete" state is seen as a control incompatible with natural human rights and choice, and with free arbitration.

Avoiding polemics and unscrutinized advocacies of the good life, can we see Hegel simultaneously as the *uncompromising* philosopher *and* as the philosopher who *compromises* man's essence and vocation, especially given the fact that "compromise" is not a political term used or sanctioned by Hegel?[5] Or instead, might it be permissible to defend Hegel against charges of invidious compromise and yet see him as the "reasonable" exponent of a politics of conciliation?

The reader will already suspect that a further exploration of these problems might result in a linguistic tour de force. Among political terms in currency, "compromise" is obviously a good example of what Hobbes called an "inconstant signification": its use-value is complicated by our preferences, *what we are trying to say or prove.*[6] For example, it may be good to know *how* and *when* to compromise — this may even be the political *ars artium* — but it is probably not good to compromise one's standards and values away, to commit "the treason of the intellectuals." But the question is not, I think, in essence the meaning of "compromise" or how it might be used in the overlapping vocabularies of modern political science. It carries into more lasting matters of political regulation and satisfaction. Still, a preliminary to these issues will necessarily be a discussion of how we intend the term "compromise."

In my ensuing remarks I would like to put aside all reference to the direct German (now worldwide) legacy of Hegelianism — that is, "anthropological humanism," "historical materialism," "Young Hegelianism," "Hegelo-Marxism," "critical theory," and the like. In America we tend to understand "compromise" in a way alien to these intellectual developments (although certainly fair game for their critique). Trading on the license of an essayist, and having only limited space, I shall confront Hegel's position, insofar as possible, only with the Anglo-Saxon notion. This means that the pedigree of "ideas" is largely forsworn; I shall neither accuse nor defend Hegel's infidelity to the expectations of his own epigoni — those writers who thought in and criticized his categories.[7]

In the Anglo-Saxon lexicon, "compromise" is basically a far more positive word in politics than it could have been for Hegel, or indeed for any writer imbued with rationalist metaphysics or the "spirit of system." English politics — rooted in a nexus of feudal and estate obligations and later in the practice of parliamentary government — proceeded by a series of compromises. The U.S. Constitution of 1787 was a vast and genial compromise between the states and the central power, the states themselves, and existing economic interests. More than once — for example, in 1820, 1850, and 1877 — the word has expressed a reality of our political history.

Essentially, for us, compromise means that politically interested groups or parties have contended, seriously but not fatally, in a relatively free market with their various strengths of argument and social power in order to reach a transient settlement that is, for a time, ac-

ceptable to most, though maximally pleasing to none.[8] This procedure is validated by an epistemology that is suspicious of all absolute
truth and regards a man's (or a society's) exposure to a wide variety of
views on reality as the *summum bonum* of education. Renan wrote of
a "plébiscite de tous les jours." Compromise in a pluralistic society
must obviously extend over more than a day's time; it needs, especially in foreign relations, to be prolonged for many years, becoming
"consensus." And yet, among us, it is always susceptible to the buffet-
ing of active political forces and subject to revisions reflecting their
relative strengths.

But political compromise cannot merely be a mechanistically determined vector of social pressures achieved through and by the
"countervailing" powers of politics. Though the accepted means of
compromise (inertia, arbitration, logrolling, etc.) often seem mechanical— a kind of quantitative hard bargaining superseding the
law of the jungle or, at very least, the "state of nature"—they require
also a different, more fundamental and cohesive, strength. They require procedural agreement—or a connivance passing for such.[9] But
the procedures, or "rules of society," themselves rest on a broad value
consensus regarding the permissible and the impermissible, the desirable and the undesirable: a party system in which there are no major
ghettos and no great shocks to the state caused by the alternance of
government and opposition; a facility of communication between labor, management, administration, and consumers; and a social polity adequately alert to the shifting demands and composition of its
major constituent groups. If the values supporting the procedures are
not present, the procedures alone will certainly fail to produce compromise, as the lesson of so many "new nations" has taught us.

This is not to say that the habit of compromise is a plateau that experienced modern states axiomatically reach once and for all. Or to
put it another way, a "disintegration theory" of politics is the substantial shadow of the optimism of "integration theories," as certain
contemporary examples among the "mature" Western polities show
us. Even in complex, relatively stable societies profound criticisms
can be launched against "establishments" that sustain the spirit of
compromise: for compromise, sometimes praised as civilized and rational, can also be seen as prejudiced and deceitful.[10] In any society
where most people are functionally literate and susceptible to being
mobilized on behalf of real or imagined grievances, the reliance on
accustomed ways of compromise can be jeopardized. Populations

may tacitly accept, and even internalize, the benefits of, say, the market or representative government. But their allegiance, especially given unforeseen shocks of economic dislocation, is conditional. Despite the power of intellectual propaganda — and sometimes because of it — populations living in "privileged" societies have not learned once and for all, especially when the shoe starts to pinch and a different drumbeat reaches their ears, to believe unflinchingly in the benevolence of the "system" or in the moral authority of the magistrates.[11] Politics, then, need not always be pluralistic compromise in "mature" societies: it can also be the ignorant right to say no, or to opt out, and it is the deduced privilege to cause damage to the "welfare of all," no matter how powerful may be the arguments against unacceptable (i.e., counterproductive) forms of social sabotage. Coherent countervalues are not necessary: delinquency can undermine instrumentally valid measures of compromise.

The French language clarifies this anomaly better than our own. French has the word *compromis,* which more or less expresses the settlement of differences within a commonly understood and acceptable framework. It also has the word *compromission,* applied frequently to dramas of the boudoir, which means a fatal sacrifice of one's virtue, or a "sell out," certainly not a trade-off. When it is said, to return to an earlier theme, that Hegel's philosophy "compromises" his dialectic, the charge is being made that he has committed a *compromission.* We have not yet made clear whether Hegel's achievement leads toward a political *compromis,* consonant with the will or genius of society *(Volksgeist),* although the critics of Hegel would probably retort here that his *compromis* was founded either on a false consciousness or on a solution negligent of legitimate rights.

In English, similarly, without the French distinction, we manipulate the word "compromise." If we use it in the passive or reflexive — for example, "The code has been compromised" or "Henry compromised himself" — we usually intend blame or criticism, at best distress. If we use the word actively, we may intend either praise or blame ("He compromised his position for the sake of his friends" or "He compromised his beliefs for expediency"). But, for the most part, when "compromise" is a substantive, unless modified by an unfavorable adjective, the usage is positive ("They reached a compromise after much give-and-take"; "He rejected the compromise offered by the other side," etc.).

"Compromise" is at least on the edge of being a virtue in Anglo-

Saxon discourse. It does not solve the world's problems once and for all, but it at least provides for the world's ongoingness. It permits us to rise the morning after knowing that certain of our complaints have been met, that the garbage will be taken, that the police will not strike, that a minority group will not reach its boiling point. Politics is, after all, the art of the possible; compromise might seem to be its code of manners. Compromise avoids disgrace, and it may reconcile. A certain sense of the worth and potential of compromise helped to occasion the shift of groups of revolutionary Marxists toward social democracy. In politics compromise seems to have links with the ancient value of prudence, combining moderation with the true art of the stateman in a way less elegant but more productive than the axiomatic principles of pure reason, which may lead to intractable conflict.

Still, it does not require much sophistication to see that a compromise tolerable in the present can lay precedents and create obligations that will defy the imagination of the future to fulfill, making for predictable rancor as the once settled present becomes a disowned past. In recent times, in the United States, issues tended to be "settled" if not "solved" by the techniques of pluralism, the bargaining of interest groups for shares of the existing national product. In pluralism, as Lowi writes, "bargaining becomes the single alternative to violence and coercion in industrial society. By definition, if the system is stable and peaceful it proves the self-regulative character of pluralism."[12] But, through "creating a discontinuity between the political world and the socioeconomic world," as the same author points out, a pluralist society also brings about "*a discontinuity between politics and government.*"[13] In compromise, groups tend to be "accommodated, not regulated." Thus the rectitude of formal government may fall victim to the process of compromise while politics becomes the pliable servant of special interests or, conceivably, the hostage of mobilized grievances.

All of the foregoing is quite alien to Hegel's design for politics, although it is remarkable how much of it can be accounted for in his theory of the modern state. Since Hegel's formal theory of politics is inseparable from other basic categories of "practical reason" such as law and morality, and since even this ensemble depends for its grounding on a metaphysical structure of reality and logic, we are compelled to make some reference to the bedrock.[14] The epistemology here is scarcely the same as the one underlying pluralistic compromise. The primary tools of Hegelian philosophy are the "concept"

(Begriff) and "dialectical reason" *(Vernunft).*

Briefly put, an entity of knowledge is fully conceptualized *(begriffen)* when it is comprehended in both its positive and negative moments and in their reciprocal realization (the negation of the positive and, in turn, its negation). This process involves not just a supersession of simple meaning but its recapturing at a higher level; not just an intellectual exercise upon the object but an interpenetration of subject and object, resulting in the reappropriation of the object by the subject in a way that is no longer merely abstract or external. *Begriff* is, among other things, the dialectical resolution of the syllogism, "the middle term between Being and Essence, between the immediately given and reflection."[15]

Vernunft is the real motion of the world, idealistically comprehended. It is implicit in all being, but it must affirm its appearance and become relevant to facts of consciousness. It is "the certainty of being all reality."[16] But it, too, is a developmental concept: it combines the oppositely manifested elements of reality, ridding it of all abstraction.[17] It is not just a regulative set of categories of "Ideas" that the mind delivers to sense perception for the purpose of intelligibility. But only mind can activate the quality of reality in things so as to combine their essence with their process. That is why all philosophy is "idealism." Hegel sharply opposed *Vernunft* to *Verstand* (scientific or causal cognition), thereby placing the rational development of the spirit above an external *ratio naturae,* "humanizing" (or, according to some readings, "theologizing") the world of phenomena, spiritualizing the *kosmos* and giving it a destiny and ultimate rational purpose.

This philosophical digression has taken us perilously far from the question of compromise; hopefully, the pathway back will be an interesting, if rocky, road. There is no hint of compromise in the procedures of the Hegelian dialectic (which, it will be recalled, is intended not as an imperative but as a hard-won description of reality), except in the banal sense that the "compromises" of world history are no doubt assorted and retained in the great Hegelian sweep. (Even if Hegel can be accused of forcing historiography into patterns or, as Hayden White would say, an "emplotment,"[18] he does not discard the *res gestae* with an utter want of discrimination.) The rationale of the world is basically created by great collisions of intractible values, not by "smoke-filled rooms," "poker playing," or "splitting the difference."

But (to remain for a few moments on the philosophical plane)

there is, imbedded in the dialectic, a Hegelian surrogate for compromise (or suspension of conflict) called "mediation" *(Vermittlung)*.
The reach of this term should not be misidentified. In pluralistic bargaining a "mediator" is often appointed, by mutual agreement or by
statute, to help conflicting parties reach a settlement. Sometimes
such mediation is considered to be binding. But this is not precisely
the scenario that Hegelian philosophy intends. For Hegel, mediation
does not bespeak arbitration (cf. "arbitrary") or compromise, as the
concept was used earlier, but rather a higher and necessary reconciliation. Nor are mediators "appointed"; mediation is a process that is
"there" in the logic of development, uniting subject with substance,
or rather the process by which the subject becomes true substance:
"that being or that immediacy which does not leave mediation outside itself but which is mediation itself."[19] The most dramatic mediation of Western culture (which Hegel took it upon himself to analyze
and explain) is that between the "substantial" demands of a political
life in common—which Hegel and many other German intellectuals
inputed to Greek antiquity—and the modern principle of subjective
will, developed from the time of Socrates on and reaching its most
expansive shape in liberal, early capitalist society. According to this
doctrine, the political order is subject to society and can be cast in
doubt by individual moral grievances. For Hegel, the mediation con-
sisted in a reflective philosophical understanding of all culture; it is
beyond the limits of this essay to indicate how. We are concerned
here only with the idea and function of "mediation."

In Hegel's logic, an entity—any object of consciousness—is, in its
most impoverished state, "immediate" *(unmittelbar)*. It is directly
perceived and accounted for, but not thought through. The immediacy of a tree in my orchard or of the political community appre-
hended as something merely external to my existence would qualify
equally. However, when dialectical reason commences to operate on
the tree (it is *my* tree, I planted it, I pruned it, it gives me shade, it
bears fruit, etc.) or on the state (I belong in *this* state and no other, it
manifests my will, it protects me and I give it loyalty, etc.), neither
remains an immediate object of perception. My consciousness and
my destiny become mixed with theirs reciprocally *(Wechselwir-
kung)*.[20] This is a progress toward my conceptualization of the world
and the concreteness of the world's reality. Finally, when there are no
alien boundaries between the object and consciousness (be it tree or
state) and the object is incorporated in my spiritual horizon, that ob-

ject has been mediated *(vermittelt):* its contradictions and alienness have been resolved in a higher reason and purpose. "Immediacy" is most obvious in the mechanical object;[21] it is overcome in the Idea. However, like all other concepts, the Idea itself has its unrealized state, which is mere undifferentiated life.[22] And the Idea (as abstract) is powerless as a mere notion, unless it appears in the world. Ultimately (for our purposes), the Idea can be collectively recovered in "mediated" form through the purification of political thought, in an ethical *(sittlich)* commonwealth.[23]

Before making special reference to the *Philosophy of Right* we can summarize as follows. Compromise is not an aspect of the Hegelian method. Without rejecting the project of previous philosophies, Hegel "totalizes" them architecturally rather than distributing them by compromise. Similarly, his conception of the state and political life depends neither on a compromise of past theories nor, as we shall see, on a compromise of the wills of the participant groups in the state. Yet Hegel does not deny that these wills have their purpose and their "right," nor does he claim that they should be stifled in a state that mediates between a "beautiful" but superseded antiquity and the centrifugal subjective forces unleashed in postclassical and Christian civilization. The clues of explanation are found chiefly in Hegel's words *unmittelbar* and *vermittelt.*

As applied to a total political conception, the Greek polis was *unmittelbar,* but also "substantial" and *sittlich.* Hegel also uses *unmittelbar* to apply to the theories of the state advanced by his natural rights predecessors, from Hobbes and Spinoza to Fichte. In such a conception the state is merely a "civil society," held together by arbitrary consent and dissoluble by the wills of its individual members. It resembles a voluntary organization and is unable to grant universal rights or demand universal duties unless it should be in the interest of all to pursue them.[24] By contrast, the state that Hegel philosophizes, while not denying the necessary existence and benefits of civil society (the *bürgerliche Gesellschaft* of property owners, contract makers, and rights-bearing individuals), is "rich" and "concrete," a universal family, *vermittelt* because modern thought is able to rationalize its articulated organs as part of a community.[25] In the *Phenomenology of Spirit,* where references to the modern state are conspicuously absent,[26] there is nevertheless the key sentence: "It is the nature of humanity to struggle for agreement with others, and humanity exists only in the accomplished community of consciousness."[27] "Struggle

for agreement"—a curious turn of phrase! But agreement and community cannot be effortless—history has proved this. If such a struggle is the prelude to "compromise," it is certainly not the recompro-
mising of the same old storehouse of wills and interests conducted by
eternally fixed procedures.

When Hegel eventually consolidated his thoughts on the state in
the *Philosophy of Right,* his systematic account of the "struggle for
agreement" and the "community of consciousness" was very much
conditioned by his acknowledgment of "the modern principle of subjectivity." Aside from his meticulous dissection of (quasi-Kantian)
"morality," the accommodation for subjectivity arises in such diverse
places as Hegel's depiction of civil society, his justification of a hereditary monarch, and his discussion of public opinion.[28] The attitude is
always bittersweet: one the one hand, "subjectivity," masking *my*
truth as the view of conduct which should be universally held, leads
to triviality, hypocrisy, error, and the sabotage of both common cus-
tom and common rationality; on the other hand, it is part and parcel
of the realization of freedom within the speculative development of
Christian civilization. Where the subjectivity of *persons* (abstract
right), of *individuals* (morality), of situated or *concrete persons* (civil
society), and of *rulers* (the constitutional monarch) has become the
content of modern politics, one cannot simply throw up his hands
and yearn for a simpler and "immediate" order or solidarity (the
polis). In a subjective culture conducive to idiosyncrasy and sectari-
anism Hegel was, to say the least, uncomfortable, and his response
was sometimes scathing. However, his philosophical design, which
involved him not only in an acceptance but a justification of the
world, committed him, against his aesthetic preferences, to rationalize the benefits of the new principle.

If "subjectivity" was the mode of conflict of human needs, desires,
and moral stances, it had also to be seen as the carrier of an as yet incomplete liberty requiring fulfillment under an evolving control: the
philosophical state in its full armature of being and becoming, unity
and diversity. Such a strategy involves a method of mastery that entails both struggle and conciliation. Whether or not we wish to call
that conciliation compromise depends on how we use the term. Interest-group bargaining cannot be the centerpiece. Hegel's instinct was
to locate basic human solidarity in organically developed units of intimate social commerce: the family, the polis, the primitive church,
popular religions, corporative work communities, and so on. Adam

Smith's division of labor, the world of profit making, the economic sphere of social combat were all unattractive. Yet Hegel's intellect brought him to terms with that world in the interest of speculative honesty.

Social contradictions coalesced in the arena of *bürgerliche Gesellschaft*. If subjectivity, first associated with abstractly posited persons and then, somewhat later, with the particular wills of groups destined to certain economic tasks in society, was rampant, it was the system in which it operated that struck Hegel as both deplorable and fruitful. No less than Marx, Hegel saw civil society as a uniquely modern development based on contract, exchange of goods for money, and the accumulation of capital, a product of the cities and not of the countryside. But, with a greater power of cultural comprehension, he saw it also as the completion of a centuries-old development of "subjectivity," a dense interaction of willing or desiring subjects. Why had civil society produced the "concrete person"? Because, according to Hegel, it had driven him not only into his professional niche but into interdependence with others.[29] To be "concrete" in Hegel's terminology means to be situated in the social system, conceivably as the member of a "corporation," mediate between the intimacy of the family and the extensive unity of the state.

Civil society might be described as the "objectification" or "universalization" of the subjective drive of Western culture. It has its dark underside. As the reservoir of "concrete persons," it is a "totality of wants and a mixture of physical necessity."[30] Moreover, it "affords a spectacle of extravagance and want as well as the physical and ethical degeneration common to them both."[31] On the other hand, civil society *universalizes* these capricious tendencies into a system of mutual dependence: "Each establishes himself and finds satisfaction by means of the others . . ."[32] This is the *external* (related to *Verstand*) condition of the common life: "Mind becomes at home with itself within this pure externality. There, then, mind's freedom is existent and mind becomes objective to itself in this element which is implicitly inimical to mind's appointed end, freedom.. . ."[33] We read also: "subjective self-seeking turns into the mediation of the particular through the universal, with the result that each man in earning, producing, and enjoying on his own account is *eo ipso* producing and earning for the enjoyment of everyone else."[34]

This is the familiar message of political economy, tempered to be sure by Hegel's pessimism about any axiomatic organization of individual social wills in a common benefit that transcends them. A gain of efficiency in society is not to be counterbalanced against a loss of morale and belongingness in its members. Yet in civil society individual freedom advances and becomes universalized. In part this occurs because Hegel concedes to civil society the mobile of education *(Bildung)*, described as a "hard struggle [note the word] against pure subjectivity of demeanour, against the immediacy of desire, against the empty subjectivity of feeling and the caprice of inclination. . ."[35] Education collides with the "immediacy" of the "system of needs." There is no ready resolution, except that Hegel planted in the context of civil society certain remedies needed to exalt its better members to "state-mindedness" or to a form of conscious behavior befitting the "universal class." Not only *Bildung* is in civil society, but the practical experience gained in the administration of the "corporations," mediate between activity as a *homo economicus* and the executive functions of the state. Similarly, a coercive agency of public authority *(Polizei)*, intended not only to protect against crime but to administer justice and oversee public works, is incorporated in civil society. When Hegel uses the phrase "public authority" it is not always simple to see where the state stops and civil society begins. No doubt this is a clue to the fact, resisted by some Hegel interpreters beginning with Marx,[36] that "state" and "civil society" are not simply posited against each other but are necessarily interpenetrating. Hegel finds reservoirs of will and solidarity, as well as institutions and personnel, in civil society that will serve the state's higher calling. Yet civil society is also the realm where the ethical order is "split into extremes and lost";[37] a "field in which the Understanding with its subjective aims and moral fancies vents its discontent and moral frustration";[38] and a *situs* where "universality is necessity only."[39]

Before passing on to Hegel's discussion of the state, we might well ponder whether there is some mode of compromise, as we previously used the term, that is transacted at the level of civil society. The answer would have to be along the following lines: (1) Individuals who are parts of civil society no doubt compromise in their private relations and as buyers, sellers, and producers through contract and exchange. (2) posited law enforces and legitimates private compromise by embodying the abstract right of *persons* (though some Hegel commentators argue that, for him, law is a rather lowly and barren category, it is actually the sine qua non of performance in society). "By taking the form of law," Hegel writes, "right steps into a determinate form of being."[40] And, "when we are dealing with human needs, it is only right as such which is steadfast."[41] But the adjudication of rights is not the compromise of group interests. (3) Corporations appear to strike compromises within their own local systems of regulation in order to "look after [their] own interest within [their] own sphere,"[42] but their possibilities of confrontation with one another — their "foreign policy" — goes undiscussed. (4) Within civil society, taken as a generality, rights and responsibilities tend to be bargained: "Civil society is . . . the tremendous power which draws men into itself and claims from them that they work for it, owe everything to it, and do everything by its means. . . . Civil society must protect its members and defend their rights, while its rights impose duties on every one of its members."[43] This legalitarian language masks some ambiguity about the voluntary or enforced nature of the reciprocity. (5) Ultimately, in civil society an anonymous "universality" of exchange and production is created where compromise becomes a class issue and where esprit de corps binds one to "gaining recognition both in one's own eyes and in the eyes of others"[44] — a competition that must end in conciliation if it is not to end in deadly quarrel, a "struggle for recognition."

The capacities and functions of the state raise additional possibilities. In introducing his discussion of the state, Hegel describes civil society as being "the phase of division."[45] By contrast, the state is "an external authority and the higher authority [of the family and civilsociety]," while also being "the end immanent within them [whose] strength lies in the unity of its own universal end and aim with the particular interest of individuals."[46] It therefore follows that the state encompasses and conciliates outstanding differences in society. Does it "compromise" them, or does it simply rule high-handedly? The guidelines of an answer are already prefigured in Hegel's discussion of civil society. The latter is apparently impotent to enact rightful solutions for the welfare of all:

The relations between external existents [i.e., private wills] fall into the infinite to the Understanding [*Verstand*]; there is, therefore, no inherent line of distinction between what is and what is not injurious, even where crime is concerned, or between what is and what is not suspicious, or between what is to be forbidden or subjected to supervision and what is to be exempt from prohibition, from surveillance and suspicion, from inquiry and the demand to render an account of itself.[47]

As Hegel concludes in his next paragraph, "universal activites and organizations of general utility call for the oversight and care of the public authority."[48] It is apparent from the progress of the argument that Hegel draws the sphere of the state's oversight a good deal wider than, say, Adam Smith, in Book V of *The Wealth of Nations:* "the differing interests of producers and consumers may come into collision with each other; and although a fair balance between them on the whole may be brought about automatically, still their adjustment also requires a control which stands above both and is consciously undertaken."[49] Paragraph 249 adds more evidence to this claim. Some interpretation is needed if we are to discover Hegel's complete intention. In the first place, these assertions furnish a prelude not just to the functions of the state but also those of the corporations, those local matrices from which state-mindedness is to emerge. This returns us to an earlier point where it was suggested that the Hegelian state has no fixed boundaries, rather that it has roots in the social reservoir. Second, it is clear from the passage just cited that Hegel regards such compromise as is within the capacity of society as largely "automatic" — the result, as Adam Ferguson once put it, of human action but not of human design. He counts on the state to add "conscious" wisdom to these settlements. This is entirely in keeping with Hegel's (to us) difficult notion of the state as a repository of wisdom, a wisdom mediated by philosophy and justified as rational.[50] The wisdom of the state is not axiomatic — bad states exist[51] — it depends specifically on: (1) a constitutional organization mediating unity and diversity and consonant with modern freedom; and (2) the enlightenment of its executants — its "universal class" — and their ability to translate the will of the culture into the will of the sovereign as incorporated in laws and decrees.

To the modern intelligence, the Hegelian solution may well seem defective for legitimate settlement of differences. In one aspect, Hegel is sympathetic because he regards the self-regulating claims — and the compromises — of liberal society as inadequate and thereby anticipates the travesties of Social Darwinism and the failures of interest-group pluralism. But, in another, Hegel's analysis appears flawed because his political mediation seems to have disagreeable elements of *force majeure,* what we might call hierarchical or vertical compromise. Such compromise assumes a valid state interest and will not only reposing above plural wills and capacities but embodying a "knowledge" that both the theory of ideology and the observation of deficient rectitude in public officials have taught us to distrust deeply.

Nevertheless, the problem remains. We could desire a state that helps us to compromise, and uses its impartial justice to this end, so as to relax the strains of the bargainers and forestall *compromission.* We may also find the "discontinuity between the political world and the socioeconomic world . . . between politics and government"[52] disturbing, and yearn for their fruitful reconciliation — not in utopia, but in "actuality." Hegel's statement of political rationality, which, not fortuitously, englobes the whole contrariety of Western culture, probes these issues. His account of community, law, and history raises man's mission from a "struggle for recognition" to a "struggle for agreement." Yet many will be instinctively hostile to a man who takes the world as it is, urges that it be subject to wisdom rather than whim, and who constantly attacks the liberal ideal of multiple moralities and life-styles with the words: "We play into each other's hands and so hang together. . . . The wisest thing here is to do as others do."[53] If we were truly wise, could compromise be anything other than conformity?

NOTES

1. G. W. F. Hegel, *The Philosophy of Right.* trans. T. M. Knox (Oxford: Oxford University Press, 1967), par. 258A, p. 157.

2. Hegel, *Vorlesungen über die Philosophie der Religion,* in H. Glockner ed., *Sämtliche Werke,* 26 volumes. (Struttgart: Frommann, Jubiläumsausgabe, 1927), 40 vol., 15, p. 80.

3. Charles Taylor, *Hegel* (Cambridge: At the University Press, 1975), p. 49.

4. Bertrand de Jouvenel, *The Pure Theory of Politics* (Cambridge: At the University Press, 1963), p. 189.

5. "Compromise" in our sense is difficult to render into German. Among the candidates we might cite are *Übereinkunft,* which has the basic meaning of "agreement" or "accord"; *Vertrag,* which means specifically "contract"; *Mithilfe,* usually rendered as (voluntary) "cooperating"; *Mitbestimmung,* "codetermination"; and *Kompromiss,* a loanword that often means "the state of being compromised." "Mediation" (Hegel's term, see ahead) is *Vermittlung.*

6. Thomas Hobbes, *Leviathan,* ed. Michael Oakeshott (New York: Collier Books, 1962), chap. 4, pp. 39-40.

7. See chap. 6 of George Armstrong Kelly, *Hegel's Retreat from Eleusis: Studies in Political Thought* (Princeton: Princeton University Press, 1978).

8. Cf. Joseph Kraft in the *Boston Globe*, April 25, 1977: "the secret of congressional leadership lies in accommodating the rival lobbies. Compromise is its essence."

9. Cf. F. A. Hayek, *Law, Legislation and Liberty;* vol. 2, *The Mirage of Social Justice* (London: Routledge and Kegan Paul, 1976), p. 15: "Our whole conception of justice rests on the belief that different views about particulars are capable of being settled by the discovery of rules that, once they are stated, command general assent." Hayek and, in a different way, Michael Oakeshott are the most dogmatic proponents of prescriptive proceduralism; cf. Oakeshott's *On Human Conduct* (London: Oxford University Press, 1975), pp. 130-58.

10. Cf. Robert Paul Wolff, *The Poverty of Liberalism* (Boston: Beacon Press, 1968), pp. 152-61; and William E. Connolly, *The Terms of Political Discourse* (Lexington, Mass.: Heath, 1974), pp. 48-53.

11. When accusations are made against "the system," it is often paradoxically true that what there was of "system" has sprung gaps or leaks. A coherently functioning "system" is rarely vulnerable or apologetic to its critics.

12. Theodore Lowi, *The End of Liberalism* (New York: W. W. Norton, 1969), p. 46.

13. Ibid., p. 48.

14. On this, see Raymond Plant, *Hegel* (London: Allen and Unwin, 1973), pp. 184ff.

15. Hegel, *Logik,* in Glockner, ed., *Sämtliche Werke,* vol. 5, p. 5.

16. Hegel, *The Phenomenology of Mind,* trans. J. Baillie (London: Oxford University Press, 1949), p. 276.

17. Ibid., pp. 279-80.

18. Hayden White, *Metahistory* (Baltimore and London: Johns Hopkins Press, 1975), pp. 123-31.

19. Preface to Hegel's *Phenomenology,* in Walter Kaufmann, *Hegel: Reinterpretations, Tests, and Commentary* (New York: Doubleday, 1965), p. 408.

20. Cf. Hegel, *Enzyklopädie der philosophischen Wissenschaften (1830),* ed. F. Nicolin and O. Pöggeler (Hamburg: Meiner, 1959), par. 155, pp. 147ff.

21. Ibid., par. 199, p. 175.

22. Ibid., par. 216, p. 185.

23. Ibid., pars. 552Aff., pp. 431ff.

24. Hegel, *Philosophy of Right,* par. 182Z, pp. 266-67.

25. Ibid., par. 260, pp. 160-61.

26. See Judith N. Shklar, *Freedom and Independence* (Cambridge: At the University Press, 1976), pp. 205-7, for comment.

27. Hegel, Preface to the *Phenomenology,* in Kaufmann, *Hegel,* p. 454.

28. Hegel, *Philosophy of Right,* par. 182, p. 122; par. 279, p. 181; par. 320, p. 208.
29. Ibid., par. 182, pp. 122-23.
30. Ibid.
31. Ibid., par. 185, p. 123.
32. Ibid., par. 182, p. 123.
33. Ibid., par. 187A, p. 125.
34. Ibid., par. 199, pp. 129-30.
35. Ibid., par. 187A, p. 125.
36. Karl Marx, *Critique of Hegel's Philosophy of Right,* ed. J. O'Malley (Cambridge: At the University Press, 1970), p. 72.
37. Hegel, *Philosophy of Right,* par. 184, p. 123.
38. Ibid., par. 189A, p. 127.
39. Ibid., par. 229Z, p. 275.
40. Ibid., par. 219, p. 140.
41. Ibid., par. 229Z, p. 275.
42. Ibid., par. 252, p. 152.
43. Ibid., par. 238Z, p. 276.
44. Ibid., par. 207, p. 133.
45. Ibid., par. 256A, p. 155.
46. Ibid., par. 261, p. 16¹.
47. Ibid., par. 234A, p. 146.
48. Ibid., par. 235, p. 147.
49. Ibid., par. 236, p. 147.
50. See ibid., par. 270, p. 165.
51. Ibid., par. 270Z, p. 283.
52. See note 12.
53. Hegel, *Philosophy of Right,* par. 270Z, p. 283.

6

MARXISM AND COMPROMISE:

A SPECULATION

PAUL THOMAS

Sink down in the slime,
Embrace the butcher.
But change the world: it needs it. . . .

> Bertolt Brecht, *The Measures Taken*

Do you? *Do* you?

> Karl Marx to H. M. Hyndman,
> on the latter's assertion that he grew more
> tolerant with age.

This is a particularly timely year for a discussion of "Marxism and Compromise." The term "compromise," thanks to the initiative of the Italian Communist party, has established itself within the official Marxist lexicon. The promulgation of the PCI's innovative doctrine of "historical compromise" *(compromesso storico)*[1] has provoked a good many searching questions, not all of which can be answered here. This essay is not primarily concerned with the pronounced tremors that the notion of "historical compromise," and the specter of Eurocommunism for which it stands, are causing, important though these reverberations may be. This essay concerns itself, rather, with what is raised by the adumbration of "historical compromise": it raises a host of basic problems about the theory and practice of Marxism that have been present for some time. To ask whether the PCI's recent policy initiative has (in a sense) compromised its standing and credentials as a Marxist party is to open up a line of inquiry with which we, as political theorists, ought to be concerned. It is the argument of this essay that the concept of "historical compromise" has deeper roots in the history of Marxism than might initially be supposed; that investigation of this concept helps us understand several important aspects of Marxist political theory and practice that for too long have been repressed; that the connection between Marxism and democracy might itself need reconsideration; and that the phenomenon of Eurocommunism, together with the compromise between communism and democracy it implies, is itself a belated expression at the *institutional* level of themes that had found expression, up till now, mainly in the *intellectual* history of Marxism. Because Eurocommunism is, in its way, the vindication of theory, its emergence, it is suggested, might prompt further reflection about the relation of theory to action in general.

HISTORICAL COMPROMISE

Few recent policies or political concepts have elicited in Italy as much comment and discussion, as many polemics and debates, as has "historical compromise." Central to most of the disputations it has evoked is the question of whether the actualization of this policy would mark the final triumph of Marxism in Italy, or whether its promulgation by the PCI provides definitive proof that the party, in accommodation itself to the existing liberal-bourgeois parliamentary system, has compromised itself as a Marxist party. Buried within this dispute is another, about means and ends: Does the PCI's unmistakable abandonment of the "classical" Leninist formula of the revolutionary seizure of power entail abandonment of its goal, the revolutionary transformation of Italian society?

These are not easy questions to answer; nor does this essay presume to answer all of them. Yet the record of what "historical compromise" has amounted to is clear enough. Since first adumbrating the need for "historical compromise" in 1973, the PCI has been softening what was once a hard-line, uncompromising opposition to successive Christian Democratic governments; it has moderated its once vicious anti-clerical polemics and has endeavored to reach agreement with

the Catholic parties on such issues as divorce and abortion legislation. At the same time, the PCI has repeatedly stressed its autonomy,
its independence from the Soviet Union, and has explicitly indicated
and reaffirmed its acceptance of a pluralistic political system, of fundamental freedoms and individual rights. It has offered reassurance
to noncommunist elements in Italian society about its proposals for
economic planning, social reform, and private property; it has argued for the acceleration of European economic integration and
dropped its objections to Italian membership in NATO. At the same
time, again, the "73 Articles" drawn up by the PCI's secretary general, Enrico Berlinguer, emphasize what the party has long been
stressing in practice — accommodation and persuasion rather than
dogmatic imposition, consensus rather than coercion, and a movement in the direction of "participatory" (as well as "parliamentary")
democracy that is being experimented with, and written about, in
Italy as elsewhere.

These shifts in policy have been accompanied by a reevaluation of
the basic rights and political liberties that have been won by bourgeois democracy. This reevaluation is, of course, common to all Eurocommunist movements, the most significant of which (the PCI; the
French PCF; and the Spanish PCE) have endured the experience of
the suppression of these rights during the fascist period. The reasons
for this reevaluation of democracy are, indeed, not hard to find.
Since the fateful Russian invasion of Czechoslovakia in 1968, Western European communists have been engaged in a critical analysis of
communism in the so-called people's democracies of Eastern Europe
from the Stalinist era to the present; they themselves are pointing to
the immense losses in personal and collective freedoms that accompanied the liquidation of political democracy there. Similarly, while
orthodox international communism has long decreed a moratorium
on all discussion of the topic, Western European communists have
begun to look back on the issues raised in and by the Twentieth Congress of the Communist Party of the Soviet Union (February 1956).
They have begun to engage in a serious and systematic study of the
causes and nature of Stalinism, together with its consequences for
communism and Marxism in the Soviet Union and elsewhere.

These reevaluations, taken in themselves, may not be, and should
not be, sufficient to dispel skepticism about whether the intentions of
the PCI, or of the Eurocommunists in general, are in fact honorable;
it is at least possible (if improbable) that even the shifts in policy con-

nected with these reevaluations of democracy amount to mere win-
dow dressing, to attempts to ingratiate by insinuation what is still a
"totalitarian" party with various European electorates. Prediction
about where these developments may all lead is, however, outside the
compass of this discussion; for our purposes, it is salutary to indicate,
not where policies and reevaluations might lead in an uncertain future, but rather what they have already presupposed. They are based
upon a modicum of free inquiry, which is itself connected with the
newly decentered character of the communist world; Moscow can no
longer be regarded as the single, fixed center of communist orthodoxy, a centre authoritatively charged with the task of final settlement of basic doctrinal questions. It is important to the argument
advanced here that this very lack of a fixed doctrinal center has long
characterized *theoretical* work among Marxists. Eurocommunism is
indeed best regarded not as a sudden, unprecedented development,
but as one that has its roots in the history of Marxist *theory*.

To establish these claims we must first take our bearings. If, following John Morley's *On Compromise*, we are to believe that "the
disciples of the relative may afford to compromise, the disciples of
the absolute, never," how can we avoid depicting Marxists in general
terms as "disciples of the absolute" if indeed this is the way they have
seen, and presented, themselves? And is it not the case that because
of this discipleship Marxists emerge by definition not only as reluctant to compromise but as actually incapable of compromising? For
on such a view the Italian communists may appear to make concessions, to surrender principles for the sake of coming to terms. They
may even act as though "compromise" in this sense of the word is indeed "the essence of politics" Macaulay believed it to be. They may
appear to compromise their deepest beliefs, their most tenaciously
held commitments; yet these very moves may belie their sincerity.
(Lenin himself once observed that there is no such thing as a sincer-
ometer.) It may be legitimate, then, to invoke the remainder of Macaulay's celebrated maxim, that "logic admits of no compromise"; for
is logic not inscribed, for the Marxist, in the process of history itself?

This question can be answered in more than one way. What *compromesso storico* means to Italian party theoreticians is straightforward enough. It means a coming to terms, an adjustment between
two points of view that is called forth by the Italian political predicament. Whether or not such an adjustment would be no more than
provisional, tactical, and ultimately insincere is one bone of conten-

tion; and whether it entails a sharp and indeed demeaning departure from principle is another. The accusation made about "historical compromise" by communist parties more orthodox than the Italian is that in coming to terms with its erstwhile "class enemies" it has called its integrity into question. The departure from principle involved in such acts of accommodation, it is held, demeans and discredits Italian communism; indeed, the PCI's recent maneuvers on this view amount to an abject surrender of everything that is supposed to distinguish it from other parties on the Italian political spectrum.

However, 'it is striking that accusations that the PCI's "historical compromise" is a sham, a smokescreen concealing the ever present threat of a Leninist *coup d'état,* conspicuously do not proceed from the same source. Official pronouncements of the Communist party of the Soviet Union have expressed grave misgivings about the likelihood of independent communist participation in Western governments. These misgivings are best interpreted as a back-handed tribute to the power of Eurocommunist ideas. The emergence of "socialism with a human face" incorporating respect for basic liberal-bourgeois freedoms might have considerable, and unwelcome, political repercussions in the "people's democracies" of Eastern Europe or even inside the Soviet Union itself. The CPSU's markedly defensive reaction to events outside its shrunken sphere of influence seem to indicate that official international communism, despite its geopolitical pretensions, is faced with as momentous a split as that dividing Moscow from Peking in the early 1960s. The orthodoxy is disaggregated. The CPSU is no longer even able to convene a conference of Western European communist parties that would support its views. Its time-honored remedy of encouraging splits in uppity national parties that display too much independence could no longer be carried out without alienating public opinion in the countries concerned. International communism is a monolith that has cracked.

What were once hallmarks of the international communist movement, and are no doubt still revered as such in Moscow, look increasingly unreal today. Unswerving loyalty to Moscow; the primary of international obligations (variously conceived) over domestic considerations; the overriding necessity to preserve the organizational core, if necessary at the cost of mass support — all these have been called into question and largely discredited. On the other hand, some measure of compromise on the part of Western European Communist parties with the forces of liberal, parliamentary democracy has long been less a matter of choice than a condition of existence, a constantly renewed *fait accompli*. Eurocommunist parties are, after all, *parties*. The PCI and the PCF are today no longer willing, or even able, to renounce mass support, whereas the Soviet-inspired "Popular Frontism" of the 1930s — with which Eurocommunism has been misleadingly compared — actually required that subscribing parties be able to do so at a moment's notice. Eurocommunism is not something administered to Western European electorates but something that will stand or fall with these electorates' acceptance or rejection of its doctrines. It seems clear that substantial parts of the French and Italian electorates are increasingly inclined to accept the entry of communist ministers "into the pilot's cabin," into the governments and cabinets of their respective countries. Communist voters in France and Italy (and also in Spain, where the Communist party, though Eurocommunist, enjoys much less electoral support) seem positively to have welcomed the same doctrinal concessions made to "bourgeois democracy" that so pain the hard-line and "orthodox" elsewhere. Even supporters of other parties in France and Italy seem less concerned with any putative threat to democracy from the PCF and PCI than with the social changes these parties, given a share of state power, might help enact: further nationalization, social and municipal reforms, and a more equitable tax system might serve as examples.[2]

Such developments should not surprise us if we consider the theoretical bases of Eurocommunist doctrine. The central belief of such Eurocommunist theoreticians as Enrico Berlinguer is that Marxism, once it is shorn of its Stalinist trappings, does not deny democracy but actually deepens its meaning and extent. It has been pointed out that the secretary general of the Spanish Communist party, Santiago Carillo's passionate attachment to pluralist, parliamentary democracy (not least in his book, *Eurocommunism and the State)* "is no mere frontist scheme, still less a tactical ploy; it is an obsession."[3] It is an obsession that may be explained in large part by the experience of fascism in Spain until so very recently. Carillo argues that "without elections, civil liberties and a multi-party system, socialism is unthinkable,"[4] that diversity of political opinion, toleration of dissent, and open confrontation of ideas, the formal rights that have emerged in the West from bourgeois democracy, must be extended and carried further forward under socialism. The question that remains to be answered is whether there is, in fact, any precedent for these views, and views like them, in the history of Marxism.

THE POLITICS OF PRESENCE

Once again, it is Italy that provides the readiest way to a discussion of this problem, even though our path will stretch much further afield. Our itinerary leads from the current notion of "historical compromise," through the policies of Palmiro Togliatti, head of the PCI until his death in 1964, to the sophisticated theories of Antonio Gramsci,[5] a Marxist theoretician of the first magnitude, and from the thought of Gramsci to that of Marx himself.

Togliatti's notion of the need for what he (with no small prompting from Gramsci) called "structural reforms" put forward as a political program a gradual transition from "bourgeois democracy" to "socialist democracy" through a process of "deepening and extending freedom and democracy" *throughout* the various institutions that make up Italian society. Togliatti, after the second world war, believed that this process of "deepening and extending freedom and democracy" away from the purely parliamentary-political level would be facilitated by the overthrow of the fascist regime in Italy and the decomposition of its residues. In this sense his thought may bear comparison with the theories of Santiago Carillo, who is faced, sometime later, with a not dissimilar situation in Spain. Indeed, the Spanish PCE has put forward a program of "national reconciliation" based on a broad alliance of parties and coalitions of popular forces that is much closer to Togliatti's "structural reforms" or Berlinguer's "historical compromise" in its conception than to the French "Union of the Left," which has taken the beleaguered form of an electoral alliance between two parties (the communists and socialists) only.[6]

Togliatti's "structural reforms" involve recourse (how much recourse is the subject of some debate) to the writings of the PCI's most distinguished theorist, Antonio Gramsci. Gramsci's distinctive and significant concept of "hegemony" *(egemonia)* is antithetical to the Leninist notion of the revolutionary "dictatorship of the proletariat," a phrase that is absent even from the statutes of the PCI. "Hegemony" has to do with the role of the party in the state and throughout society. While this is not the place to attempt to establish with any degree of precision the extent to which Enrico Berlinguer's "73 Articles," and the notion of "historical compromise" that underlies them, are outgrowths of Gramsci's conception of hegemony, certain points do need to be made. The PCI's current pronouncements and policies refer to, and bear the imprint of, Gramsci with remarkable frequency. At this level, at least, the continuity between Gramsci's beliefs and the practice of the PCI is marked.

According to Gramsci, "hegemony" is to be opposed to "domination" *(dominatio);* hegemony, "the most important face of power throughout society" is concerned with cultural and moral directive power and with the adaptation and transformation of social institutions and practices from within. Domination, by contrast, remains at the level of *political* institutions and depends on force and coercion rather than on consent and persuasion. Hegemony and domination are alternative principles of party organization, the former emphasizing transformation from below as well as above, the latter fixing its sights on transformation from above, as an exclusive initiative and perquisite of state action. The Leninist notion of the dictorship of the proletariat, which Gramsci considered to be wholly inappropriate to Italian conditions (no matter how appropriate it may have been to those in Russia), is an instance of a belief in the power of domination, a belief Gramsci did not share. Gramsci's concern was with the *esprit général* of Italian society taken as a whole and with what he believed was its impermeability to state directives handed down from on high. Hegemony, instead of emphasizing the intense, if temporary, preeminence of the state over society that is attendant upon a Leninist coup, emphasizes something quite different: the continuous buildup and accretion of proletarian counterinstitutions, under the influence of the party, throughout society at large. Without such prior counterinstitutionalization, Gramsci believed, any purely political or merely institutional change, any mere shift in control at the helm, would be either stillborn or unlikely to survive.

The creation of proletarian hegemony is expansive and proceeds by diffusion throughout society; and in this respect it is most unlike what Gramsci called a merely "corporative" ideology or organization, which, he feared, would be narrowly and exclusively class-bound. What emerges from Gramsci's contrasts—the contrast between hegemony and domination as principles of revolutionary organization, and that between hegemonic and corporative ideology as an intellectual weapon—is a prescription for the necessary and sufficient conditions of successful revolutionary transformation. Without prior effectiveness on the various social and (broadly) cultural fronts, and without the diffusion (by means of persuasion rather than coercion) of radical ideas throughout society, no seizure of power, and no mere victory at the polls, can be anything more than transitory and insecure.

The point here is not only that Gramsci's regenerative concept of hegemony, extending as it does into what he called a "war of position" throughout society, is distinctly anti-Leninist. It is also that Gramsci's cognate conception of "the politics of presence" has had a pronounced effect on the current theory and practice of the PCI. The party, very much as Gramsci suggested, has been concerned, not to distinguish itself in the Leninist manner from the working class, but to integrate itself within all available aspects of the everyday lives of working people, whether these are, on the strictest of definitions, proletarians or not.

What Gramsci provided is best seen as a theoretically attractive alternative to all the drawbacks of a prevailingly Leninist mode of party organization: the decay of internal democracy, organizational stasis, institutional ossification, and stultifying bureaucratization. Gramsci's alternative— the buildup by consensus and persuasion of "hegemonic" counterinstitutions and processes as the main task of the party—has additional advantages. It regards coercion and dogmatic imposition as unworkable and is unafraid of taking society as it is and of working within its institutional structure. Society's own dynamism, together with whatever democratic tendencies society may exhibit, are in this way respected, not denied, or argued out of existence. A "corporative" definition of the tasks of the party, by contrast, would add, somewhat disdainfully, another, nondemocratic, bureaucratized institution to society's superstructure in the hope either that the very existence of such a doubtful alternative would somehow serve as an example to the rest, or in the equally unlikely hope that society could be at some stage dramatically transformed in the Leninist manner, *de haut en bas*. The difference between a hegemonic and a corporative approach is, on one level, the difference between a strategy and a blueprint. On another level, it is the difference between a desire to come to terms with whatever inherent democratic tendencies society may display, and a high-handed insistence upon regarding society as mere *matériel* to be drastically transformed, no matter what democratic elements may happen to be present within it. In many ways, the difference between these alternative approaches comes down to a difference between two ways of looking at democracy itself. Gramsci's approach, which has found only partial and belated expression since his death (for in many ways the organization, if not the ideology, of the PCI and the PCF has remained Leninist), nevertheless provides an increasingly influential alternative to Leninism; it remains to be shown that its roots in Marxist theory actually strike deeper than those of Leninism itself.

"POLITICAL" AND "HUMAN" EMANCIPATION

Most accounts of Marx's theory of the state follow Lenin's *State and Revolution* in emphasizing its character as a "ruling-class" theory. By the same token, such accounts largely overlook some crucially important arguments about the modern, democratic state that Marx advanced for the first (though not the last) time in an article he wrote in 1843 against Bruno Bauer, "On the Jewish Question."[7] The neglect of this essay is unconscionable, for it can be shown that its arguments indicate a way of looking at the modern state that cannot be accounted for by a purely "Leninist" reading. Marx's "ruling-class" theory of the state, taken in and of itself, can be made to lead into Leninism; the idea of the state as being no more than an "engine of class despotism" feeds more or less directly into the Leninist version of the "revolutionary dictatorship of the proletariat" toward which Leninist party organization is to be directed. It is no accident that Gramsci and his Eurocommunist heirs have discounted the Leninist argument and have set out to provide an alternative; for the Leninist argument itself remains on a purely institutional level, on that of *dominatio* rather than *egemonia*. The relevance of Marx's early essay "On the Jewish Question" to this alternative and to the theme of Marxism and compromise can readily be shown, since it demonstrates that Marx's theory of the state has a greater depth, resonance, and continuity than a purely Leninist reading would allow.

The argument of "On the Jewish Question" addresses the issue of the displacement, or alienation, of men's communal capacities, their social potential for arranging their own lives, as to the purely institutional level of the modern state—the very level Lenin restricts himself within, but Gramsci conspicuously does not. The modern bourgeois state in its "democratic" form is seen by Marx as the representation of the alienated communal abilities of men that need to be reappropriated. What Marx calls "political emancipation", which stands for bourgeois revolution, has the political effect of bifurcating human life in a brutal and unprecedented way. Private and public realms of being become separated; they are no longer contiguous realms as they had been in earlier forms of society. Man's political significance, as a citizen of the modern state, becomes detached from his private condition. Citizenship and private life become mutually exclusive spheres of activity. A man's vocation, or occupation, in civil society and his political status are no longer organically linked. What is meant by the separation of the political state from civil society, of citizenship from everyday activity, is that the citizen belongs to the state, whereas he actively participates only in civil society.

The distinction is one of roles that become mutually exclusive; the bourgeois state is grafted onto a realm of private, self-interested economic activity. What men do politically is no longer coterminous with, and indeed no longer even involves, what men do productively, in the everyday conduct of their lives. Political behavior seals itself off from social and economic activity; the liberal theory of the night-watchman state, which stands aside from the self-interested pursuits of men in civil society, is an ideological expression of the fact that politics no longer refers to, or has any bearing upon, economic activity, which is said to be capable of regulating itself. Social and economic life have undergone depoliticization; "political emancipation" heralds the emancipation of society from any conscious control over the operation of the impersonal forces of the market. It is nothing less than alienation in the labor process (as outlined in Marx's *Economic and Philosophic Manuscripts)* writ large, or expressed at a higher level. Individuals are powerless faced with the outcome of their own actions. Marx himself draws the connection between alien politics and alienation in the labor process quite explicitly:

> In the political community [man] regards himself as a communal being; but in civil society he is active as a private individual, treats other men as means, reduces himself to a means and becomes the plaything of alien powers. The political state is as spiritual in relation to civil society as heaven is in relation to earth . . . . In the state where he counts as a species-being, he is the imaginary member of an imaginary universality, divested of his real individual life and endowed with an unreal universality.[8]

The problem posed by "political emancipation" is, however, one that lends itself to a certain kind of solution, which Marx terms "human emancipation." Depoliticization implies repoliticization—the reassertion of conscious social control over men's conditions of existence. If citizenship in the modern state is indeed, as Marx thinks, the fantasy of universality, it is a fantasy that can be made real; the reintegration of political forces to which Marx refers under the heading of "human emancipation" is, in one sense, the realization of the fantasy of citizenship, and in another sense, its extension into areas of life left untouched and sacrosanct under capitalism and laissez-faire.

> Only when the actual individual man takes back into himself the abstract citizen, and in his everyday life, his individual work, and his individual relationships has he become a species-being, only when he has recognized and organized his own powers as social powers so that social force is no longer separated from him as political force—only then is human emancipation complete.[9]

What makes "On the Jewish Question" strikingly relevant to the current wave of Eurocommunist doctrine is, in the first instance, the way in which Marx counterposes "political" to "human" emancipation, bourgeois revolution to communist revolution, liberal democracy with its corollaries of universal suffrage and formally defined individual rights to the yet to be attained stage of social as well as political freedom. "Political" and "human" emancipation are not mutually exclusive, nor yet are they straightforward polar opposites; they are historically related categories. Neither one *denies* the other. Political emancipation is a presentiment of human emancipation; it hints at the possibilities of human emancipation in advance of the attainment of human emancipation. To put the same point in another way, the achievements of liberal democracy are real, if incomplete, gains; they are not to be dismissed or devalued out of hand. Political emancipation is an uncompleted or insubstantial form of emancipation, to be sure, but it does hold out a promise; and seen in this way it becomes a necessary part of, or prelude to, full "human emancipation." In Hegelian terminology, the modern democratic state is an "abstract universal" that demands to be made "concrete." Yet, for our purposes at least, the relevant terminology is not Hegelian so much as Gramscian. The individual rights and liberties that are attendant upon "political emancipation"—Marx himself cites those of the "Declaration of the Rights of Man and Citizen" that ushered in the French Revolution in 1789—are in no way to be written off as meaningless or discounted by virtue of their formality. Marx himself is clear on this point; such rights and liberties, unimpeachably "bourgeois" though they may be, are to be *extended,* not replaced, in and by the process of "human emancipation" in such a way that they will actually embody some real, general meaning once the alien political realm has been brought back to the level of real, conscious social control.

The relevance of Marx's essay of 1843 to current Eurocommunist reevaluations of the nature and scope of democracy is, however, more pointed than this observation, taken in itself, might suggest. Marx's counterposition of "political" to "human" emancipation in no way implies Leninism as a mode of party organization, as a means, let alone *the* means, of attaining "human emancipation." On the contrary, what Marx had to say might be taken as an immanent critique of Leninism. There is with Lenin a problem of means and ends, a problem with which Marx himself grappled (not always successfully), which has been raised again in orthodox critiques of Eurocommunism, and which Gramsci valiantly attempted to cut through at its source. It can be specified—admittedly with the benefit of hindsight—that rigid party organization, with its concommitants of a discernible elitism and a discipline *ac cadavar* is not the likeliest means of bringing about emancipation. The relationship between the two might seem to an unbiased observer more Manichaean than dialectical. The problem is, of course, a complex one and can hardly be resolved here; but what can be said is that Eurocommunist reevaluations of basic democratic rights and liberties, rights and liberties that are to be respected, not undercut as Leninism has in the past undercut them, point in a quite different direction from the Leninist orthodoxy. Eurocommunism, to reiterate, poses a threat to the orthodoxy in this sense as in other senses.

But how orthodox *is* the "orthodoxy"? Marx's own theory of the state, it has been argued, has more than one face to present; the aspect appropriated by Lenin is but one of them. Marx himself constantly insisted that the alien state cannot be the instrument of its own reintegration; if it is an institutional expression of human alienation, such alienation cannot be overcome within the sphere of alienation. The implications of this denial are distinctly anti-Leninist and lean much more readily in the direction of Gramsci; the disjuncture of the state from society, which Marx investigated most thoroughly in *The Class Struggles in France* and *The 18th Brumaire of Louis Bonaparte,* is a problem Marx always insisted could not be solved by the *further* disjuncture of the state from civil society—a further disjuncture of the kind, we might add, that would be attendant upon a Leninist coup. "The working class," as Marx put it in *The Civil War in France,* "cannot simply lay hold of the ready-made state machinery and wield it for its own purposes";[10] and it would not be fanciful to regard Gramsci's theories, at least those aspects of Gramsci's theories that have been touched upon here, as a kind of extended commentary on this text.

The Civil War in France specifies that the alien bureaucratic state, which disfigures and distorts as well as reflects the society that gives it birth, signifies the separation between citizens and the means of their common action, the progressive extension of the sphere of alien regulation of life in society. As a means of checking this extension, Marx emphasizes as the primary achievement of the Paris Commune its deinstitutionalization of political power. This, Marx argues, will cut through the usurpation and mystification of men's conscious control over the social conditions of their lives. Deinstitutionalization of political power amounts to an act of reappropriation of what had been alienated away; and the prescription that underlies it is that men should become "masters of their own movement." This suggests not only that Marx, for all his occasional disdain for parliamentarism and, indeed, gradualism, did indeed have an understanding of democracy in another of its aspects—the extension of genuine social control over the conditions of existence, which is given incomplete and distorted expression by the political systems he knew. Does the point need to be labored that it is also given incomplete and distorted expression under the aegis of "Marxist-Leninist" political forms? Or that Gramsci, who points forward to "historical compromise" as well as backward to Marx, at least had (or envisioned) an alternative— "the politics of presence"?

The parallelism between what Marx said in 1843 about "political" in its relation to "human" emancipation and current Eurocommunist doctrine centering around the need for "historical compromise" with liberal-democratic forces in Western Europe today may not be exact; but it is nevertheless striking. The idea that the various features of liberal democracy, or, *mutatis mutandis,* of "political emancipation" are not to be denied by virtue of their partial, "abstract," uncompleted character, but rather treated as way stations on the way to a substantive broadening of the definition and meaning of democracy, has rather deeper roots in the history of Marxist doctrine and method (if not in the actual practice of communist parties) than might initially be supposed.

What this suggests is first that a reevaluation of the relationship of

Marxist theory and practice might be in order, particularly at a time
when the PCI might be on the verge of actively participating in the
Italian government. Shlomo Avineri's remarkable study, *The Social
and Political Thought of Karl Marx,* [11] has indicated persuasively
some of the dangers involved in refracting the thought of Marx
through the lens of an "orthodox" Marxist-Leninist doctrine, and political practice, that postdated Marx's death. Avineri has argued con-
vincingly that Marx's writings, if examined with as unjaundiced an
eye as possible, often turn out to be rather more open-ended and suggestive than some of the traditional "Marxist-Leninist" formulas,
taken at face value, might suggest. What Marx himself had to say often does not square with later accounts and interpretations of his
work that were written, with an official imprimatur, in the name of
dogmatically sanctioned *positions déjà prises.* The "official" version
of Marx's theory of the state as a straightforwardly ruling-class theory
that leads directly into the received Leninist formula of the revolutionary dictatorship of the proletariat is a case in point; it is no accident that Eurocommunist movements have had to drop the dictatorship of the proletariat from their programs and manifestos. Nor is it
accidental that they have been frontally attacked for doing so by
those whose sights are set by orthodox "Marxism-Leninism." Nevertheless, the accusation that has accompanied these attacks, the
charge that to drop such slogans as "the dictatorship of the proletariat" is to compromise oneself as a Marxist committed to revolutionary
change, cannot be sustained. Marx himself, as Avineri has pointedly
reminded us, advocated proletarian alliance with liberal-democratic
forces in society whenever such a step was possible, and by the same
token reserved his bitterest scorn and invective for those who instead
of doing this would entertain the possibility of alliance with the forces
of autocracy and reaction in the name of "progress." This, of course,
was one of the issues separating Marx from Lassalle. The least that
this suggests is that Marx's own opposition to the status quo, though
forthright, was less than uncompromising. The revolutionary proletariat's choice of allies according to Marx was likely to make some
considerable difference to the nature of the revolutionary movement
and, indeed, to the contours of future society itself. Times have
changed, and revolutionary hopes have often been dashed; yet it is
difficult not to discern an echo of Marx's point in current Eurocommunist doctrine, even though the Marxist-Leninist tradition has
done much to stifle the resonance of Marx's thought.

To Marx, democracy in the sense of communality *(Gemeinwesen)* and communism as he envisaged it were not necessarily antagonistic. The latter could, and should, be seen as the extension and continuation, the fulfillment and consummation of the former. Yet promises can turn into threats, and either term can undergo change. Democracy can betray the promise attendant upon its emergence, as Marx recognized remarkably quickly. Democracy, as Marx warned, may become identified with a self-perpetuating and self-preserving institutionalization of men's alienated communal capacities and needs that will make the extension of rational human control over the free play of inhuman mechanisms in society less, not more, likely. Communism, for its part, may turn in the direction of yet another inhuman mechanism to be added to the rest. It may take the form—and of course *has* taken the form—of a rigid, doctrinaire series of ritualistic formulas that may be dusted off from time to time in order to provide dubious "explanations" of whatever happens to be taking place.

The melancholy reflection is indeed prompted that both Marxism and democracy have in fact betrayed us. Both remain opportunities rather than accomplishments, and Marxist theory—*some* Marxist theory—helps us see why. We have lost sight of the connection between Marxism and democracy; the question whether they rise and fall together is still an open one. The Eurocommunist doctrine of "historical compromise" might serve, at the very least, as a belated reminder of their connection. Its aims, however, are of course more ambitious; they are those of translating into political action a connection that for too long has been relegated and domiciled within the realm of theory. All the more reason, then, why we as political theorists should pay attention to an important attempt to reconstitute what our century has succeeded in rending asunder.

NOTES

1. The English-language literature on the Italian Communist party's "historical compromise" is meager; but see Giacomo Sani, "The PCI on the Brink," *Problems of Communism*, 25 (November-December 1976), 27-51, for an excellent survey. For a more extended treatment, see Donald Blackmer and Sidney Tarrow, eds., *Communism in Italy and France* (Princeton: Princeton University Press, 1975); and a review of this and other recent books by Giuseppe di Palma, "Eurocommunism?" *Comparative Politics* (April 1977), 358-75.

2. See D. B. Golden, "Communism in France and Italy," *Political Studies,* 25, no. 3, pp. 431-36, for a discussion of these points.

3. Carl Boggs, review of Santiago Carillo, with Régis Debray and Max Gallo, *Dialogue on Spain,* translated from the French by A. M. Elliott (London: Lawrence and Wishart, 1976), *Telos,* 32 (Summer 1977), 233-41.

4. In the accurate paraphrase of Boggs, Ibid.

5. Very few of Gramsci's voluminous writings have been translated into English. The most readily available exceptions are *The Modern Prince and Other Writings,* translated from the Italian by Louis Marks (New York: International Publishers, 1975); *Selections from the Prison Notebooks of Antonio Gramsci,* ed. and trans. Quintin Hoare and Geoffrey Nowell-Smith (New York: International Publishers, 1971); and *Letters from Prison by Antonio Gramsci,* ed. and trans. Lynne Lawner (New York: Harper & Row, 1973).

6. On the PCF, see Ronald Tiersky, *French Communism 1920-1972,* (New York: Columbia University Press, 1974), passim, and a suggestive review by George Ross in *Telos,* no. 24 (Summer 1975), 193-202. On the PCE, see Jon Wiener and Temma Kaplan, "The Spanish Left," *Working Papers for a New Society* (January-February 1978), 20-24.

7. Karl Marx, *Early Writings,* ed. and trans. T. B. Bottomore, with a foreword by Erich Fromm (New York: McGraw Hill, 1964), pp. 1-40.

8. Ibid., pp. 13-14.

9. Ibid., p. 31.

10. Karl Marx and Frederick Engels, *Selected Works in Two Volumes* (Moscow 1962), vol. 1, p. 516.

11. Shlomo Avineri, *The Social and Political Thought of Karl Marx,* (Cambridge: At the University Press, 1970).

PART III

COMPROMISE
AND POLITICS

7

COMPROMISES IN POLITICS

JOSEPH H. CARENS

Ordinary attitudes toward compromise are marked by a fundamental ambiguity which is reflected in the definition of the term itself. The first definition of "compromise" offered by *Webster's New Collegiate Dictionary (1951)* is a "settlement of differences by arbitration or by consent reached by mutual concessions." This suggests that compromise is simply a technique for settling conflicts, in itself morally neutral and perhaps even praiseworthy insofar as it involves a peaceful, mutually acceptable resolution. By contrast, the second definition of "compromise" is "a concession to something derogatory, hazardous, or objectionable; a prejudicial concession; a surrender; as, a *compromise* of character". Clearly this definition indicates that compromise is something undesirable, perhaps even morally wrong. If the two types of compromise were clearly distinguished in practice, this difference in definitions would pose problems only for clarity of expression. The problem, however, is that a given act may well be regarded as a compromise in *both* senses of the term.

Nowhere is the ambiguity of attitudes toward compromise more profound than in the realm of politics. As Professor Golding observed, "The politician or diplomat is on the one hand, expected to make compromises and, on the other, is condemned for doing that very thing."[1] If the same people are doing the expecting and the condemning, then their behavior seems at best paradoxical and at worst hypocritical. Yet even politicians and political theorists who extol the virtues of compromise in politics often draw lines demarcating areas where they think compromise inappropriate. Different people draw different lines, however. Edmund Burke, for example, argued rather sweepingly that "all government, . . . every virtue, and every prudent act is founded on compromise and barter,"[2] yet he was unwilling to compromise with his constituents in Bristol by adjusting his stands on certain controversial public issues to coincide more closely with their views. Former Senator Eugene McCarthy wrote an essay in 1957 that also praised the virtues of compromise in politics.[3] Indeed, he seemed willing to go somewhat further than Burke, since he argued that it might be proper for a representative to compromise by taking a position that the representative himself did not personally accept if the position reflected the informed, strongly held views of his constituents. (Senator McCarthy suggested that the actions of some southern members of Congress on racial questions might be justified in this way.) In another area, however, he saw no room for compromise: "We all agree that applying intrinsically evil means to attain intrinsically good ends cannot be justified."[4] An earlier advocate of compromise, T. V. Smith, disagreed. Politics, he argued, is "the institutionalized art of compromise," and "the limit of compromise is . . . not fixed primarily by appeal to conscience."[5] Compromise is justified, he argued, so long as it is necessary, it promotes peace, and it advances progress. Even for Smith, however, compromise had its limits. The 1938 agreement at Munich did not meet his criteria for justifiable compromises.

As this brief introduction suggests, views about the proper role of compromise in politics are numerous, conflicting, and often confused. This essay will attempt to sort out some of the issues by addressing the following questions: Why is compromise so common in politics? (section I.) What kinds of political compromise are desirable and how can such compromises be achieved? (sections II-IV.) Why do people have such ambiguous attitudes toward compromise in politics? (section V.)

I

One reason why compromise is so common in politics is that in politics we are required to *act*.[6] Suppose that two eminent scientists offer conflicting theories about the causes of cancer. Each is convinced of the correctness of his own theory. No one would suggest that they compromise in order to reach agreement on what causes cancer. Compromise would be out of place in this type of theoretical investigation. Each should pursue his research until his theory is either proved or refuted. Of course, some scientist might find the causes of cancer by combining elements from both theories. But if he does, his new combined theory will have merit, *not* because it is a *compromise* between the two previous theories, but *rather* because it is *correct*.

By contrast, suppose that an individual has $2 million to donate for cancer research and that each of our eminent scientists has requested $2 million to conduct his research. Suppose also that the individual has no way to tell which of the two scientists is more likely to be correct. He might well decide to give $1 million to each. This decision would clearly be a compromise, and yet it is by no means so obviously inappropriate as a compromise between the scientists on the content of their theories would have been. Each of the scientists may regard the decision as a compromise in the second, pejorative sense of the term, because each is convinced of the correctness of his own theory. The donor is convinced by neither, however, or is equally convinced by both. From his perspective, therefore, a compromise may be the fairest and most prudent action in the face of uncertainty.

In sum, theoretical inquiries permit us to suspend judgment until we are satisfied that we have reached the truth. In such inquiries compromise is neither necessary nor appropriate. By contrast, in practical affairs we are often forced to act in the face of uncertainty before we are confident that we have reached the truth. Under such conditions, compromise may offer the best solution.[7]

Action often requires compromise for reasons besides uncertainty. A given individual may have many goals, some of which conflict with others. For example, pursuit of one's career may conflict in various ways with an important personal relationship. While it is theoretically possible to pursue either the career or the relationship to the exclusion of the other, it is also possible and perhaps more common to sacrifice the full pursuit of each goal to some extent. In the language of economists, one makes marginal trade-offs among the available alternatives. This kind of choice is a compromise, even if a purely internal one. The individual genuinely wants both the career and the relationship. He would prefer not to sacrifice any aspect of either one. Nevertheless, the need to act in a particular situation may force him to make some sacrifice, and frequently an individual will choose a smaller partial sacrifice of both of his goals in preference to a larger sacrifice of one.

So far we have identified two common features of human action —

uncertainty and conflict among goals—which may incline a single individual to compromise in deciding what to do in a given situation.
The tendency to compromise is greatly increased when it is a question of political action because politics is a *collective* enterprise.
Other things being equal, the more numerous the people who have to
act together, the greater the likelihood of uncertainty and disagreement about whether or not a given action will lead to a given goal,
and the greater the likelihood of conflict among the goals people seek
and disagreement about the relative priorities that should be at-
tached to different goals. The less coercion is used to insure coordination, the more necessary compromise may be as a technique for se-
curing the cooperation of those who are to engage in the collective
action. For example, Apter notes that a strong tendency to compromise is built into consociational pluralist systems because of their voluntary character.[8] The alternative to compromise in such a context
may be inaction.

II

If the nature of collective action seems to make compromise inevitable in politics, it does not follow that compromise is always desirable. Let us assume for the moment that politics is exclusively concerned with conflicts of interest and that no questions arise about the
legitimacy of the interests that are in conflict. Given this context,
what would make compromise desirable?

If two parties are in conflict, a compromise that permits them to
reach agreement is clearly desirable whenever the agreement permits
both of them to gain more (or lose less) than they would from the failure to reach agreement.[9] This is a common situation in politics. For
example, different people might have different and conflicting interests they would like to promote in a tax bill, but all might agree on
the need for tax legislation. Two countries may have conflicting interests on certain questions of trade policy, but a trade agreement
might leave both countries better off than no agreement at all.

While a compromise that leaves both sides better off is desirable,
one should not assume that only one compromise solution for any
given conflict of interests is possible. There may be many possible
compromises that would be better for the parties than no agreement,
but some of them may offer much greater benefits to both parties
than others. Indeed the range of possible solutions may be seen as a

continuum. At one end is the distributive compromise, which is only slightly more satisfactory to both sides than failure to reach agreement at all. At the other end is the integrative compromise, which provides great benefits to both parties.[10] Clearly the more integrative the compromise, the more desirable it is, given our initial assumptions.

The literature on bargaining and negotiation mentions at least three factors that seem likely to lead to more integrative compromises.[11] First, if the parties are in conflict over many issues, they may gain by considering several issues at once, because each party may not attach the same degree of importance to every issue. Thus, they can gain by making trade-offs among the issues. One party can make a large concession to a second party on an issue the first regards as relatively unimportant and the second regards as relatively important in return for a large concession by the second party on an issue the first regards as relatively important and the second as relatively unimportant. In politics this type of procedure is called logrolling. It *is* a form of compromise (pace Golding) because each party must give up something he wants, but it leads to highly integrative compromises because each party gets more of what he cares most about than would have been possible if each issue had been considered separately. Psychological experiments with artificial conflict-of-interest situations have confirmed the theoretical argument that logrolling will lead to more integrative solutions.[12]

Second, parties are more likely to reach more integrative compromises if they adopt what Pruitt and Lewis call a "problem-solving orientation" rather than an "individualistic orientation."[13] With a problem-solving orientation, parties view their conflict as a problem to be solved rather than as a battle to be won or lost. Each adopts the goal of trying to find a mutually satisfying solution instead of simply seeking a solution which satisfies his own concerns. Each party continues to seek what is best for himself, but satisfaction of the other's concerns becomes a positive (if secondary) goal. By contrast, with an individualistic orientation, a party will regard the interests of the other merely as constraints that must be overcome through minimal concessions in order to achieve one's own goals. This leads the parties to adopt a "distributive approach" to their bargaining. They will use threats in an attempt to secure concessions; they will adopt positions purely for tactical reasons; and they will withhold information about their real preferences.

A problem-solving orientation leads parties to make positive proposals rather than threats and to trust the information provided by the other party. This can lead to more integrative compromises in two ways. First, each party can adopt a trial-and-error approach, seeking the reactions of the other party to many tentatively advanced alternatives. Since each party can believe the reactions of the other to the various offers, the proposals should converge at a point that will be more satisfying to both than would be possible if they had been using threats and adopting positions purely for the sake of bargaining. Second, the parties can exchange information about their basic goals and preferences. From this, a party may gain new insight into ways in which the goals and preferences of the other may be combined with his own and may be able to propose entirely new options that had not occurred to either party before and that would not emerge from a simple trial-and-error process. The more complex the problem, the more likely it seems that the most integrative solution will emerge only from this kind of creative thinking. The effectiveness of this approach obviously depends to a large extent on the reliability of the information about the goals and preferences of the conflicting parties and thus on the trust that is characteristic of the problem-solving orientation. Again, an experimental study tends to confirm the theoretical argument that a problem-solving orientation will lead to more integrative solutions than an individualistic orientation.[14]

Finally, parties are likely to reach more integrative compromises if each party has high aspirations, that is, if a party will settle for an agreement only if the agreement provides a high degree of satisfaction. This may appear paradoxical, given what we have just said about the importance of a problem-solving orientation, but in fact the two points are complementary. The more integrative solutions to conflicts are usually not the most obvious ones. People will look beyond the obvious compromise solutions only if they are extremely reluctant to make any unnecessary or costly concessions. Indeed, the experimental study previously mentioned found that the problem — solving orientation offered only a slight advantage over the individualistic orientation when levels of aspiration were low, because agreement would be reached through obvious compromises even though solutions that were more satisfactory to both sides were potentially available. By contrast, when levels of aspiration were high, an individualistic orientation simply led to failure to reach agreement, whereas the problem-solving orientation led to the more integrative solutions.[15] Thus, a firm commitment to one's own interests enhances

the prospect for more integrative compromises as long as it is combined with a problem-solving orientation toward the conflict.

Throughout this section we have assumed that politics is concerned only with conflicts of interest and that no questions are raised
about the legitimacy of the interests in conflict. If we are to consider
in any adequate way what role compromise *ought* to play in politics,
however, we must now reexamine that assumption.

III

One obvious objection to the assumption adopted in the previous
section is that questions do sometimes arise about the legitimacy of
conflicting parties and/or about the legitimacy of their interests. For
example, questions about legitimacy are at the heart of the current
conflicts between the PLO and Israel, between blacks and whites in
Southern Africa, and between the Communists and Christian Democrats in Italy. One is scarcely likely to adopt a "problem-solving orientation" to a conflict if one considers the goals of one's antagonist to
be fundamentally illegitimate. Indeed, it is by no means clear that an
integrative compromise would even be a desirable solution to such a
conflict, since an integrative compromise is one that is highly beneficial to both sides. Why would one seek to advance interests one regards as illegitimate?

This does not mean that compromise can play no role in conflicts
in which questions of legitimacy are at stake, but it does mean that a
different type of compromise will be regarded as desirable. If one is
engaged in a dispute with another party that one regards as illegitimate, one may find it necessary to make some concessions in order to
achieve some of one's own goals, but one will surely try to minimize
those concessions. In short, an individualistic orientation and a distributive approach would be appropriate. Moreover, one would use a
radically different standard to measure the desirability of a compromise in this context. The ideal would not be an integrative compromise but a skewed distributive compromise in which one achieved
great benefits in exchange for small concessions.

One consequence of this is that it is far more difficult to find compromise solutions to conflicts in which questions of legitimacy are at
stake. One should not infer from this, however, that parties in conflict should always be willing to recognize the legitimacy of the

other's interest. To do this would be to assume that all interests are equally legitimate, which is clearly not the case. Hitler's interest in ruling Europe was not as legitimate as the interest of the Europeans in ruling themselves. The interest that whites in Southern Africa have in maintaining their hegemony over the blacks is not as legitimate as the interest of the blacks in achieving self-determination. In conflicts of this type it might be necessary for the party with the more legitimate interests to compromise at times simply because the other party has more power, but it would be a political and a moral error to accept the other party's interests as legitimate simply because of this power.

Compromise is not an end in itself. To extol the virtues of compromise simply because it resolves conflicts peacefully and satisfies both sides to some degree is to exalt means over ends and to judge the merits of a conflict purely by the method used in settling it. The method of settlement is not irrelevant to moral judgments about conflicts, but it should not be the sole criterion. The question of legitimacy is prior and more fundamental. Where the interests in conflict are equally legitimate, an integrative compromise is clearly good and a problem-solving orientation is desirable. By contrast, where the interests of one of the parties in conflict are not legitimate, the party with the legitimate interests should try to concede as little as possible to the other, even if this approach reduces the chances of a compromise solution.

A second and related objection to the assumption adopted earlier is that political conflicts are not limited to conflicts of interests. Political conflicts may involve conflicts of principles, of rights, or of ideologies. As Professor Golding noted, it is not obvious that conflicts of this type can be settled by compromise. But the objection goes still deeper. Interests and morals are often intertwined in politics. Consider, for example, a conflict over tax legislation; this involves obvious conflicts of interest among different groups, but it may also involve a conflict over justice, that is, over the question of what tax policy is *fair*. Since Marx, we can hardly fail to be aware that there is often a strong link between a person's views about justice and his economic interests. Nevertheless, this does not mean that debates about justice are reducible to conflicts of interest. Indeed, this implicit reductionism is precisely what is most objectionable about our earlier assumption. To assume that political conflicts are conflicts of interest and that integrative compromises are desirable solutions is to subvert the process of discussing issues on their merits. One of the reasons why plea-bargaining is so offensive to our sense of justice (however useful it may be for administration) is that it relies on compromise for the settlement of a dispute that ought in principle to be settled on the basis of our best judgment about guilt or innocence. In short, the process relies on relative strength rather than on the truth. Evidence about guilt or innocence is one of the factors affecting the relative strengths of the parties, but only one. Financial resources, the skills of the lawyers, and the costs or benefits which delay may entail are only a few of the other factors which may affect the relative strengths of the parties and thus the outcome of a compromise, even though these factors have nothing whatever to do with innocence or guilt. In politics, too, an orientation toward compromise as the solution for conflicts is apt to undermine the deliberative process. Logrolling may result in highly integrative solutions for parties with conflicting interests, but the process of logrolling appears to leave no room for consideration of what is right or just in a given case. Hallowell puts the argument this way:

> Compromise, as a self-sufficient principle divorced from all considerations of truth and justice, is simply, in the last analysis, the ancient Thrasymachian doctrine that might makes right.[16]

Hallowell's judgment is a bit too harsh. As we have seen, the problem-solving orientation toward conflict is one that attempts to minimize reliance on bargaining power to attain one's goals and to increase the search for mutually beneficial solutions. To that extent, it orients conflicting parties toward solutions that are in their common interest. Nevertheless, the type of reasoning that characterizes the problem-solving orientation is still fundamentally different from that which characterizes moral argument. No common standard apart from the interests of the conflicting parties themselves is appealed to; and to the extent that the conflict does not admit of a mutually beneficial solution, the compromise solution is likely to reflect relative strength in bargaining power.

In the previous section of this paper I argued that integrative compromises would be desirable solutions to political conflicts if one assumed that political conflicts were conflicts of interest and that no questions arose about the legitimacy of the interests in conflict. In this section, I have now considered two objections to this assumption and to the related inference that integrative compromises provide desirable solutions to political conflicts. Both of these objections stress the importance of distinguishing moral judgments from calculations of interest. Someone might respond, however, that compromise should play a major role in political life *even if* one does not think that all interests are equally legitimate or that all political conflicts are reducible to conflicts of interest. One need not be a positivist to recognize that people of goodwill may often disagree about what is right. Cohen puts it this way:

> Some hold that conscious adoption of compromise as a political method is morally wrong. It is wrong, they say, because it is hypocrisy to compromise when one knows — or at least firmly believes — one's principles to be altogether right and just. Only by resolute support can these principles be expected to emerge triumphant, and such resoluteness is undermined by any disposition to compromise.
>
> To this I reply: one's knowledge of the truth and justice of his principles, or his firm belief in them, is counter-balanced within the community by others who also know, or firmly believe, that other principles, in direct conflict with his own, are just and true.[17]

Unwavering commitment to principle, Cohen suggests, threatens to turn every disagreement into a violent confrontation. This would hardly be a victory for reason and moral argument. For many, including Cohen, the solution to this dilemma lies in a commitment to democracy as the means for resolving conflicts within a given community and, as part of the commitment to democracy, a commitment to compromise. The focus on political conflicts within a given community narrows the scope of our investigation somewhat, while raising new issues. In the next section, therefore, we shall consider questions about the role of compromise in a democracy.

IV

Much of the debate over the desirability of compromise in politics is set within the context of democratic theory. The role of compromise in democracy is complex and disputed. Some claim that compromise is incompatible with a true democratic spirit. Tussman argues, for example, that the notion "that compromise is a reasonable and democratic way of dealing with controversy" has its roots in "cognitive skepticism" and "moral relativism" and "goes hand in hand with the belief in consumer sovereignty, competitive individualism, and the invisible hand."[18] He contends that a disposition to compromise emerges from a "bargaining spirit" and undermines the "art of common deliberation" that is essential to truly democratic decision-making.[19]

Tussman's strictures against the "bargaining spirit" and his pleas for "common deliberation" constitute an important antidote to the tendency to view all political conflicts within a democracy as mere conflicts of interest to be settled through give-and-take. On the other hand, it is by no means clear that one can or should seek to eliminate bargaining and consideration of private interests from democratic politics as completely as Tussman wishes. J. R. Lucas notes, for example, that:

> The great merit of bargaining is that it is external. Bargaining presupposes that the parties are separate beings, each with his own identity, and own interests, not absorbed in some Hegelian whole, nor with his actual wishes subordinated to a Rousseau-like general will.[20]

Furthermore, Tussman's critique of compromise never seems to consider the possibility that citizens might fail to reach agreement even after common deliberation.[21] Much of the argument for compromise in democracy is based precisely on the assumption that failure to reach agreement will be a common occurrence. Indeed, the procedure of majority rule can itself be seen as a compromise technique for resolving such disputes, a compromise that people accept because it is fair.

To see why majority rule might be viewed as a compromise technique, consider the following familiar argument for democracy.[22] On matters requiring collective action (or collective restraint) within a given community, each member of that community would presumably want to have the community adopt the policy he regards as best. If all are agreed on the best policy, there is no problem. But if discussion cannot resolve all disagreement, there must be some method for deciding what will be done. For most issues, it may be presumed that a peaceful method of resolution will be preferable to a violent one. What procedure offers the best chance for each individual to have the policy he regards as best adopted by the community? Equality of voting rights and majority rule.[23] Singer argues that this makes a simple democracy "a paradigm of a fair compromise" because

> the nature of the decision-procedure makes it possible for everyone to refrain from acting on his own judgment about particular issues without giving up more than the theoretical minimum which it is essential for everyone to give up in order to achieve the benefits of a peaceful solution to disputes.[24]

Note that the procedure does entail a compromise even if all agree to the procedure, because each individual can presumably expect to be outvoted some of the time and thus to have a policy adopted that he would prefer not to see adopted. In effect, the procedure is one of compromise by succession: individuals take turns in getting their own way on issues instead of compromising on each particular issue. This type of argument presupposes, of course, that individuals *do* take turns in getting their own ways. In other words, it assumes that there will be no permanent minority whose views and preferences are consistently overridden by the majority.[25] Otherwise, the procedure is not a compromise but a victory for those who find themselves always on the majority side and a defeat for those who find themselves on the minority side.

One striking feature of the account offered thus far of the role of compromise in democracy is that it makes no mention of any need for compromise on particular issues. Indeed, it seems at first glance as though the principle of majority rule requires no compromise other than the one entailed in committing oneself to a decision procedure that may lead to policies one opposes. In fact, compromise plays a much larger role than this simple majority-rule model suggests.

First, the majority on a particular issue must often be *created* through compromise. The simple majority-rule model seems to imply that issues are clear-cut and dichotomous. One is either for or against a particular proposal. In fact, there is a range of opinions on most issues, and it is rare than any single opinion will command a majority. Instead, majorities are apt to be coalitions of people with different, somewhat conflicting views who have all made some concessions in order to attain a majority position on the issue. Moreover, the process of creating a majority allows feelings of relative intensity to play a role that is obscured by the simple majority-rule model. People can trade their votes on issues about which they have less intense opinions in order to gain support on other issues which they regard as crucial. This logrolling does not necessarily entail acceptance of the view that political conflicts are reducible to conflicts of interest. Different people often have different opinions about what constitutes an important moral issue, and they might be willing to trade votes because of these differences in moral judgment. It should be noted, however, that those who trade votes have effectively abandoned the attempt to decide *particular* issues on their merits.

Some people would also argue that a stable democracy requires a strong, widely shared sense of community and that such a sense of community can be maintained only by a commitment to compromise that goes much deeper than the acceptance of the principle of majority rule. As Cohen puts it:

> The growth and endurance of any democratic community will much depend upon certain intangibles — the spirit of union, the feeling of the members that their common membership is somehow deeper and more important than any issue over which disputes may arise among them. . . . The commitment to union largely explains why compromise can prevail among widely divergent views within a democracy but often does not prevail between democracies.[26]

This line of argument suggests that in a democracy people should make concessions to their opponents even when the concessions are not needed to create a majority. Barker explicitly describes compromise of this sort as one of the fundamental principles of democracy:

> The will of a majority does not prevail when it is merely the formal will of a mathematical majority. It prevails when it has been attained in spirit and when it has thus attained a content . . . which does justice to the whole of the community. . . . The *spirit* which does justice to the whole of the community is a spirit which induces the majority to make concessions to the views of the minority.[27]

At the extreme, this idea leads to the view that consensus should replace majority rule as the decision procedure within a democracy. Here compromise would play a major role indeed. The problem with this view, however, is that it undermines the political equality that formed part of the initial justification for democratic resolutions of disagreements. If consensus is required for action, those who prefer the status quo enjoy a considerable advantage.[28]

Despite this objection, the concept of a "commitment to union" can help to explain the major role compromise should play within an ideal democracy, even if one does not depart from strict majority rule. We saw earlier in the section on conflicts of interest that the attitudes adopted by the parties affected their chances of finding an integrative solution. A similar point can be made about the effects of attitude upon the chances of reaching agreement in conflicts of principle or conflicts of rights. Formally, such conflicts can be settled only by reasoned arguments in which one side persuades the other. Thus, a willingness to compromise might seem irrelevant and out of place. In practice, however, the chances for agreement depend heavily on the extent to which each party is *disposed* to listen to the other's argument. A sympathetic listener is much more likely to adopt favorable interpretations of uncertain points and to see the other's point of view, than is an unsympathetic listener. Even in moral arguments, one approaches disagreements quite differently if one is seeking areas of mutual agreement and if one is willing to be persuaded than if one merely wishes to score a few logical points and to refute the other's case. In effect, the willingness to be persuaded represents a disposition to compromise. Moreover, the line between conflicts of interest and conflicts of principle is often unclear and subject to interpretation. A "commitment to union" may dispose people to interpret such ambiguous conflicts as conflicts of interest that can be settled by an integrative compromise. (The alleged tendency of Americans to transform all conflicts of principle into conflicts of interest is, however, a bit excessive.) In short, it is impossible to abstract conflicts of any kind from the attitudes of the parties in conflict. Other things being equal, conflicts in which the parties share an underlying and fundamental commitment to union are far more likely to be resolved through mutual concessions regardless of the nature of the conflict. Thus, the commitment to union that is essential for the endurance of a democracy will promote a tendency to compromise. In sum, compromise is closely linked to democracy in several respects, and therefore many arguments for democracy are also, in effect, arguments for compromise as a method for settling disputes.

V

So far the analysis has shown why compromise is widespread in politics and why it is desirable under some circumstances and not so desirable under others, but this does little to explain why people are so suspicious of political compromises and so critical of politicians for compromising. One possibility is that people might agree on certain general principles about the desirability of compromise but disagree on the applicability of these principles to particular cases. For example, people with similar interests might agree that a compromise advancing these interests would be desirable, but they might disagree about whether a particular compromise is the best that could be obtained for their side. Or people with similar values might agree that they should not compromise on questions of fundamental principle, but they might make different judgments about whether fundamental questions of principle are at stake in a given conflict. If attitudes toward compromise merely reflected disagreements about particular cases, however, we would expect people to agree with the politicians' judgments at least as much as they disagreed with them, and we would not expect to find politicians condemned for compromising per se. Instead, as I noted at the beginning, people do seem to expect politicians to compromise, and yet they also seem to condemn them for being compromisers. What explains the ambiguity of the popular attitude toward compromise?

To some politicians the answer may seem simple: hypocrisy. Those who condemn political compromises are like meat eaters who condemn butchers because they slaughter cattle. They want the benefits of the process, but they are not willing to get their own hands dirty or even to recognize the necessity for others to do so.

This complaint of politicians has some merit. Some people demand legislative action and then condemn their representatives for making concessions needed to get a bill through. (Particular cases can be disputed, of course.) Many people claim to want politicians who will be honest and who will tell them the truth and then vote against those candidates who attempt these things even in small ways. Nevertheless, the hypocrisy of the electorate is not the whole answer.

The ambiguity of popular attitudes toward political compromise cannot be understood in isolation from the ambiguity of the politician's situation. On the one hand, people expect the politician to compromise because it is often in their interest for him to do so. On the other hand, it is often in the interest of the politician to compromise more than the people might wish. Most politicians, especially those already in office, share certain interests regardless of their political positions. For example, most benefit from arrangements that make it easier for an incumbent to get reelected. Similarly, most will benefit from arrangements that promote compromise as a means for settling disputes. Compromise tends to contain political conflicts within those arenas where the professional politican can exercise the greatest knowledge and control.[29] For politicans, the primary "commitment to union" is often a commitment to union with other professional politicians. They do give their peers a sympathetic hearing. They pay attention both to their interests and to their beliefs. But they seek to keep debate and negotiation within the professional community. This maximizes the flexibility and freedom of each of them. Thus, they have a bias toward interpreting all conflicts as conflicts of interest. They dislike and fear issues (such as abortion) that animate and divide the public, since such issues can have important but unpredictable effects on their chances for reelection.

Logrolling by professional politicans is a familiar element in political life for the reasons mentioned earlier. Through this compromise technique, each politician is able to get more of what he wants than he would if each issue were considered separately and on its merits. But what each politican wants is not necessarily what his constituents want. For one thing, most politicians want to get reelected, but given the imperfections of knowledge, communication, and control between the politician and his constituents (and many of these imperfections are unavoidable), the policy that enhances the politician's chances of reelection may often not be the policy that best meets the needs of the immediate community he serves (to say nothing of the larger community). This leads to a kind of logrolling with which we are all familiar and that is far less benign than the types discussed earlier.

Furthermore, hypocrisy is not exclusively the property of the ordinary citizen. If the voter thinks that politicians are too ready to compromise on questions of principle, that is partly because the politician often presents a position as a question of principle in a speech but treats it as a negotiable interest in the making of policy. The false expectations are his own creation.

Finally, the politician may face an even more fundamental dilemma than the one posed by the conflict between his own interest and the interests of those he serves. According to some, it is impossible to govern effectively and to remain innocent in a moral sense. The nature of the task a politician faces often requires him to do things that are morally wrong. If he fails to do these things, he shirks his duty. If he does them, he is guilty. This is what Michael Walzer has called the problem of dirty hands.[30] In our terms, it points once again to the close links between the first and second definitions of compromise. The concessions one makes in a political compromise are indeed often hazardous or objectionable. If Walzer is correct, this problem is a common and often inescapable feature of the politician's life, and yet it is one for which there is no solution. We must all take responsibility for the consequences of our actions and, to some extent at least, for the consequences of inaction in cases where we could have acted. For the politican this responsibility is often much greater than for the rest of us because the politician exercises public power. The consequences of his action or inaction are usually much greater than the consequences of the action or inaction of the ordinary citizen. To compromise one's principles is wrong by definition. Yet Walzer argues persuasively that that is what the responsible politician must sometimes do. How can it be wrong to do what one ought to do? To this question there is no satisfying answer. Yet we ought neither to ignore the principles nor to deny the obligation. In the final analysis the ambiguity of our attitudes toward compromise may be rooted in the nature of political life.

NOTES

1. Martin P. Golding, "Compromise," in Chapter 1 of this volume. Former Senator Eugene McCarthy expressed a similar complaint in his essay, "Compromise and Politics," in R.M. MacIver, ed., *Integrity and Compromise* (New York: Institute for Religious and Social Studies, 1957), p. 19.

2. Edmund Burke, "On Conciliation with the Colonies," in *Speeches and Letters on American Affairs* (London: J. M. Dent & Sons, 1908), pp. 130-31.

3. McCarthy, "Compromise and Politics."

4. Ibid., p. 23.

5. T. V. Smith, "Compromise: Its Context and Limits," *Ethics,* 53 (October 1942), 2; 4.

6. Aristotle distinguishes between theoretical sciences such as metaphysics and mathematics whose goal is knowledge, and practical sciences such as politics and ethics whose goal is action. Compromise may be more appropriate in the latter than in the former. My thanks to Charles Miller for this point.

7. For more on the appropriateness of compromise in the face of uncertainty see John E. Coons, "Compromise as Precise Justice" in Chapter 11 of this volume.

8. David Apter, *Introduction to Political Analysis* (Cambridge, Mass.: Winthrop, 1977), p. 319.

9. Compare Golding's description of the "compromisable conflict situation" in Chapter 1 of this volume.

10. The distinction between integrative and distributive compromise derives historically from Mary Parker Follet, "Constructive Conflict," in H. C. Metcalf and L. Urwich, eds., *Dynamic Administration: The Collected Papers of Mary Parker Follett* (New York: Harper, 1940). At the limit, an integrative solution might be found that would satisfy both parties so completely that it would no longer be appropriate to speak of compromise (or conflict).

11. The analysis in the rest of this section draws heavily on Dean G. Pruitt and Steven A. Lewis, "Development of Integrative Solutions in Bilateral Negotiation," *Journal of Personality and Social Psychology,* 31 (1975), 621-33.

12. See Lewis A. Froman and Michael D. Cohen, "Compromise and Logroll: Comparing the Efficiency of Two Bargaining Processes," *Behavioral Sciences,* 15 (1970), 180-83.

13. Pruitt and Lewis, "Integrative Solutions", p. 622. In my view, much of Professor Golding's essay should be understood as an analysis of the problem-solving orientation toward conflict rather than as an analysis of the compromise process per se. The kind of hard, strategic bargaining that goes on between a used-car dealer and his customer often leads to a compromise solution. Golding arbitrarily excludes this kind of bargaining from his description of the "compromise process" and, in consequence, obscures useful distinctions between different types of compromise and between different methods for reaching compromise solutions to conflicts.

14. Pruitt and Lewis, "Integrative Solutions," p. 632.

15. Ibid.

16. John H. Hallowell, "Compromise as a Political Ideal," *Ethics,* 54 (April 1944), 173.

17. Carl Cohen, *Democracy* (Athens, Ga.: University of Georgia Press, 1971), pp. 181-82.

18. Joseph Tussman, *Obligation and the Body Politic* (New York: Oxford University Press, 1960), pp. 114, 117.

19. Ibid., p. 117.

20. J. R. Lucas, *Democracy and Participation* (Harmondsworth: Penguin Books, 1976), p. 35. Lucas notes as well that the advantage of bargaining is simultaneously a disadvantage, since it undermines the sense that we exist in a community of shared interests.

21. Tussman is aware of the possibility that discussion might not lead to agreement, as he makes clear in his discussion of majority rule in *Obligation and the Body Politic,* pp. 25-27, but he never connects this to his discussion of compromise.

22. This version of the argument for democracy draws on Peter Singer, *Democracy and Disobedience* (New York: Oxford University Press, 1974).

23. For a formal demonstration of the point, see Douglas Rae, "Decision Rules and Individual Values in Constitutional Choice," *American Political Science Review,* 63 (March 1969), 40-56; and Douglas Rae, "Political Democracy as a Property of Political Institutions," *American Political Science Review,* 65 (March 1971), 111-19.

24. Singer, *Democracy and Disobedience,* p. 32.

25. Ibid., pp. 42-45. See also Henry B. Mayo, *An Introduction to Democratic Theory* (New York: Oxford University Press, 1960), pp. 206-9.

26. Cohen, *Democracy, p. 47.*

27. *Ernest Barker, Reflections on Government* (London: Oxford University Press, 1942), p. 67.

28. See Robert Dahl, *A Preface to Democratic Theory* (Chicago: The University of Chicago Press, 1956), esp. chap 1; and Douglas Rae, "The Limits of Consensual Decision," *American Political Science Review,* 69 (December 1975), 1266-94.

29. See Louis C. Gawthrop, *Administrative Politics and Social Change* (New York: St. Martin's Press, 1971), pp. 43-50.

30. Michael Walzer, "Political Action: The Problem of Dirty Hands," *Philosophy and Public Affairs,* 2 (Winter 1973); reprinted in Marshall Cohen, Thomas Nagel, and Thomas Scanlon, eds., *War and Moral Responsibility* (Princeton: Princeton University Press, 1974), pp. 62-82.

8

COMPROMISE IN THE REALIZATION OF IDEAS AND VALUES

EDGAR BODENHEIMER

Webster's Third New International Dictionary sets forth several meanings of the term "compromise." One of the definitions equates compromise with "a settlement by arbitration or by consent reached by mutual concessions." Professor Golding's contribution to this volume has undertaken an inquiry into the nature of compromise conceived in this sense. Another definition describes compromise as "a thing intermediate between or blending qualities of two different things." The present essay will take up this broader and less common meaning of the term "compromise" and endeavor to clarify its significance in a circumscribed area, namely, that of realizing ideas and values in the building of human societies. Since the number of ideas and values that are instrumental in guiding the social process is a large one, a treatment of this subject must necessarily be of a selective nature. The choice of illustrative problems from the domains of politics, economics, education, and law has been made in light of the contemporary importance of the issues discussed.

COMPROMISES BETWEEN FREEDOM AND ORDER

In a book entitled *A Guide for the Perplexed,* E. F. Schumacher has made a distinction between two types of problems with which human human beings living in society will have to contend. The distinction he proposes is one between *convergent* and *divergent* problems.

Solutions offered for the first type of problems come together in a final design that will remain essentially uncontested and stable over time. The second type of problems calls forth answers that do not converge but move in different directions because of certain contradictory elements inherent in the problem. There exists no solution to these problems that is required by straight logical thinking or that can be reduced to the form of a precise instruction covering all phases of the subject matter. A satisfactory solution will often call for a high degree of wisdom and effort, and it may have to be limited to some special aspects of the problem.[1]

Under the theory of classical liberalism, the dichotomy of freedom and order presented a problem of a convergent nature. The purpose of the political order established by government was to insure that each person's range of freedom was consistent with the exercise of every other person's freedom. The notion of freedom was conceived as independence from the constraint of another's will, and the term "constraint" was interpreted to include violence.[2] Inasmuch as freedom was considered a supreme and universal value, it was to be secured for all human beings, not only for some. This goal, as Locke and Kant pointed out, could not be accomplished without an order of law, which would aim at preventing each citizen from encroaching on the liberty of every other citizen.[3] It is obvious that under this view there is no inherent contradiction between freedom and order, inasmuch as it is the very purpose of legal ordering to guarantee the reign of universal freedom.

The increasing complexity of social conditions and the emergence of grave social problems, such as proliferation of crime, deterioration of the environment, inflation, unemployment, and racial unrest have produced a crisis in the ideology of classical liberalism. The fight against crime and political subversion has engendered demands by conservative groups for restrictions on the right to be free from warrantless arrest and electronic surveillance. On the other side of the political spectrum, the right of business organizations to conduct their operations without governmental interference has been subjected to challenges predicated on the need to reduce water and air pollution. Affirmative action programs and other measures adopted in the interest of disadvantaged minorities have made a dent in the liberties to hire employees, rent homes, and provide accommodations according to one's choice. Restrictions on a person's right to build are not designed to preserve or enlarge the freedoms of other persons; their purpose is to protect public safety or to promote aesthetic values.

While it may be possible to subsume some of the new social and economic rights under a greatly enlarged conception of freedom (including the freedoms from fear and want, freedom to find work and achieve one's goals, freedom to breathe clean air and enjoy good health), it is clear that the new categories of rights involve values different from, and potentially contradictory to, the classical freedom to be protected from constraint. Under the classical doctrine of liberalism, legislation was designed to safeguard everybody's right to bodily integrity, freedom of movement, and power to acquire property and enter into contracts. These rights do not clash with other, opposing rights, since challenges to them, such as acts that inflict bodily injury, interfere with another person's property, or constitute a breach of contractual commitments, are considered to be exercises of non-rights that normally result in delictual sanctions.

On the other hand, when the right of employers to hire according to their choice is confronted with the right of employees not to be discriminated against on account of race or sex, when the right to charge a price for the sale of a commodity is limited by a legislative maximum, when the right to conduct one's business operations free from interference faces environmental restrictions, a clash or potential clash of conflicting interests occurs. While under classical liberalism the interests of all in the preservation of life, liberty, and property were, in Schumacher's terminology, of a convergent, that is, noncontradictory nature, this is no longer true, as a general proposition, under present-day conditions. When subtle accommodations are to be made between the values of freedom, equality, and security, when private concerns become pitted against the public interest, the problems often take a sharp turn toward divergence, so that the possible answers to them will tend to pull the decision-makers in different directions. One must therefore agree with the statement by Carl Friedrich that "as the patterning of rights and freedoms has unfolded in the Western world, the conflict between freedom and order has become more pronounced."[4]

The solution of such a conflict finally adopted may entail either a sacrifice of one interest for the sake of another or an accommodation between opposing interests. When all of the interests involved are deemed to be worthy of protection, some reconciliation between them will ordinarily be attempted. For example, when the freedom

to hire employees according to one's choice is confronted with the
right to be free from discrimination, the former right, without being
abrogated, may merely be limited by a mandate that an applicant
for employment shall not be turned away solely because of race or
sex. When the right to operate a business is made subject to environmental safeguards, such ecological restrictions are often reduced in
scope by considerations of their impact on costs and profitability. A
regulation of maximum hours will usually not set an absolute limit
on the number of hours an employee may work (although some states
have established compulsory ceilings in certain industries) but will
discourage excessive overtime work by prescribing compensation at
higher rates of pay. A curbing of certain procedural rights in the interest of crime control, such as has occurred in recent Supreme Court
decisions, thus far has left the core of these rights intact.

A structuring of order that seeks to harmonize individual freedom
with social and economic rights, and with other dispositions held to
be in the public interest, requires qualities such as understanding,
maturity of judgment, and public dedication, which Schumacher
considers to be preconditions for the solution of "divergent" problems. The future of mankind appears to portend an increase, rather
than a diminution, of the number and gravity of such problems.

COMPROMISE BETWEEN PERMISSIVENESS
AND AUTHORITY

In the field of education, the contrast between permissiveness and
authority corresponds to the freedom versus order pattern in politics.
A radically permissive system of education allows the children a far-
reaching degree of autonomy in conducting their lives as soon as they
are capable of independent action. Authoritarian education, on the
order hand, proceeds from the assumption that during the period of
minority children and adolescents are in need of a large measure of
definite guidance and disciplinary control, though to a decreasing
extent as they advance in age.

Many parents and educators will feel that no unbridgeable gulf between these two pedagogical methods exists, and that they can be
reconciled by what might be called a compromise. If this position is
adopted, it will be assumed that the ability to use one's judgment and
make one's own decisions should be developed in children from an

early period of their lives, and that an unlimited dependence on parents or educators is likely to hamper the growth of the young person. It will be realized, on the other hand, that in many respects young persons lack the experience for making well-considered judgments and that they need (and normally desire) firm guidance in many areas relating to the conduct of life.

Examples of fields in which such authoritative guidance may be deemed necessary are nutrition and the relations between the sexes. The mass media have reported that children eating lunches provided by their schools frequently throw away food items they do not like and purchase junk food in their place. Since the proper kind of nutrition is an indispensable factor in the healthy growth of young persons, some exercise of authoritative control in this area by parents and educators would appear to be highly desirable. Although a strange "right to be unhealthy" has been advocated by at least one scholar, it is not certain that this writer would wish to extend this "right" to persons in the stage of growth who may not as yet realize the serious consequences of nutritional neglect.[5]

There is widespread agreement that the relations between the sexes, because of their strong emotional impact upon individuals, present special dangers for young persons. In spite of the pronounced change of sexual mores in contemporary society, few informed persons will argue that a policy of pure permissiveness will be the most satisfactory approach for all ages. The sharp increase in teenage pregnancy, for example, has demonstrated the need for the exercise of some control by the home and the school.

In recent times, serious questions have arisen with respect to the need for moral education in a broader sense, involving the observance of a general code of social conduct. Many persons hold a belief in a situational ethic that makes the formulation of moral directives a matter of personal judgment. But it can hardly be denied that there is an objective element in morality, evidenced by the fact that the most basic norms of ethical behavior are incorporated into the law. Ignorance of the law is no excuse from liability under the law of crimes and torts, and this fact alone makes it mandatory for responsible parents and educators to insist on compliance with those standards of conduct not considered to be matters of individual choice.

It is by no means easy to combine the fostering of independence and self-reliance in the minds of the young with a reasonable measure of disciplinary control. It requires much less display of discriminating judgment if we are either in the habit of giving strict orders or refrain altogether from providing firm guidance. But the fact cannot be overlooked that even in the free societies of this world, the majority of people are often required to carry out imposed tasks in their daily work, while at other times they are expected to use their own judgment intelligently.[6] Here again we are confronted with a "divergent" problem that cannot be solved by a set of simple, "correct" formulas.

COMPROMISE BETWEEN COMPETITION AND COOPERATION

A simultaneous pursuit of mutually opposed aims also comes into play when we consider the interaction of the competitive and cooperative principles. The very nature of contemporary society makes it inevitable that attention be paid to both of these attitudes.

In those sectors of the economy that are dominated by a relatively small number of giant corporations, the principle of competition has given way to a blending of competitive and cooperative policies. Although competition continues to exist with respect to the kind and quality of goods produced, a substantial degree of cooperation prevails in the determination of prices. There is a community of interest among enterprises that have attained some independence from impersonal market forces to prevent price-cutting wars among them by informal understandings with respect to prices, and the antitrust laws have not been successful in stemming this tide.[7] Recent private and governmental studies have also shown that corporate cooperation is fostered by the fact that the nation's largest corporations are often linked together by officers who serve on one another's board of directors.

It is also to be taken into account in drawing up a balance sheet on this problem that a great deal of collaborative effort among employees is required within the four corners of an enterprise. To be sure, substantial competition for promotions and raises in salary will continue among employees and officers. This need not detract from the achievement of the economic goals of the enterprise as long as it does not degenerate into an intramural war by everybody against everybody.

Similar observations are applicable to academic life. With particular reference to the concerns of the students, in recent times some reservations have been put forward as to the desirability of a fierce struggle for good grades. As long as grade competition is kept within proper ethical bounds and does not absorb all of the energy of the students, it can be defended as inevitable as well as salutary. There are, on the other hand, areas of university life in which reasonable men and women will agree that a cooperative spirit guided by the educational goals of the institution ought to take precedence over struggle between groups, especially struggle between faculty and students. This would hold true especially for the work of committees consisting of faculty members and student representatives. While the voicing of sharp disagreements may frequently be desirable and wholesome, an unremitting attitude of antagonism between groups that are supposed to work toward a common institutional objective can easily produce deleterious effects.

The distinguished biologist Dobzhansky has said that "the relationships between organisms based on cooperation are in general more stable and enduring than relationships based on struggle and conflict."[8] Although a certain amount of conflict may be a sign of societal vitality, a state of severe social crisis will emerge when combat between competing interest groups takes on an internecine character. The achievement of a proper balance between competition and cooperation is a "divergent" problem whose solution in the United States is not yet in sight.

COMPROMISE BETWEEN EQUALITY AND DIFFERENTIATION

In a work by Sir Ernest Barker entitled *Principles of Social and Political Theory*, the following statement is found in a chapter dealing with the problem of equality:

> Burke's dictum, "All men have equal rights, but not to equal things," is a truism, and not a sophism. Law is a giver of legal capacities, and of legal capacities only. If it gives such capacities even-handed, it has obeyed to the full the principle of equality, and done all that in it lies to observe and follow that principle.[9]

The principle of "legal equality" thus defined is contrasted by Sir Barker with the notion of "social equality."[10] While he identifies legal equality with a nondiscriminatory assignment of rights, social equality aims, in his opinion, at the removal or amelioration of conditions that produce de facto inequalities between individuals or groups, especially in the economic and educational fields.

No sharp line of demarcation can be drawn between legal and social equality, as Barker admits. First of all, the granting of legal capacity to all persons, irrespective of race, sex, or religion, to vote, hold office, use accommodations and other facilities, and be eligible for any kind of employment also increases social equality, at least if the term "social" is understood in a broad sense. Second, the reduction of gross inequalities in economic status or educational opportunity can often be achieved only by means of the law. Examples are minimum wage legislation, food stamp programs, progressive taxation, educational grants-in-aid to indigent students. While such measures may result in the allocation of specific legal rights, their main purpose is to promote greater equality of condition, especially in the area of basic human needs.

The extent to which a narrowing of the gap between the rich and poor is desirable from the point of view of sound economic and social policy is a matter of controversy in this country. Furthermore, the issue is one that is generally judged differently in countries with a free enterprise system and those operating a socialist economy. What is important from the perspective of the approach taken in this essay is the fact that some compromise between the ideas of equality and differentiation is deemed desirable in all contemporary societies, regardless of their economic system. This means that the idea of radical egalitarianism is everywhere rejected in theory as well as in practice.[11]

Sharp differences in the wielding of power and influence exist in all countries in the areas of political and economic decision-making. In parliamentary democracies, members of legislative bodies exercise powers that far transcend those of ordinary citizens. The laws enacted by them affect the lives of those citizens in many important ways, and it is well known that these laws often do not merely reflect popular consensus. The executive branch in these countries possesses prerogatives in the field of foreign policy whose exercise — depending on the international power status of the country in question — may not only shape the destiny of the country but touch upon the lives and fortunes of people throughout the globe. The decisions of a ruling elite in autocratically governed countries may be of even greater impact upon the well-being of the citizens and of mankind at large. Economic decisions made by the managers of large enterprises, whether they are privately or publicly owned, may decisively influence the prosperity and standard of living in a society. Great inequality of decision-making also exists in those educational institutions whose governing boards of regents or trustees have the final word on the hiring and firing of instructors and the programmatic direction of the institution.

Disparities in salaries and other forms of remuneration exist, albeit in substantially different ratios, in all countries, regardless of their ideological preference. Some imperative rule of reason accounts for this phenomenon. Although it can be argued that the basic needs of human beings are essentially equal, it is obvious that merit, talent, and accomplishment are unequal. All healthy societies wish to maximize productivity and superior performance in the realization that incentives are usually necessary to promote this goal. For this reason there is, in the words of Amitai Etzioni, a need for a sector of social life "in which individual achievement can be exercised for differential rewards."[12]

It would not seem farfetched to maintain that, throughout the world, an increasing consensus is developing on the following three propositions: (1) that some equality of condition should be realized on the lower level, in the sense that the most urgent needs of human beings ought to be satisfied; (2) that human beings should have sufficient equality of opportunity to enable each to reach the place in society for which he or she is best fitted; and (3) that equality of basic need satisfaction and equality of opportunity should be complemented by a natural hierarchy of ability and leadership, to be promoted by proper economic and noneconomic incentives.

COMPROMISE BETWEEN SECURITY AND RISK

In his theory of human needs, Abraham Maslow has assigned the second place in his scale of basic needs to the desire for security and safety:

> If the physiological needs are relatively well gratified, there then emerges a new set of needs, which we may categorize roughly as the safety needs (security; stability; dependency; protection; freedom from fear, from anxiety and chaos; need for structure, order, law, limits . . .).[13]

Maslow goes on to say that the safety needs are particularly strong in the child but that they persist, perhaps in an attenuated form, in the adult person. Every human being wishes to be protected from criminal assault, murder, chaos, and tyranny. Everybody also has a preference for security of employment and, in the contemporary world, for insurance of various kinds.[14]

It is clear that large sectors of the legal system are designed to satisfy the human urge for safety. It is the purpose of criminal sanctions to discourage the commission of acts that endanger or violate the integrity of life, limb, and property. The law of torts pursues the same goal by different means of redress. The rules and principles of contract law are meant to safeguard the performance of agreements so that a party to a contract can safely rely, in the normal situation, on the proper execution of commitments by the opposite party. Old-age insurance, unemployment insurance, and disability insurance have the purpose, among others, to allay the potentially paralyzing fear of being overwhelmed by economic disaster in situations beyond the control of individuals. In these particular areas of the law, the public determination to guarantee a maximum degree of safety is not counterbalanced by arguments pointing in the opposite direction.

In some domains of life, on the other hand, the desire for security is overshadowed, in many individuals, by a propensity to take risks. Dangerous mountain climbs, expeditions to unknown or unsafe parts of the world, and hazardous sport activities are illustrations. Entrepreneurs and financiers will sometimes decide to engage in speculative ventures that may spell financial doom if they turn out to be unsuccessful.

While the assumption of risk in these examples is voluntary, strong arguments can also be made in favor of compelling persons to endure certain hazards they would much prefer to avoid. Maslow mentioned job protection as an example of a coveted area of safety. It is undoubtedly fair and just to adopt legal provisions prohibiting the arbitrary dismissal of employees on grounds of racial, sexist, or political prejudice, or on other grounds unrelated to performance or economic necessity. But every person must be held to the risk of job termination by reason of incompetence or substandard work, and even the rules governing tenure in academic institutions afford no protection against judgments of clearly inadequate performance.

Another field in which the complete elimination of risk may lead to socially disadvantageous results is accident insurance. If an individual or company, by taking out such insurance, can wholly relieve itself from legal responsibility for causing an accident or injury, this may produce carelessness or lack of concern in the observance of safety standards. This problem is receiving increasing attention in this age of insurance, and there are many legal experts who believe that insurance should leave intact some measure of civil and criminal liability for injury-causing acts.

COMPROMISE BETWEEN PAST- AND FUTURE-ORIENTED RATIONALES OF PUNISHMENT

The last example of an accommodation between seemingly contradictory ideas is drawn from a more specific area of societal concern than the illustrations offered earlier. It is, however, an area of great importance for the well-being of society. As was pointed out in the preceding section, the desire of men and women to be protected against assaults and depredations belongs to the most basic needs of human beings. When this desire is frustrated by attacks on one's person or property, all societies resort to the institution of punishment for the purpose of providing sanctions against such attacks. In spite of the universality of this institution, the identification of its specific objectives has been a matter of intense controversy and debate.[15]

Kant was convinced that legal punishment should never be administered in order to promote a future good, either with regard to the criminal himself or to civil society generally, but that penal measures must in all cases be imposed only because the offender has committed a crime in the past.[16] Hegel indicated his essential agreement with this view when he stated that the infliction of punishment was aimed at the annulment (negation, in his own words) of the offense.[17]

Bentham took an entirely different approach to the problem. To him, the chief purpose of punishment was the prevention of crime. He distinguished between general prevention, directed at the discouragement of wrongdoing by other members of the community, and particular prevention, intended to deter the punished offender himself from the commission of further crimes.[18] The same position was taken by Beccaria, who declared that the function of punishment "can only be to prevent the criminal from inflicting new injuries on the citizens and to deter others from similar acts."[19]

This last-mentioned view of punishment was accepted in the nineteenth century in many countries, and particularly by those in the Anglo-American orbit. It was complemented by another future-oriented rationale of punishment, the theory of rehabilitation, which was mentioned by Bentham as a secondary justification of penal sanctions.[20] Ferri was the first writer to elaborate a penal philosophy of rehabilitation, to be put into effect by the application of social and medical hygiene.[21] In more recent times, Lady Wootton has advocated reformation of the offender as the sole aim of a criminal system.[22] In contrast to Bentham, Ferri and Lady Wootton pushed the deterrent objectives of the criminal law into the background, and they completely rejected the retributive element in penology, which they thought was based on an untenable doctrine of moral responsibility. Both believed that they were thereby serving the cause of humanitarianism.

Today we are witnessing a decisive retreat from purely future-oriented conceptions of punishment. It is simply not considered judicious to deny that the perpetration of a crime in the past, the manner in which the action was executed, and the mental state accompanying the commission of the offense constitute important ingredients of the sentencing process. Even such a convinced utilitarian as H. L. A. Hart has pointed out that a position that relies exclusively on the potential future benefits of punishment cannot offer a full justification of the institution. "A necessary condition of the just *application* of punishment to a particular individual includes the requirement that he has broken the law."[23]

Another reason why the past offense must figure prominently in any sound system of penology is the necessity for establishing some modicum of proportionality between the offense and the punitive sanction imposed. From the point of view of good consequences to be expected in the future from punishing an offender, the fact that the penalty should reflect the gravity of the crime does not appear to be of major importance. A policy of crime prevention does not militate against overpunishment. If we take into account considerations of justice, on the other hand, the requirement of commensurateness can be ignored only at great risk. Severe punishments should not be imposed for trivial crimes. Furthermore, the experience of the last few decades demonstrated that widely discrepant sentences for similar offenses created a serious morale problem among prison inmates and, along with other factors, impeded their rehabilitation.[24]

Extreme divergences in the length of confinement have occured particularly under the system of indeterminate sentencing. It was also found that the indeterminate sentence — contrary to the initial belief that its use was more in accord with humanitarian principles than the determinate sentence — has actually increased the time spent in prison by convicted offenders.[25] This is attributable to the fact that the administrative authorities in charge of the system have been reluctant to release convicts because of fear that they might repeat the commission of crimes, while at the same time little was done to modify their criminal inclinations.[26]

Because of such adverse experiences with the indeterminate sentence, the California legislature passed the Uniform Determinate Sentencing Act of 1976, which went into effect on July 1, 1977. The chief purpose of the new law is defined by the legislature as follows:

> The Legislature finds and declares that the purpose of imprisonment for crime is punishment. This purpose is best served by terms proportionate to the seriousness of the offense with provision for uniformity in the sentences of offenders committing the same offense under similar circumstances. The Legislature further finds and declares that the elimination of disparity and the provision of uniformity of sentences can best be achieved by determinate sentences fixed by statute in proportion to the seriousness of the offense as determined by the Legislature to be imposed by the court with specified discretion.[27]

Under the act, sentencing, within narrow, legislatively fixed limits, is entrusted to the trial judge, who must choose one of four possible sentences: probation, a mitigated prison term, a normal prison term, or an aggravated prison term. If the judge chooses prison, he must select the middle term unless facts in mitigation or aggravation of the sentence are presented. He must state the reasons for his sentence choice at the time of sentencing.

The new law combines the past-oriented objective of creating proportionality between crime and punishment with the forward-looking goals of deterrence and rehabilitation. In a number of situations the judge — primarily for reasons of deterrence and societal protection — is directed to enhance the length of the terms provided by the regular tariff of sentences. Furthermore, the department of corrections is authorized by the act to reduce determinate sentences set by the judge by a maximum of one-third for good behavior and participation in rehabilitative programs. It is likely that the California attempt to reconcile traditional notions of commensurateness in sentencing with crime prevention and rehabilitative ideas will be imitated by legislation in other states.[28]

In addition to the reasons already mentioned, a further consideration supports the combination of penological rationales pointing in different directions. The classical past-oriented theory of punishment placed a strong emphasis on the element of moral blameworthiness. It was thought that the more willfulness and conscious planning in the execution of a crime was demonstrated, the more severe should be the mode of punishment. However, the method of adjusting the penalty to the degree of moral guilt exhibits a substantial weakness in certain types of cases. These are cases in which an accused person, although not legally insane, was reduced in his capacity of self-determination to such an extent that his action must be viewed as predominantly unfree. In such situations, where the perpetrator was impulse-ridden, saddled with an unfortunate hereditary endowment, and predisposed toward antisocial conduct, moral blameworthiness might be slight, but the need for protecting society might be great. Here it will be necessary to rely upon rationales of punishment other than commensurate desert, rationales that look to the future of society's well-being and that of the offender himself, provided he is capable of being resocialized.[29]

VII. NO COMPROMISE BETWEEN VALUES AND DISVALUES

The foregoing reflections were concerned with accommodations between values and ideas which, generally or at least by a substantial number of persons, are viewed affirmatively as building stones for a successful society. A different problem is presented when the relevant antithesis is not between conflicting values, but between values and disvalues. It appears that every value stands in contrast to a corresponding disvalue, which is appraised negatively as a potentiality to be avoided or resisted. Thus good is opposed by evil, fairness has its negation in unfairness, truthfulness is set against untruthfulness. We do not favor compromises between values and disvalues.

The reason why, in individual as well as social life, we generally insist upon adherence to certain basic values and avoidance of their corresponding disvalues has its roots in the natural reactions of human beings to the conduct of others. Human beings normally desire preservation of their lives as well as protection of their bodily integrity and reputation, and actions which evince disrespect or contempt for these values are viewed as "evil." If standards of fairdealing in trade, commerce, and other forms of social intercourse were radically displaced by their opposites, life in society would be poisoned by an unbearable amount of anger, frustration, and chaos. Since human beings wish to know the truth about physical and social reality, science and learning would become an absurdity if they were dominated by a general preference for untruth.

Recent anthropological research has demonstrated that all societies that have emerged from the most primitive state exhibit a great deal of congruency with respect to the recognition of the most fundamental values relating to organized social life.[30] The decisive preponderance of such moral principles of conduct in the relations between human beings is deemed so essential that, in the opinion of reasonable men and women, they should not be "compromised." This means that is is considered inappropriate to seek some sort of "middle ground" between good and evil, fair and unfair, truthful and dishonest. It does not mean that there may not be exceptional situations in which a departure from a fundamental value is permitted. Thus, some types of intragroup killing, some unfair methods of trade or competition, some lying by governmental authorities and private citizens may be sanctioned in a society.[31] Such exceptions do not detract from the presumptive and predominant validity of the fundamental principles, while genuine compromises between conflicting values presuppose an approximate parity of rank for these values.

A SEMANTIC POSTSCRIPT

This essay has used the term "compromise" in a sense that differs from its more traditional meaning. Most of the time when we speak of compromise we refer to an arrangement between parties with conflicting interests by which each party yields some ground to the other for the purpose of arriving at a settlement satisfactory to both sides. The chief difference between this more customary usage of the term and the one explored in this essay is that the compromise underlying the settlement of a controversy between individuals or groups is arrived at reluctantly and in the face of necessity or expediency. The compromises between conflicting ideas and values here discussed, on the other hand, are advocated on grounds of sound and desirable public policy.

It is one of the principal laws of semantics that different phenomena should be identified by different linguistic terms. Although, as was pointed out at the beginning of this essay, the broad use of the term "compromise" here employed is consistent with the conventions of the English language, it is submitted that the term "synthesis" is preferable as an alternative when we enter the domain of adjustments between conflicting ideas and values. In the area of the law, the word "balancing" is frequently used to denote accommodations between clashing constitutional or other legal principles.

NOTES

1. E. F. Schumacher, *A Guide for the Perplexed* (New York: Harper & Row, 1977), pp. 120-28.
2. See Immanuel Kant, *The Metaphysical Elements of Justice*, 1797, trans. J. Ladd, (Indianapolis: Bobbs-Merrill, 1965), pp. 43-44; John Locke, *Two Treatises on Civil Government*, 1689, book II, ch. 6, sec. 57 (London: Everyman's Library Edition, 1924).
3. Locke, *Two Treatises, book II, chap. 6, sec. 57;* Kant, *Metaphysical Elements of Justice*, pp. 34-35.
4. Carl J. Friedrich, "The Dialectic of Political Order and Freedom," in Paul G. Kuntz, ed., *The Concept of Order* (Seattle: University of Washington Press, 1968), p. 350.
5. Samuel I. Shuman, "The Right to Be Unhealthy," *Wayne Law Rev,* 22 (November 1975), 61, 81-82.
6. See in this connection Alfred N. Whitehead, *The Aims of Education* (New York: Macmillan, 1929), chap. 3. Cf. the following statement by the psychiatrist Hans J. Eysenck, *Crime and Personality* (London: Routledge & Kegan Paul, 1977), p. 172: "Clearly, the path to follow is through a middle ground, to treat children with a sufficient degree of severity to achieve the conditioning required by society, but not to treat them so severely that they fall prey to neurotic disorders."
7. See John K. Galbraith, *Economics and the Public Purpose* (Boston: Houghton Mifflin, 1973), pp. 114-15, 216.
8. Theodosius Dobzhansky, *The Biological Basis of Human Freedom* (New York: Columbia University Press, 1956), p. 65.

9. Ernest Barker, *Principles of Social and Political Theory* (Oxford: Clarendon Press, 1951), p. 151.

10. Ibid., p. 153.

11. On radical egalitarianism, defined as the notion that "all social inequalities are unnecessary, and unjustifiable, and ought to be eliminated," see Hugo A. Bedau, "Egalitarianism and the Idea of Equality," in J. Roland Pennock and John W. Chapman, eds., *Equality, NOMOS IX* (New York: Atherton Press, 1967), pp. 13-16.

12. Amitai Etzioni, *The Active Society* (New York: The Free Press, 1968), p. 640.

13. Abraham H. Maslow, *Motivation and Personality*, 2d ed. (New York: Harper & Row, 1970), p. 39.

14. Ibid., pp. 40-41.

15. For a good general survey see Stanley E. Grupp, ed., *Theories of Punishment* (Bloomington, Ind.: Indiana University Press, 1971).

16. Immanuel Kant, *The Philosophy of Law, 1797*, trans. W. Hastie (Edinburgh: T. & T. Clark, 1887), p. 195.

17. G. W. F. Hegel, *The Philosophy of Right*, 1821, trans. T. M. Knox, (Oxford: Clarendon Press, 1942), p. 73.

18. Jeremy Bentham, "Principles of Penal Law," 1778, in John Bowring, ed., *The Works of Jeremy Bentham* (New York: Russell & Russell, 1962), vol. 1, p. 396.

19. Cesare Beccaria, *On Crimes and Punishment*, 1764, trans. H. Paolucci, (Indianapolis: Bobbs-Merrill, 1963), p. 42.

20. Bentham, "Principles," p. 396.

21. Enrico Ferri, *The Positive School of Criminology*, 1901, ed. Stanley E. Grupp (Pittsburgh: University of Pittsburgh Press, 1968), pp. 98-103.

22. Barbara Wootton, *Social Science and Social Pathology* (London: Allan and Unwin, 1959), pp. 227-28, 250-52; Barbara Wootton, *Crime and the Criminal Law* (London: Stevens, 1963), pp. 79-81.

23. H. L. A. Hart, *Punishment and Responsibility* (New York: Oxford University Press, 1968), p. 80. Hart makes it clear in his discussion that a penal policy exclusively geared to deterrence is not per se inconsistent with the punishment of innocent persons. See also Alfred C. Ewing, *The Morality of Punishment* (Montclair, N.J.: Patterson Smith, 1970), pp. xiii-xiv, 44-45.

24. See the valuable study of Judge Marvin E. Frankel, *Criminal Sentences: Law without Order* (New York: Hill and Wang, 1972).

25. See Merrill T. Eaton, "Treatment for the Criminal," in Richard W. Nice, ed., *Criminal Psychology* (New York: Philosophical Library, 1962), pp. 223-24; Francis A. Allen, "Criminal Justice, Legal Values and the Rehabilitative Ideal," in Grupp, *Theories of Punishment*, pp. 324-25; Sol Rubin, *The Law of Criminal Corrections*, 2d ed. (St. Paul, Minn.: West 1973), pp. 758-59.

26. An extreme instance of an excessive prison term imposed under the indeterminate sentencing system is presented *In re Rodriguez,* 16 Cal. 3rd 638, 122 Cal. Rptr. 552 (1975), where the California Supreme Court released a prisoner who had served twenty-two years for a rather minor sex offense.

27. See West's Annotated California Codes, Penal Code, Sec. 1170 (a) (1).

28. A foreign code inspired by ideas similar to those expressed in the new California legislation is the West German Penal Code of 1975. See Hans-Heinrich Jescheck, *Lehrbuch des Strafrechts: Allgemeiner Teil,* 3d ed. (Berlin: Duncker & Humblot, 1978), pp. 51-54, 703-5.

29. For a balanced account of the purposes of punishment see F. J. O. Coddington, "Problems of Punishment," in Grupp, *Theories of Punishment,* pp. 333-53.

30. See Ralph Linton, "Universal Ethical Principles: An Anthropological View," in Ruth N. Anshen, ed., *Moral Principles of Action* (New York: Harper & Bros., 1952), pp. 645-60; Clyde N. Kluckhohn, "Ethical Relativity: Sic et Non," *Journal of Philosophy,* 52 (November 1955), p. 663; Margaret Mead, "Some Anthropological Considerations Concerning Natural Law," *Natural Law Forum,* 6 (1961), p. 51; Lawrence Kohlberg, "From Is to Ought," in Theodore Mischel, ed., *Cognitive Development and Epistemology* (New York: Academic Press, 1971), pp. 155, 174-80.

31. See Linton, *supra* note 30, at 652-58; Edgar Bodenheimer, *Jurisprudence: The Philosophy and Method of the Law,* Rev. Ed. (Cambridge, Mass.: Harvard University Press, 1974), pp. 217-29; Sissela Bok, *Lying: Moral Choice in Public and Private Life* (New York: Pantheon Press, 1978).

PART IV

COMPROMISE AND
THE LAW

9

COMPROMISE AND LITIGATION

MARTIN SHAPIRO

There are two senses in which speaking of compromise *and* litigation rather than compromise *or* litigation appears somewhat strange. First, compromise is customarily viewed as diadic — involving negotiation between two parties.[1] Litigation is triadic, involving two disputants and a third party. Thus, to compare compromise and litigation might be considered an apples-and-oranges problem. There is, however, a triadic form of compromise. That form is usually known as mediation. Mediation employs a third party who tries to devise a compromise or mediate solution mutually satisfactory to the disputants. This paper will deal with both mediation and negotiation as related forms of compromise.

The second sense in which compromise appears different from, and indeed the direct antithesis of, litigation is that litigation is commonly conceived to demand a winner-take-all outcome. Either in its diadic or triadic form compromise is, almost by definition, seen as having mediate outcomes. As other papers in this volume make clear, if compromise is purely a function of the relative bargaining power of two or more parties, it may not achieve mediate outcomes. For one of the parties may be so powerful as fully to determine the outcome of the bargaining. In short, whether or not the process of compromise yields an outcome that may fairly be called a compromise partly depends upon factors outside the process. For a number of reasons that will appear shortly, this paper will set aside as a special case instances in which a disproportionate power vested in one party leads to a nonmediative outcome for the mediation process.

It is the other side of the coin that is of concern to us here. That is, assuming that mediation does produce mediate outcomes, is it really antithetical to litigation. The notion that winner-take-all outcomes are an essential feature of litigation is deeply embedded in Western legal thought. In his contribution to this volume and in his earlier work cited there,[2] Professor Coons has noted and challenged this legal preoccupation with winner take all. He proposed a number of litigational situations in which courts ought to abandon winner-take-all for compromise outcomes. His challenge, however, is to what he sees as a very solid winner-take-all tradition, and his proposal is conceived as a rather radical reform. While I would second his proposal, I question the solidity of the tradition. In order to do so, I shall take a rather roundabout path that leads through the notion of consent in order eventually to return to that of compromise.

In another place I have argued that triadic conflict-resolution structures may be ordered along a continuum running from go-between through mediator to arbitrator and finally judge.[3] This continuum is ordered by the proportion of consent to coercion found at each point. The go-between operates in an almost purely consensual matrix. He will succeed at resolving conflict only if both parties freely consent to employ him as a conflict resolver and both freely arrive through his services at a meeting of the minds about an outcome to their dispute. The go-between coerces only to the very limited degree that his rephrasing of the messages he carries back and forth moves the parties in the direction he desires. The real-estate broker who turns "ninety thousand and not a cent more for that dirty shack" into "He feels he can't go higher than ninety thousand" is exercising what little coercive power the go-between has.

The higher and higher levels of coercion that we encounter as we move along the continuum are achieved by the increasing substitution of office and law for consent. Where go-betweens or mediators are involved, typically two conflicting parties choose both the third person and the legal rule, if any, according to which the conflict is to be resolved. It is possible to conceive both the go-between and the mediator situations as involving "pure" negotiation simply assisted by a third party. That is, it is possible to conceive these forms of triadic conflict resolution as being ultimately governed only by the relative bargaining power of the two conflicting parties without regard to any moral or legal rule. As Eisenberg has shown, however, even negotiation often involves the invocation of rules.[4] And the very presence of a third party introduces an influence other than that of the two disputants. A mediator, for instance, exercises more coercive authority than a go-between in the sense that he is expected to propose solutions as well as simply carry messages. While he must find a solution to which both parties consent, he as well as they is a legitimate source of proposed solutions. And mediation frequently occurs in the context of contract disputes in which the parties made the law that will govern the dispute by consenting to the terms of the contract.

The progressive substitution of law and office for consent along the continuum is even clearer when we reach arbitration, and particularly binding arbitration. The parties must both still consent to the particular arbitrator. But he is more likely than the mediator to come from a preset list and to hold special legal or religious qualifications. Arbitration very frequently is provided for in contracts that also provide rules of decision. The arbitrator is close enough to the mediator to be expected to arrive at a somewhat more mediate solution than a court of law but close enough to the judge to be expected to reach a solution in accord with the rule governing the dispute. Where a contract requires binding arbitration, elements of consent remain, given that both parties consented to seek and abide by arbitration and both consented to the subtantive provisions of the contract that supply the arbitrator's rules of decision. Nevertheless the level of coercion has risen very high, since one of the disputants may be forced to abide by a decision that is far more favorable to his opponent than to himself. Where a law requires submission to binding arbitration, arbitration merges into litigation.

The procedures of the ancient Roman law show us quite clearly the gradual substitution for office and law for consent in the litigation process. In the earliest times two Roman heads of family who wished to litigate first had to agree to a rule of law to govern the resolution of their dispute and then to a particular person to serve as iudex. Gradually the Romans fell into the habit of going to government officials to assist them in formulating a rule for their case. Eventually those officials ceased to tailor-make a rule for each dispute and instead published a catalogue of ready made rules. Finally the catalogue became the law of the state, and state officials also were substituted for the private iudex. (The common law writ system evolved in roughly the same way). Now if the two parties wished to litigate they had to submit to the law made by the state rather than to a rule upon which they had personally agreed. And they had to submit themselves to the state judge rather than to a judge of their own choosing.

That judges wield more coercive power than do other triadic conflict resolvers because they hold government office and apply government law is clear. That, nevertheless, they are firmly placed within a continuum all points along which represent various mixes of coercion *and* consent is not so clear. Yet to see courts as purely coercive institutions is to neglect much of what they do and even more of what they say. For even while applying coercion, courts constantly touch base with the consensual element of triadic conflict resolution. For instance, Stenton tells us that the judical ideal of Anglo-Saxon justice was not litigation but mutual agreement confirmed and recorded in judicial proceedings.[5] And for centuries after the Norman Conquest English landownership, which was the central concern of English law, was largely established by mock litigation in which what was really a consensual transfer was given the form of a judicial decree awarding the land to the victor, AKA purchaser.[6]

Winner take all naturally follows from this consent-eliciting rationale, because if one party is legally right and the other legally wrong then one must win all and the other lose all. Even granting the utility of the law rationale, however, why could the judge not say, "The law decides that each of you is half right?" No doubt a number of reasons are embedded in basic Anglo-American law-ways. Professor Coons notes some of them in the pieces cited earlier. A major reason is that mediate solutions are bound to expose judicial discretion. Perhaps we can believe that the judge is a mindless servant of a law that clearly dictates that one party broke it and the other did not. It is far more difficult to believe that he imposes nothing of his own will when he says that the law dictates that both parties broke it a little bit and each is entitled to some remedy. It is hard to wrap the judical discretion involved in deciding just who gets how much remedy in the majesty of black-letter law.

It is indicative of the risk that compromise poses to the judicial guise of nondiscretion that Professor Coons, even while championing judicially imposed compromise, is especially attracted to a very peculiar form of compromise—the 50-50 split. For this kind of compromise appears almost as non discretionary as winner take all. If the judge determines that certain conditions exist, he switches from winner take all to 50-50 split, and this latter rule determines the remedy just as automatically as winner take all. Since there is no actual determination of who ought to get exactly how much, no judicial discretion is apparent, only the automatic working out of a legal rule.

This is one of the keys to the distinction we make between judging and arbitration, even binding arbitration. The arbitrator is supposed to decide according to law — where relevant law is to be found. But in a way not absolutely clearly specified in Western jurisprudence, he is supposed to enjoy somewhat more leeway than the judge in shaping a legal solution that gives at least some satisfaction to both parties. This extra leeway exists because the arbitrator has reached his triadic position on the basis of a higher quantum of consent and a lower quantum of state imposition than the judge. Both parties have consented to arbitration — even if only in advance and in general. Only one party may have sought the judge's services. Both parties have chosen the arbitrator, even though that consent may have been only to a general list. Neither party has chosen the particular judge.[7] Because the arbitrator taps the consent of both parties more fully, he is less in need of the rationale that it is the law, not the conflict resolver who decides. Because he needs the law cover less than the judge, he need not adopt the winner-take-all stance that is a corollary of the law cover. To put the matter differently, conflicting parties are more willing to accept a discretionary intermediate resolution from someone they have chosen than from someone they have not.

Winner take all is associated with judging because judging lies at one extreme of a continuum of conflict-resolution devices that mix consent and coercion. The judge uses winner take all because he is imposing resolutions, but he does so precisely because he seeks to elicit as much consent as possible to his impositions. Thus, we encounter the paradox that compromise, a general technique for eliciting mutual consent, is read out of litigation because winner take all is seen as a particularly effective technique for eliciting consent by both parties to judicial conflict resolution. This paradox arises because, where office is substituted for consent, the government officer must proclaim some special virtue or legitimacy. Judges do so by proclaiming themselves the independent servants of winner-take-all law.

Is there a resolution to this paradox? In fact, courts are often willing to reveal a bit of their discretion in order to achieve mediate solutions. We have already noted how that favored remedy of Anglo-American law, money damages, involves a good deal of sub rosa compromise. Where Anglo-American courts move from money damages to specific performance or injunctive remedies, they say they are

moving from common law to equity. In fashioning equitable remedies, judges have always proclaimed their duty to "balance the equities" and shape a remedy that makes the winner whole while doing
the least damage to the loser. Indeed, where the remedy that would
be best for the winner would do disproportionate injury to the loser,
the winner may have to settle for a second- or third-best remedy. In
short, while equity declares that one party wins and the other loses, it
has always insisted that winner does not necessarily take all.

Contemporary lawyers dress their abhorrence of *ex parte* proceedings in the rationale of conflict. The truth shall emerge from the
clash of litigants. The traditional reluctance of Anglo-American
courts to proceed in the absence of one of the parties, however, is historically linked to the experience of judges that it is extremely difficult to elicit the consent of the loser to a proceeding in which he did
not even participate. One of the most striking features of most court
systems is their underdeveloped enforcement mechanisms. Most of
the world's judges have largely depended upon eliciting sufficient
consent to their verdicts to insure voluntary compliance with their
decrees. Here we see the typical judicial mixture of consent and coercion. Every lawyer knows that getting the judgment is one thing and
collecting it another. Yet he knows that should the losing party refuse
voluntarily to comply with the court order, further court proceedings
are available to force him to do so.

The traditional reluctance of common law courts to grant any
remedy other than money damages illustrates rather well this mixture of coercion and consent. No doubt money damages was a remedy that entailed fewer enforcement problems than specific performance, but its consensual roots lie much deeper than that. For the
money-damages remedy is in origin essentially a compromise or mediate solution to conflict. In tort it begins as the substitution of *Wer-
gelt* for physical retribution. Having struck out the eye of another, it
is surely more agreeable to pay money than to suffer the relatives of
the injured party to strike out your eye in return. In contract money
damages is a compromise solution when compared with specific performance. Having agreed to deliver the horse, if you cannot bear to
part with it, then keep it, but compensate the party who has suffered
loss through your failure to deliver. For the loser in a lawsuit, better
money than his eye or his horse. Moreover, is it sheer coincidence
that the common law wishes in the final analysis to translate all disputes into disputes over how much X should pay Y? Money is, after

all, the ideal medium for mediate solution. For it is almost infinitely divisible, and any money award is likely to fall somewhere between what the plaintiff feels he deserves and what the defendant feels he ought to pay.

One could go on multiplying these examples of judicial mixing of coercion and consent endlessly. For our purposes here it is enough to say that while the Anglo-American legal system typically contemplates winners and losers, even where those labels are not shams behind which agreements are registered, winners do not necessarily take all.

Indeed the winner-take-all image of courts is itself part of an attempt to preserve consent even as law and office are substituted for the direct and immediate consent of the parties. Much of the institutional myth of courts, which laywers and judges work so hard to build, is directed to persuading losers that the triadic structure of courts has not degenerated into two against one. Thus, as official judges are substituted for those picked by the parties, the independence and neutrality of judges must be stressed until they become the touchstone of true courtness. For unless litigants are persuaded that the judge is not a proponent of their opponents' interests or of interests of government contrary to their own, they are unlikely to given even minimum consent to the court's judgment. That in reality most of the world's courts have been neither neutral nor independent does not prevent these qualities from being built into the very definition of court purveyed by those concerned to elicit consent for judicial proceedings. Precisely because the judge is a government official who necessarily favors the interests of government over those of the litigating parties, and precisely because he acts according to a law that is likely to favor one of the parties over the other, we constantly insist that he is independent of government and favors neither party.

Similarly, precisely because the judge in reality exercises considerable discretion, we insist that he does not. It is from this insistence that the winner-take-all phenomenon arises. As an officer imposed by government rather than chosen by the parties, the judge prefers to rely on something above and beyond his self-proclaimed bona fides — the law. Thus, the judge says to the losing party, "It is not I but the law that decides against you. You were legally wrong. He was legally right. Of course, as a good citizen you consent to your loss because you believe in the rule of law."

Equity can take this position because historically equity judges always admitted that they exercised discretion. Common law remedies were available as of right, but equitable remedies were special remedies available at the discretion of a special set of judges who, indeed, were carefully denied even the title of judge. (The two great equity judges of England were the Chancellor and the Master of the Rolls.)

Those familiar with judicial activity in the school desegregation area have often heard the trumpeting of the traditionally wide discretionary power of judges in fashioning equitable remedies. Under those discretionary powers U.S. judges today draft our children for the army of social justice and bus them off to battle. They also decide which teachers will teach what and where and which schools will and will not teach auto shop. This very experience, however, also reveals the potential danger of mediate judicial solutions. For these judges have long since lost any resemblance to neutral triadic conflict resolvers and stand forth fully exposed as administrators wielding the coercive powers of government to achieve its policy goals.

In addition to money damages and equitable discretion, one could go on to identify a number of other channels of mediate decision or compromise that exist even within the mainstream of the litigation process.[8] These are, however, usually interstitial and often cleverly disguised. Instead we might turn to the principal role played by litigation in facilitating compromise, a role that is played out not strictly within the litigational process but in the relation between that process and the processes of mediation and negotiation.

Perhaps this relation is best illustrated by a brief look at the legal system of imperial China. It has long been observed that the Chinese were very prone to mediation of their disputes. Indeed it is often urged that winner-take-all solutions were as antithetical to Chinese law-ways as intermediate solutions are alleged to be to Western law-ways. Yet the Chinese had a long, very detailed code of law which prescribed the most severe form of winner-take-all solutions. The winner received restitution and the loser penal sanctions even in what we would call civil cases. The existence and enforcement of this code[9] might be taken as giving the lie to those observers who insist on seeing mediation as the dominant mode of traditional Chinese conflict resolution. Or it might be taken as constituting a paradox requiring explanation. Why does a society so bent on mediation develop an extreme, winner-take-all legal system?

The explanation lies not so much in closer examination of Chinese litigation as in a more general appreciation of the dynamics of mediation. Mediation obviously tends toward split-the-difference rather than toward winner-take-all solutions. It is precisely in its split-the-difference aspect that mediation encounters its principle barrier to success. Both parties may consent to the mediation and consent to the person of the mediator but nonetheless sabotage the mediation by overstating their claims. For overclaiming is the natural response to anticipation of split-the-different resolution. If we are going to split the difference, then the more I ask for the more I get in the end. Mediation may be killed simply by the competitive escalation of claims. More often no doubt it is killed through a two-step process. The escalation of claims leads to so many false or offensive claims by each party against the other that the minimum of mutual goodwill necessary to achieve a successful mediation disappears.

It is customarily argued that the Chinese solved the overclaiming problem ideologically. Confucian thought denigrated overclaiming and declared the superior virtue of the person who yielded most. While Confucianism may have provided a favorable climate for mediation, it can hardly have solved the overclaiming problem single-handed. For Confucianism denigrated conflict itself. It it had really dominated men's minds and behavior thoroughly enough to prevent overclaiming, it would have prevented the occasion for overclaiming, that is, a conflict sufficiently bitter to require resort to a mediator.

The key to the Chinese solution to the overclaiming problem lies in the interaction between Confucian inclination to mediation and a Draconian code. A lawsuit was expensive. Its outcome was unpredictable. Once begun it might well end in the ruin of both parties and was very likely to end in the beating or exile, if not the execution, of one. The frightening prospect of a lawsuit not only moved conflicting parties to consent to mediation but inhibited their tendency to overclaim. For if one of the parties so overclaimed as to drive the other to adamantcy, then the disaster of a lawsuit might follow.

Thus, the existence of an elaborate code of strict law side by side with an essentially mediatory system of conflict resolution constitutes not a contradiction or paradox but a natural combination. It is the strict law that cures the overclaiming problem and thus makes split-the-difference mediation work.

The Chinese experience points us to a central fact of Western legal experience, which has always been known but somehow has not penetrated very far into our theoretical understanding of law, courts, and litigation. The bulk of our conflict resolution according to law today is done not by litigation but by mediation or negotiation conducted under the shadow of litigation.[10] This is not the simple and quite true statement that most people settle their disputes without resorting to law. Rather it is that in most instances in which the conflicting parties do wish to resort to law, they nevertheless reach a compromise rather than winner-take-all resolution, and they do so while under the expectation that, should they fail to compromise, winner-take-all litigation will occur.[11]

It is necessary to emphasize, as Eisenberg has done,[12] that such negotiation is not purely a matter of registering the weight of the interests and their comparative bargaining power. Where litigation is potentially present, negotiated outcomes will reflect the values expressed by the law. Often both the negotiating or mediating parties will have accepted the basic values expressed by the law relevant to their dispute. At the very minimum the ability of either party to go on to assert his legal rights by litigating makes the legal position of each highly relevant to arriving at a mutually satisfactory outcome. We solve our overclaiming problem exactly as the Chinese do, by the implied or articulated threat to litigate if the other side claims too much. Thus, a very high proportion, not only of disputes in general, but of what fairly may be called legal disputes are settled by compromise under the threat of, and in contemplation of the outcome of, litigation.

To separate out this whole mass of mediated and negotiated compromise and set it in opposition to litigation is to do violence to the day-to-day experience of lawyers and judges. For they live in a world that emphasizes, not the opposition, but the interrelation between compromise and litigation. Attempts at mediate solution typically begin before the lawsuit is filed and go on right up to the courthouse door. Indeed, they go right through the courthouse door. The outcome of many a litigation well under way before judge and jury is the announcement of a settlement by the parties.

Thus, to see a legal system or even a judicial system as requiring winner-take-all outcomes is to focus on a single static factor rather than to perceive the dynamics of the system. It is true that, from the perspective of any single disputant, mediation (or negotiation) and litigation may be seen as alternatives. But from the perspective of the legal system they constitute mutually supporting processes each of which is necessary to the success of the other.

As we have noted, litigation makes mediation work by solving the overclaiming problem that is central to split-the-difference solution. I wish to focus now on the other side of the coin, the extent to which mediation and negotiation contribute to the health of the courts that conduct litigation. For the widespread practice of mediation and negotiation under threat of litigation allows courts to have their cake and eat it too. As we have noted, even with the progressive substitution of law and office for the direct consent of the conflicting parties, courts continue by various means to elicit consent as well as wield coercive authority. Yet they must seek to do so within the context of imposing the law of the forum. Negotiation or mediation under the threat of litigation is a rather nice solution to this problem. The larger quantum of mutual consent that exists in mediation or negotiation as opposed to litigation is partly preserved. At the same time, the law the court seeks to enforce will be an important determiner of the outcome.

Admittedly this is not an ideal solution. The parties do not come together in an absolutely consensual way, since either or both may come to the bargaining table and then be forced into concessions by threat of litigation. On the other hand, so long as they can reach agreement, they need not settle their dispute exactly as the law in court would have settled it. In short, mediation or negotiation under threat of litigation lies along the continuum we sketched earlier at a point somewhere between mediation and litigation. It is a point at which courts can exercise their coercive legal powers by implication or anticipated reaction in a context that involves a considerable amount of real consent and an even greater appearance of consent by the conflicting parties. Thus, it provides for courts an optimal solution to the problem of imposing law while maintaining their legitimacy as conflict resolvers rather than as purely coercive governmental authorities.

Mediation or negotiation under threat of litigation is also optimal in another way that returns us to our main theme—the opposition between mediate outcomes and the winner-take-all outcomes to which courts are inclined. We have noted that a court that itself shapes mediate outcomes runs the risk of exposing its judicial discretion. When the legal system shifts a high proportion of outcomes from trial to the mediation or negotiation preceding possible trial, it encourages mediate solutions without unmasking judicial discretion.

In summary, then, we ought not to see compromise as antithetical to legal or even judicial resolution of conflict. In the first place, lurking within such judicial institutions as money damages and equitable discretion are major elements of compromise. Our tendency to ignore these elements derives from a false picture of courts as purely coercive mechanisms when in fact they seek to preserve significant elements of mutual consent by the conflicting parties to the legal outcomes they prescribe. In the second place, and perhaps more important, mediation and negotiation under threat of litigation are a central feature of Western legal systems. Such mediation or negotiation typically will produce intermediate or compromise outcomes. To be sure, they are compromise outcomes partly determined by anticipation of the winner-take-all outcomes that might result should litigation occur. Unless we limit the term "compromise" to "pure" compromises in which the bargaining power of both participants is absolutely equal and neither can threaten to call upon outside resources or allies should negotiation fail, this kind of prelitigation settlement is surely entitled to the name "compromise." And if such a settlement is entitled to be called compromise, then we must say that compromise is as central a mode of Western legal systems as is winner-take-all litigation. Indeed we must say that far from being in conflict, an intimate interrelation between compromise and winner-take-all must exist if either mediators or judges are to enjoy any substantial success as conflict resolvers.

NOTES

1. This paper deals with compromise only as a device for dispute settlement. In the policymaking context, of course, compromise typically involves many parties.
2. John E. Coons, "Approaches to Court Imposed Compromise—The Uses of Doubt and Reason," *Northwestern Univ. Law Rev.*, 58 (1964), 750-805.
3. "Courts," in Fred Greenstein and Nelson Polsby, *Handbook of Political Science*, (Reading, Mass.: Addison-Wesley, 1975), Vol. 5, pp. 321-70.
4. Melvin Eisenberg, "Private Ordering Through Negotiation: Dispute-Settlement and Rulemaking, "Harvard Law Rev., 89 (1976), 637-81.
5. Doris Stenton, *English Justice, 1066-1215* (Philadelphia: American Philosophical Society, 1964), pp. 7-8.
6. See A. Simpson, *An Introduction to the History of Land Law* (London: Oxford University Press, 1963), pp. 44-224.
7. There is, of course, the problem of sub rosa forum shopping, but it is sub rosa precisely because neither party is supposed to pick the judge.

8. Here we have emphasized the adoption of legal rules that provide formal avenues for compromise. In addition, of course, courts may achieve compromise on an ad hoc basis by stressing the equities of a particular fact situation over the formal dictates of law. The choice of money damages as an instrument of common law neatly combines the two. It provides a new formal vehicle through which intermediate results may be achieved, and in particular cases it permits judges or juries to give one of the parties something less than what might formally be his winner-take-all due.

9. That it was enforced is clear from Derk Bodde and Clarence Morris, *Law in Imperial China* (Cambridge: Harvard University Press, 1967).

10. For one of the few studies to explicitly treat legal negotiation in this way see Robert Mnookin and Lewis Kornhauser, "Bargaining in the Shadow of the Law: The Case of Divorce," *Yale Law Journal* (April 1979).

11. Binding arbitration is usually not subject to subsequent litigation in the regular courts. Binding arbitration, however, is itself a form so close to litigation that parties to a binding arbitration agreement typically will seek to negotiate their differences. Only if they fail are they likely to invoke the arbitration clause.

12. Eisenberg, "Private Ordering Through Negotiation," passim.

10

CUMULATION AND COMPROMISES OF REASONS IN THE LAW

ALEKSANDER PECZENIK

Introductory Remarks

Legal norms are, generally speaking, a result of various compromises. The law aims at achieving an equivalence of conflicting interests. The law is itself a result of a compromise of various political and other interests, both in legislation and in adjudication. Trials in most countries are more or less consistently arranged as a dispute between the parties; sometimes one of the parties wins; sometimes a compromise is achieved.

In ordinary usage, "compromise" means settlement of dispute by mutual concession, or adjustment of conflicting opinions, demands, and the like, by modification of each.

Let us say a little more about compromise of *reasons.* Assume that a given decision is to be made and that there are two competing reasons, both aiming at influencing the decision. It is typical of compromise that none of the reasons is recognized as totally decisive; on the other hand, all of them are to some extent taken into account.

Compromise is not incompatible with giving one of the reasons a relative priority; a compromise of two reasons, x and y, may "include" 90 percent of x and 10 percent of y. Compromise is incompatible only with a total disregard of a given reason or with ascribing to any reason an absolute value.

Compromise is impossible if there is no way of taking the competing reasons simultaneously into account. Imagine the following scale:

A	B	C
X	X	X

Assume that x stands at the point B. One reason supports moving closer to A, another reason indicates moving closer to C. One can say that the compromise is impossible, since moving closer to A implies becoming more distant from C and vice versa. In another sense, a kind of compromise *is* possible: even if the first reason is stronger and thus one moves toward A, one does not go very far in that direction, since the second reason functions as a brake.

This kind of impossibility can be very complex. It can result from a logical (deductive) incompatibility of the reasons or merely from an empirical incompatibility. Let us mention only one, important example concerning penal law. There are reasons for trying to improve the offender, and there are reasons for trying to achieve general deterrence. A compromise is difficult (impossible?) to achieve, since what is good for the improvement is bad for deterrence and vice versa. This is an instance of empirical incompatibility.

Compromise is a subspecies of "weighing" reasons. "Weighing" of conflicting reasons may result either in a compromise or in a total victory of one of them and a total defeat of the other. "Weighing" of non-conflicting reasons results in their cumulation. Such a cumulation is interesting if its total argumentative power is greater than the power of each of the cumulated reasons.

In my opinion, compromise and cumulation of reasons is much more important in the law than an "all-or-nothing" choice between them. No legal reasons are totally convincing. It is natural that they are cumulated with each other and that one makes a compromise between them.[1]

COMPROMISE AND THE PURPOSE
OF LEGAL PROTECTION

The following values — and corresponding reasons — compete with one another in the law of torts.[2]

(1) Security from damages. The plaintiff's security is to be en-

forced, but on what conditions? Should the tort-feasor's negligence be required, or should strict liability be introduced? Also, one must choose among the following aims:

a.   restitution of a situation existing before the damage;
b.   satisfaction of the plaintiff's needs;
c.   compensation depending upon the degree of the risk the plaintiff has taken.

There is a compromise between a, b, and c, although *in principle* a goes before b, while c is controversial.

(2) The defendant's security. He should not be economically destroyed by payment of damages.

(3) Justice. Losses should be spread equitably. The law should not lead to the practice of the poor paying for the rich.

(4) Promotion of morals. The law of torts should be so arranged that it would cause the growth of a moral order demanding care, condemning negligence, and so on.

(5) General deterrence. People should be afriad of causing damages.

(6) Economic efficiency. The law of torts should be arranged so that it would diminish the social costs of accidents and so on.

None of these values has absolute priority. The compromise between them is probably both logically and empirically possible, but it is an open question to what extent all of them can simultaneously be taken into account.

The compromise of values is technically achieved via another compromise — one among requirements of liability. Such requirements as the tort-feasor's fault, proximate causation between his conduct and the harm done, and absence of various excuses are not independent of one another but are interpreted in terms of their mutual connection. They are also interpreted in connection with such ideas as the purpose of the legal protection, the scope of the tort-feasor's duty, and so on. The resulting compromise is extremely complex. Finally, it must be kept in mind that the law sometimes introduces the same considerations in many ways. The same limitations of liability can thus be discussed under the heading of "adequacy," "fault," "necessity," "the purpose of protection," and the like.[3]

The fact that different requirements sometimes cover the same considerations does not mean, however, that the requirements in question are only apparently different and are actually identical. For example, fault is *not* the same as adequacy, and adequacy is *not* the same as the purpose of protection. The requirements are different because they only partly cover the same considerations; they also partly cover quite different ones.

Compromise is more essential for legal thinking than is generally recognized because some compromises are *hidden*. Consider the following example. According to the Swedish system of "day-fines," instead of being sentenced to pay, say, five hundred crowns, one is sentenced to pay, for example, five so-called day-fines. How much a day-fine is worth depends upon the income of the sentenced person; it can be, let us say, fifty crowns; or it can be two hundred crowns, which makes the final payment two hundred and fifty crowns, or one thousand crowns, respectively. Take the following story, unfortunately not at all fictitious. A prominent member of a legislative committee argues that punishment should be adapted *solely* to the crime and not at all to the personality of the offender or other factors. However, he accepts the system of day-fines. He argues that when deciding the punishment, one should take into account only the crime, not the offender. Each offender should be sentenced to pay five day-fines for the same crime. Any differentiation according to the offender's income is first introduced after the punishment has been decided. In other words, the compromise has been concealed via dividing of the decision into two stages. At the first stage, the idea of taking only the crime into account is respected. At the second stage it is not respected. When discussing only the first stage, one can say that no compromise occurs. But when it comes to paying the fine, two hundred and fifty or one thousand crowns for the same offence — the offender sees very clearly that his income as well as his crime has been taken into account.

COMPROMISE, CUMULATION OF REASONS, AND "SCIENTIFIC" REQUIREMENTS IN THE LAW

Returning to the law of torts, not only is there a compromise and cumulation of various requirements of liability but also each of the requirements is a result of a very complex process of compromise and cumulation of ideas. It applies even to such "scientific" requirements as that of a causal connection between that act and the harm done.

A cause of a given event is obviously a kind of a condition of it—necessary, sufficient, or more complex. However, not all conditions of a given event are its causes, but only those that a law of nature, or a common sense quasi-law of nature, connects with the effect. These laws of nature distinguish the causally relevant conditions from the causally irrelevant ones. The latter constitute the *normal background* of the effect in question.

It cannot be said simply and elegantly what a law of nature is. The laws of nature are recognizable only as parts of science as a whole; they must satisfy many technical requirements—for example, that of simplicity, invariance, analogy between one another, appropriate use of the inductive or hypothetically dedutive method, etc. None of those requirements alone seems to be decisive; but an evaluative compromise and cumulation of them is.[4]

The role of compromise and cumulation increases when we pass to the juristic part of the problem. The causally relevant elements of a condition of the‎ effect in question are causes. The legally relevant causes should lead to liability.

The legal criteria of relevance mainly concern two problems: remoteness of damage (adequacy, etc.) and the choice between the requirement of sufficient, necessary, or redundant cause.

The legal decisions concerning the first problem are often influenced by a compromise and a cumulation of many criteria.[5] An adequate (legally relevant, not too remote, etc.) cause of a harm must consist in a human act or in an extraordinary event,[6] must be direct,[7] immediate, proximate,[8] or typically foreseeable,[9] must increase probability[10] or risk of harm or make the harm inevitable,[11] must be apt to cause the harm;[12] must comprise the dangerous properties of a negligent act;[13] and so on.

Legal decisions concerning the second problem of the choice between the requirement of sufficient, necessary, or redundant causation constitute a very complex normative system, which cannot be discussed in the present paper.[14]

COMPROMISE AND CUMULATION OF "MATERIAL" AND "PROCESSUAL" RULES

Let us follow the example of causation in torts still further. "Procedure is the heart of the law," as it is often said. In order to understand the functioning of the requirement of causation, one must consider its compromise and cumulation, not only in terms of such requirements as fault, the purpose of protection, and the like, but also in terms of such matters as the rules of evidence and the burden of proof.

Although the rules of evidence cannot replace a differentiation of the rules of causation in torts, they should be *added* to them, *inter alia*, because of the following advantage: the requirement of proof can be *graded*, from 100 percent certainty via various degrees of probability down to zero probability. Nonprocedural rules are, on the other hand, rather formulated in terms of all-or-nothing terminology: the act in question was or was not a necessary condition of the harm; it was or was not a sufficient condition of it; and so on. It is true that some gradual evaluations are already important for the nonprocedural rules, for example adequacy, can be graded, and the very distinction between the cause and the normal background is gradual. But the rules of evidence in torts make transition from liability to non liability still more successive, gradual, and thus better adapted to social evaluations.

The nonprocedural rules of torts are not complete. They say that compensation should be paid in a given type of situation if there is a given type of causation between the act and the harm. This, however, is only a part of the legal requirement in question. The complete requirement contains rules about judicial decision-making. The complete rules about judicial decision-making in the law of torts may be called, following Olivecrona's terminology, "judicial law of torts."[15] The judicial law of torts is a product of two incomplete systems of rules: the law of torts in the traditional sense and the law of evidence. The law of evidence, completing the traditional law of torts, constitutes *eo ipso* rules that *correct* it. It is, after all, *not* so that compensation should be awarded if, and only if there is a given type of causation. Instead, compensation should be awarded if it is certain that there is a given type of causation, or in some cases if it is merely probable that there is a given type of causation, it should not be awarded even if causation of this type was present but if there is sufficient evidence of exonerating circumstances.

The law of torts in the traditional sense — that is the "material," nonprocessual law of torts — gives, in other words, only *approximative and idealized* guidelines for judicial decisions, to be completed and corrected by the law of evidence. Nonprocessual rules of the law of torts and the rules of evidence are to be *cumulated* in order to reach the decision. However, not only is their cumulation but also a *compromise* between them is possible, *inter alia,* because the *interpretation* of both kinds of rules is mutually connected. The literal interpretation may lead to incompatibility, to be removed by compromise of the rules in question.[16]

A HARD CASE. HYDMAN V. HANSA INS. CO. AND AXELSON, NJA 1961, p. 425

Let us illustrate all the compromises and cumulation of reasons, I have mentioned with an example of a hard case. In 1947, B was beaten up by C and became disabled. In 1952, after having been healthy for half a year, B was knocked down by A's car and became disabled once again. A was held liable for all the harm, including the part possibly attributable to C. The reasoning of the Supreme Court constituted a compromise of arguments concerning multiple sufficient causes, cumulative causes, adequacy, *novus actus interveniens* (the so-called break of causation), cumulation of the victim's illness with the tort-feasor's wrongful conduct, the so-called accomplished harm, and the burden of proof.[17]

One can imagine the following division of the harm:

a.   the harm caused only by the assault;
b.   the harm caused only by the accident;
c.   the harm to which both the assault and the accident were independently sufficient;
d.   the harm to which both the assault and the accident were necessary, as cumulative causes.

A, responsible for the accident, is not liable for the harm caused only by the assault; this harm was *accomplished* before he had acted; A and C are liable *in solidum* for the harm to which both the assault and the accident were independently sufficient. A and C are also liable *in solidum* for the harm to which both the assault and the accident were necessary. Finally, only A is liable for the harm caused solely by the accident. However, neither A's nor C's liability for any of the parts of the harm occurs if the causation (exclusive, cumulative, or alternative) between his act and the part in question was not adequate. Inadequacy can result from many circumstances. A's *novus actus interveniens* can, for example, break the chain of causation from C's act to the harm, and thus make C's act a merely inadequate cause of the harm. On the other hand, the causation between A's act and the corresponding part of the harm is not rendered inadequate by the fact that B—because of C's assault—had been extraordinarily vulnerable. However, A's liability may be reduced to some extent by the fact that C's assault had been the *main* cause of the harm. All those rules, intricate enough, are, however, not sufficient and must be completed by the rules of evidence.

The majority of the Supreme Court, Justices Hellquist, Hedfeldt, and Y. Söderlund, pointed out that ". . . .[I]t cannot be established, to what extent the traffic accident and the assault . . . contributed to the harm . . . . In such a case, in order to protect the injured person, . . . each tortfeasor . . . should be liable for all the harm . . . to which he contributed." For this reason full compensation should be awarded from A and his insurer.

The main problem is whether the decision should be interpreted *e contrario*. What would have happened if it had been possible to establish the extent to which the traffic accident and the assault had contributed to the harm? If that had been the case, would A's liability have been limited to a part of the harm? Some writers have pointed out that such a conclusion *e contrario* would be incompatible with the principles of the law of torts, especially with the principle that the tort-feasor takes the victim as he has found him.[18] Full liability must thus be recommended even for the cases in which the evidence is clear. A should be liable for all parts of the harm except the part caused by C's assault.

We have already pointed out that full liability agrees both with the rules about independently sufficient causes of the harm and with the rules about cumulative causes. Hence, it is not important to discuss the question whether A's and C's acts were independently sufficient or cumulatively necessary to the harm, or to a given part of it.

Why did the Supreme Court emphasize the uncertainty of the evidence? The most plausible explanation seems to be that the Court did not want to state its reasoning, precisely, but wished merely to eliminate any possibility of reducing the compensation.[19] The full reasoning would be something like the following. According to the nonprocessual rules, A would have been liable even if C's assault had—independently or cumulatively—contributed to a given part of the harm. Even if the nonprocessual rules had been different, that is, even if the influence of the assault had constituted any excuse, A would still have been liable. Since the harm and the weak causation had been proved by the victim, the tort-feasor had to prove an excuse. He did not do it, and for this reason he had to pay, quite independently of the first reason, that is, independently of the fact that the "excuse" was not good at all.

The case shows two things. The first is that the decision can be reconstructed as a result of a cumulation and/or a compromise of many legal rules. The second is that this compromise has not been expressed clearly but concealed behind a very unclear, general, and "synthetic" justification. We can ask whether this way of writing decisions does not open the door to additional compromises. The Court did not want to express its reasoning in clear terms, since it admitted that other imaginable reasons could also be components of the compromise; a too clear formulation of the precedent would prevent the use of those additional reasons in the future cases, and this should be avoided.

COMPROMISE AND CUMULATION OF THE SOURCES OF THE LAW

I would now venture to make some general comments. It is obvious that the content of the law often results from a cumulation or a compromise of different reasons. Less obvious but equally important is that *legal thinking* always is a result of a cumulation or of a compromise of different ideas, reasons, and lines of thought.

Which norms belong to, and which ones do not belong to, a legal system? This is, indeed, the question of what is "valid law." Several lines of thought compete in this context. All of them constitute the language game about legal validity.

A positivist believes in the possibility of distinguishing the legal norms (positive norms, legally valid norms, call them what you like) from other norms, without any reference to morality. A natural law adherent believes the opposite to be true. Practicing lawyers may be positivists more often than not, but they are inconsistent. In fact, they play a language game[20] involving instances of both positivism and natural law.

The positivist part of the language game about validity also contains many lines of thought. A predictionist sees positive law as the norms the courts are going to apply.[21] A normativist sees positive law as the norms made consonant with higher norms. Practicing lawyers play a language game containing some elements of predictionism and some elements of normativism.

The complexity, however, does not end here. The language game about the law contains not only the line of thought about the, so to speak, officially valid law, but also line of thought about its *interpretation*. The materials included within the interpretative context may or may not be positive, officially valid legal norms. The language game about the materials in question consists of two lines of thought. The first one concerns the question how to *make* a legal decision; the second concerns the question how to *write* a legal opinion.

The line of thought concerning the question of how to write a legal opinion includes all the classical problems of interpretation and construction of statutes. Propositions concerning the interpretation of law can be seen as an "output" of a chain of operations, starting from the recognized sources of the law. The sources of the law comprise material that must or should or may be taken into account,[22] although the distinction is not sharp, and a number of comments are necessary. The material that *must* be taken into account comprises statutes and, in common law countries, precedents. The material that *should* be taken into account comprises — in continental law — precedents, in many countries *travaux préparatoires,* and sometimes other sources as well. Finally, some sources *may* be taken into account — for example, legal writing, draft statutes, repealed statutes, foreign statutes, evaluations that are considered to prevail in some relevant groups in the society, and others.

An important part of legal thinking consists in a cumulation, a compromise, or a choice among different legal materials, that is, different sources of the law and different methods of legal thinking. Legal thinking oriented toward some materials must take into account other materials as well.[23] A construction *of statutes* consists in looking at a statute in its context, which includes precedents and other extrastatutory sources of the law. Since the compromise between the sources of the law is, to a great extent, determined by the traditional legal arguments (i.e. the traditional operation rules in law), legal thinking can develop the law creatively and, *at the same time,* contain strict, methodologically well-defined, and *in this sense* scientific elements.

COMPROMISE AND THE DOCTRINAL STUDY OF LAW

The creative element in the doctrinal study of law is traditionally treated in one of the following ways:

(1) *Begriffsjurisprudenz (conceptualism)*. Legal rules are generalized and broad principles are formulated. Deductive consequences from the principles provide answers to any legal questions. *Begriffsjurisprudenz* is generally regarded as incorrect. It is incorrect, in my opinion, because of the overoptimistic, exaggerated nature of the supposedly inductive generalization of legal rules from which it starts.

(2) *Intuitionism*. Legal rules are freely corrected by vague speculations about the purpose of the law, the advantage to society, and so on.

(3) *The purely descriptive method*. Legal rules are passively described. A legal scholar refuses to deal with the hard cases, those not covered by the rules. Such a doctrinal study of law is not very useful for a judge.

It is clear that all those "pure" methods have a common weakness. Each of them is one-sided; each takes into account only one part of the compromise entailed by legal thinking, that is, only logical reasoning, only evaluations, or only descriptions of the sources of the law. We have already seen that lawyers actually use a "mixed" method, a method of compromise. It begins with a description of many sources of the law involved in lawyers' work: statutes, precedents, preparatory materials, and the like. The sources of the law are adapted to one another by means of several legal arguments.

COMPROMISE AND APPLICATION OF PHILOSPHICAL TERMINOLOGY IN JURISPRUDENCE

The law is a product of compromises, and the doctrinal study of law is an art of compromise. This makes the classical philosophical terminology inapplicable to the law. This observation has constituted the decisive factor in my approach to the problem of the juristic method. I call the approach juristic operationism.[24] I have also used

other terms, such as "juristic theory of law" and "neo-realism in law."
The main point of juristic operationism is as follows. A traditional
philosopher of law asks many "either-or" questions. For example, is
the doctrinal study of law value-free or evaluative? Since it is obviously not value-free, it must be evaluative, and this leaves the following alternatives. Either our philosopher must admit the existence of
true propositions expressing values, or he must reject the idea that
the study of law can express true propositions. My approach is different. I say that the study of law contains both evaluative and value-
free propositions. And I *refuse* to answer the question of whether juristic propositions possess truth values or not.

If one hundred gallons water are mixed with one gallon of dirt, all
the water is dirty. If one hundred descriptive operations are added to
one evaluative operation, all is, from a semantic point of view, evaluative. But an operationist never forgets the descriptive operations. A
juristic proposition, which constitutes a product of many descriptive
operations and some evaluative operations, should not be — *simplic-
iter* — labeled evaluative, but should be seen in relation to *all* the operations involved. Consequently, the question whether the typical
propositions, stated by jurists about the law, have any truth value
(i.e., are either true or false) cannot be answered with a simple yes or
no, but only with a *yes but* . . . or a *no but* . . . . The word "but" is
crucial to juristic operationism. The words "true" or "false" are too
simple to be used in the doctrinal study of law.

For very similar reasons, many other classical philosophical terms
are equally difficult to use in the context of the law. Consider two distinctions, *scientifically verified* versus arbitrary, and *descriptive* versus normative. I have argued here that legal thinking is to some extent arbitrary and to some extent scientific in the sense of being determined by operational rules. Instead of the sharp distinction — scientific versus arbitrary — we thus have a compromise between the scientific element and the arbitrary element. Moreover, my own approach expresses a compromise. I have contended that legal thinking
is determined by some operational rules. But is it *actually* so determined? My answer is: to some extent. Our view of legal thinking and of
the doctrinal study of law is an *idealization*,[25] that is, it contains elements of both description and arbitrary reconstruction. The elements of description are there because the actual work of lawyers and
jurists in fact contains the operations about which I have written.
The elements of an arbitrary reconstruction are also present since I

have arranged juristic activities systematically in order to understand them and in order to show their similarities to scientific activities.

Parenthetically, let me point out two elements of the reconstruction: (1) a maximal use of reasoning as accepted within an idealized—positivist—philosophy of science; (2) a maximal use of arguments from authority, quoting the sources of law that *must* or *should* be taken into account. "Maximal" here means as extensive as possible without making the reconstruction too different from actual legal reasoning. The term "too different" is obviously evaluative, and means "too different for the reconstruction to be valuable in legal theory." What is left, after the correct scientific and juristic operations have been performed, consists mainly of free evaluations. In this idealization, these juristic evaluations are put as far at the back of the picture as possible. But the evaluations are unavoidable, and thus compromises between various values are unavoidable.

CONCLUDING REMARKS

To summarize, an interesting theory of law need not be consistently normative or consistently descriptive but may also express an idealization, this is, a compromise between a normative and a descriptive point of view.

Compromise and cumulation of different ideas, reasons, approaches, and so on, dominate legal practice, legal thinking, doctrinal study of law, and legal theory. Any effort to replace this cumulation and compromise by a "pure," "monistic" approach leads to dogmatism, simplism, and poverty of description.[26]

NOTES

1. Chaim Perelman, "Self-evidence and Proof, *Philosophy*, 33 (1958), passim.
2. See Jan Hellner, "Värderingar i skadeståndsrätten," *Festskrift til Per Olof Ekelöf* (Stockholm: Nordstedt, 1972), passim.
3. See Aleksander Peczenik, *Causes and Damages* (Lund: Acta Societatis Juridicae Lundensis, 1979), chap. 9.
4. See ibid., chaps 1 and 10.
5. See ibid., chap. 6.

6. H. L. A. Hart and A. M. Honoré, *Causation in the Law* (Oxford: Clarendon Press, 1962), pp. 2, 26ff., and passim.

7. See A. M. Honoré, "Causation and Remoteness of Damage," *International Encyclopedia of Comparative Law* (Tübingen, Paris, New York: Mohr, Mouton, Oceana, 1971), vol. 11, chap. 7, pp. 40ff., with references.

8. Ibid., pp. 44ff., with references.

9. Ibid., pp. 55ff. Cf. Jan Hellner, *Skadeståndsrätt*, 3d. ed. (Stockholm: Almqvist and Wicksell, 1976), p. 153.

10. J. v. Kries, *Die Prinzipen der Wahrscheinlichkeitsrechnung* (1886); cf. Honoré, Causation, pp. 49ff.

11. Lennart Aqvist, *Kausalitet och culpaansvar inom en logiskt rekonstruerad skadeståndsrätt* (Uppsala: Almqvist and Wicksell, 1973), passim.

12. Hjalmar Karlgren, *Skadeståndsrätt*, (Stockholm: Nordstedt, 1969), p. 41.

13. A. Vinding Kruse, *Erstatningsretten* (Cophenhagen, 1971), pp. 93ff., 219, 223. Cp. also a refined formulation by Stig Jorgensen, *Erstatning for personskade og tab af forsorger*, 3d. ed. (Copenhagen: Juristforbundets forlag, 1972), p. 119.

14. Cf. Peczenik, *Causes and Damages*, chap. 3.

15. Karl Olivecrona, *Rätt och dom*, 2d ed. (Stockholm: Nordstedt, 1966), pp. 146ff.

16. Cf. Peczenik, *Causes and Damages*, sec. 9.6.

17. Cf. ibid.

18. Halvar Lech, *Skadeersättning för personskada* (Stockholm: Nordstedt, 1973), pp. 41ff.; Anders Agell, "Orsaksrekvisit och beviskrav," *Festskrift till Per Olof Ekelöf* (Stockholm: Norstedt, 1972), p. 33.

19. Agell, Festskrift.

20. The application of Wittgenstein's idea of language games to the law has been elaborated in a very comprehensive way by Aulis Aarnio in *On Legal Reasoning* (Turku: Turun Yliopisto, 1977), pp. 47ff., 86, 126ff., and 296ff.

21. Alf Ross, *On Law and Justice* (London: Stevens, 1958), pp. 38ff.

22. Aleksander Peczenik, "The Structure of a Legal System," *Rechtstheorie*, 6, no. 1 (1975), pp. 6ff. For more comprehensive treatment see Peczenik, *Juridikens metodproblem* (Stockholm: Almqvist and Wicksell, 1974), esp. pp. 48ff., with references.

23. See Peczenik, "The Structure of a Legal System," pp. 9ff.; and Aarnio, *On Legal Reasoning*, pp. 282ff.

24. Seeks under Peczenik, "Juridisk Operationism," *Tidskrift, utgiven av Juridiska Föreningen i Finland*, 3, (1977), pp. 122ff.

25. Cf. Aarnio, *Or Legal Reasonsing*, passim.

26. Cf. Stig Jorgensen, "Årsagsproblemer i forbindelse med personskade," *Nordisk forsäkringstidskrift* (1960), p. 185.

11

COMPROMISE AS PRECISE JUSTICE
JOHN E. COONS

Introduction

My responsibility is to assist the principal paper in defining compromise; I will confine myself to one major area — civil litigation.
This is not my maiden voyage in these waters, and I will avoid need-
less repetition. Briefly summarized, the earlier work proposed 50-50
apportionments by courts in certain cases of indeterminacy of fact or
value. The even split was said to follow from the common assumption
of equality before the law. Given a balance of conflicting proof or of
conflicting policies, an all-or-nothing judgment would seem to violate the equality principle.

That earlier work left the underlying conception of equality unex-
amined. Most of this paper will be devoted to filling that gap. At
least a start can be made toward a new meaning for equality, a contribution which seems sorely needed. The final sections will briefly
outline how viewing equality as here defined might help to clarify the
notion of compromise as embodied in a system of apportioned civil
justice.

LIMITING THE SCOPE

No definition of compromise would be "true," but one could be
more useful to our purpose than another. Ambiguous definitions can

be functional; law, for example, employs paradox and riddle when they suit the goal of doing justice. Here, however, the aim is not to do justice but to understand a certain aspect of it in order that others may do it better; hence clarity is a principal objective.

For clarity's sake, then, let us limit the scope without sacrificing the essence. Two brief examples will help. First, a robber demands my hundred dollars; I tell him my troubles, and he settles for fifty. Second, Jones offers me a thousand dollars for my car, and I counter-offer to sell for two thousand; eventually we agree on a price between. These could be thought examples of compromise, but I exclude both. Each involves what is common to all possible definitions of compromise — the apportionment of some good or burden between persons. But such a concept is too broad. We must whittle the domain of apportionment to suit our purposes. Our primary interest is the relationship of compromise to justice; hence we eliminate the halfhearted robber whose "sharing" is scarcely an example of a just outcome. By contrast, the transaction with Jones achieves a just apportionment, but it too drops out, though for a different reason. It is but a common higgle, the maximizing of utilities under conditions of relative freedom. It is the everyday experience of markets, politics, statecraft, and personal relations. If compromise were to include every trade-off of one good for another, it would incorporate most of life and forfeit the power to distinguish. For the sake of parsimony we will limit the term to cases of conflict, and conflict of a certain variety — namely, those which involve incompatible claims of right.

The scope can be further narrowed. Suppose this variation of the previous example: Jones and I each claim to be the sole owner of the car. However, we reach a settlement; I keep the car and pay him half the value. Here are clashing claims of right, and common usage would view the outcome as a compromise. Once again, I exclude it. Though in itself a just outcome, the example teaches little about compromise as a form of justice. A free accord between adversaries yields but their private view of justice in the particular case; more, it is contingent upon their peculiar preference, circumstance, and necessity. Social science may someday derive a behavioral definition of compromise from such private settlements, but it will learn what phenomena to count only when nonempirical sources have provided a standard of relevance. The hope here is to move toward such a standard.[1] Bargained settlements thus are excluded not as irrelevant to a schema of compromise but as premature.

What is left are apportioned outcomes of conflict such as would be imposed by an authoritative third party—a judge or arbitrator. This is the world of jurisprudence, and its traditions place us under a healthy discipline. To simulate the role of judge not only sustains our concern for justice but forces us to articulate reasons for chosen outcomes. It commits us to seek a view of compromise that is principled in the sense of being drawn from identifiable values. Here this will mean arguing for a certain view of human equality and inferring from it a system of decision.

Let us, then, begin with the following framework, which we will explain and defend. In private dispute resolution compromise is a species of ordered justice inferable from the fact of human equality. Absent a relevant factor peculiar to one disputant, justice is governed by a presumption of equal desert, and an even apportionment is required. Likewise, where relevant distinctions exist, the degree of departure from an even apportionment must be justified by the distinctions; for example, a bare preponderance of evidence for A does not by itself justify an unapportioned award to A.

COMPROMISE AND EQUALITY

Mere equality cannot serve as a basis for deserving anything. Two stones may be indistinguishable, but a difference in their treatment triggers no presumption of injustice. To be important as a consideration of justice, equality must hold for some quality that is distinctly human and ethically relevant. In identifying that quality here there is no need to reinvent human ontology. It is sufficient to enlist the traditional Western view that at its core our identity is moral; if there be a distinctly human equality, it is one associated with the making of ethical choices. Borrowing from Jaspers, "The essential equality of all men resides solely in that depth where to each one freedom opens a way to approach God through his moral life . . . ."[2] (Nor need it concern us here whether the object of the moral life is defined as God.)

One consequence of locating human equality in moral worth or dignity is that we part company with the determinist, for to deal in morality is to deal in liberty. I regret the separation, but if equality does not lie in effective moral parity—if it does not consist somehow in human freedom—I fear it will not be found at all.

The essential quality proposed as the ground of the presumption of apportionment is, then, equal moral desert. It is a feature of the experienced person—deep, subjective, essential, identifying—the real me, not the one you see. It is a quality not given but achieved—the formed character, not mere moral capacity. It is to be distinguished from what one "deserves" superficially in the external order such as reward or punishment for particular choices or acts; desert in such cases is the judgment of an exterior event in an exterior forum. To borrow from the language of the law, such a forum lacks jurisdiction of the person. The world does not judge character; it judges acts.

This claim of the moral parity of all persons, like every egalitarian assertion, must confront the contradictions of experience. It may be that (like stones and bees) we human beings share certain qualities, but we also differ from one another in such a multitude of important ways as to make any claim of fundamental equality seem on its face fatuous. In fact, some human beings more resemble stones and bees than the norm of their own species. Prima facie there seems no reason of justice to forbid our treating such creatures as members of an inferior order of nature.

This is a primary hurdle for any theory of justice (at least any based in equality), and the problem is not limited to cases of extreme difference among human beings. Within the range of "normality" there are many differences that may justly be considered in distributing benefits and burdens. John and Mary are equally intelligent, but Mary can run faster, excels in mathematics, and has a prison record, while John speaks better French, is ten years older, and has a low income. Equality seems to fail as a description of our experience of one another; in turn, it fails as a basis for equal treatment. This has been the besetting weakness of egalitarian theories; equality exists only as aspiration, and then only among particular human beings. There is no equality even of the aspiration of equality.

Is equality of moral desert also but a yearning peculiar to a certain culture or personality type? At first it would appear so. No voluntarist holds that people are in fact equally "good"; how could such a view consist with liberty? Our philosophies, culture, and history emphasize that virtue and depravity are alternate possibilities for Everyman. Societies, past and present, have passed judgment upon individual character, drawing inferences from behavior, genealogy, caste, and religion. Character, like blindness and age, has been a common juridical classification for rewards and penalties. It thus seems as flimsy a basis for equality as any other.

194   JOHN E. COONS

Rawls would solve this problem by locating equality in the mere
capacity for moral choice, ignoring the manner of its exercise. "The
capacity for moral personality is a sufficient condition for being entitled to equal justice."³ This view, which is an appealing assumption
for a philosophy concerned essentially with distributive justice, is
problematic if applied to conflicts between individuals. We can
agree with Jaspers, as with Rawls, that moral capacity is "an essential
equality of men"; the trouble is that capacity seems no basis for one's
deserving anything beyond the *opportunity* to make ethical choices.
It does not clarify dyadic conflict; there the issue is not the general
opportunity to choose among options but special rights to be enjoyed
exclusively by one person. In conflict situations one party does not
become more deserving than the other to enjoy a particular good, say
an automobile, simply by *having* the potential for moral activity, but
only by its exercise. If moral personality counts toward entitlement,
one deserves by freely *becoming* a certain kind of person through
choices actually made. To base human desert in the mere capacity
for morality would be to admire the philanthropist for being rich and
punish the strangler for being strong. The relevant quality for a theory of commutative justice is not an unexercised moral liberty be-
stowed by nature but the actual character forged by the individual in
deliberate response to the challenge of his experience.⁴ That character is anything but equal from person to person, and that reality of
moral inequality seems to put our presumption of equal treatment in
deep trouble.

Fortunately, we are rescued by our own weakness. Once we surrender the impossible claim that the moral desert of individuals is
equal, we uncover the plausible claim that it is unmeasurable. Inscrutability—if that is the fact—will distinguish individual moral
desert from age, race, income, intelligence, criminality, and the
multitude of other factors by which human beings discernibly differ
and that are employed by the state to justify distinction of treatment
in the civil order.

Is moral desert inscrutable? The question could be put at several
levels. First, as a root problem in epistemology, is reliable knowledge
ever possible on this issue, or is moral identity so disconnected from
behavior as radically to elude inference? Is the moral condition even
of a Judas or a Hitler knowable? That enduring issue is beyond this
brief comment and beyond me. I will, therefore, assume what I
doubt—that there is no absolute barrier to assessment of individual

moral worth. I will further assume that under certain conditions this possibility of knowledge may be actualized—that, for example, it is possible to perceive moral worth through intimate and prolonged private relationship, and I will even grant that gifted individuals sometimes are able to read character in transient encounters. (This is in spite of my own experience, which is that of mystery and implacable complexity; the injunction to "judge not" seems to me a caution of epistemology as much as of charity.)

The issue for us, however, is not the possibility of insight by individuals under ideal conditions but the capacity of a decision-making bureaucracy to achieve systematic penetration of individual character in the course of dispute resolution. Judges and arbitrators must decide between strangers who appear before them briefly in stereotyped adversary roles; in this setting the mediating links of intimacy and rapport—of confidence given and received—are not only unavailable but forbidden to the decider. All disclosure is guarded. No one is expected or even entitled to appear as himself but only as the reporter of an external historical reality that is his "case." Under such conditions individual moral worth is radically inaccessible. Its perception by a Solomon might be imaginable in a polity based upon family or even extended family; but, once society has passed beyond tribalism, the moral worth of persons becomes inscrutable to government.

Objection may be made that in certain cases—for example, in passing criminal sentence—even modern society purports to judge factors that are virtually indistinguishable from moral desert; for example, the convict's personal history of misbehavior is considered in sentencing. One response is that these occasions for considering moral status are more theater than legal process. They help maintain both the system's function as moral educator and the judges' preferred view of their own roles. It is important that the system be observed to judge character; therefore, it purports to do so. This is not, however, because it penetrates the criminal's heart. The decision is all surface. It is a quasi- or ascriptive judgment that involves judicial anguish precisely because real worth remains mystery. This indeterminacy is central to the current criticism of inequality in sentencing practices; the law relies upon social sciences that are incapable of distinguishing sheep from goats. Caleb Foote finds the tools so weak that the only fair resolution is flat equality of sentences for the same objective act.[5]

Nevertheless, for purposes of argument I will make still another concession and assume that, where there is a history of flagrant and egregious misbehavior, the finder of fact may draw the inference of relative moral depravity; I will likewise assume that a life of objective blamelessness and self-sacrifice would justify a contrary inference. There would remain the mass of human conflicts in which the character of the parties—even if put in issue—would be utterly impenetrable. As a further tactic of economy, I will exclude the criminal process and speak only of conflict resolution in civil matters between private parties.

Assuming that the decision-maker in such cases remains invincibly ignorant of moral desert, what follows? A great deal follows, at least if it be moral desert alone that can raise the issue of justice. If it is only in the exercise of our moral freedom that we forge a distinct character and thus come to deserve something more or less than merely an opportunity, it is in the inscrutability of that character that we deserve equally. Ironically it is the very absence of a yardstick for individual moral worth that permits us to accord each an equal dignity; for, if we could know that of two disputants only one was virtuous, we would be entitled to reward him just as the tax code rewards philanthropy. It is society's ignorance of our chracter that liberates it from yet another distinction among human beings and thereby provides the basis for a descriptive equality.[6]

Thus, the epistemological barrier is crucial to the argument. Only when individual desert is accepted as important and real but inscrutable to public process does it cease to be a ground of discrimination and become transmuted into a basis for a civil order purged of arbitrary distinctions. But note both how much and how little this claim of effective moral parity represents. It is on the one hand the only descriptive basis for the presumption of equal treatment of conflicting parties—the crucial starting point for any theory of commutative justice. On the other hand, it is something most everyone would have admitted on faith without hearing the argument from indeterminancy; human equality and the presumption of equal treatment may be a surprise to jurisprudes, but everyone else—including the law— already knew about them. The practical question has been, rather, what weight to give the equality presumption when it stands against particular values, proofs, and conflicting presumptions argued by each of the parties to offset the original equilibrium.

The law has a traditional answer to this question. It has been developed in its most refined form in the exegesis of the "equal protection" clause, but it is implicit in all civil litigation as well.[7] It is a minimalist position favoring no particular objectives for the system. The decisive fact, value, or presumption that overcomes the presumption of equality need only meet a test of rationality; it must plausibly serve *some* legitimate objective of the decision-making system. This need not always be the objective of justice between the parties. Thus, in a factual dispute over ownership of a chattel, a rule favoring the party with possession would be justified if credibly linked to the end of discouraging false claims by others; the opposite rule might be justified on the ground that it discourages self-help. Whether the rational relation criterion is in any case a trivial or significant hurdle is not revealed by this formal description but can be discerned only in practice; from its use by the courts, it is plain that one man's rational connection is another's non sequitur. Furthermore, it is crucial to know what objectives the decision-maker is permitted to pursue that conflict with the objective of justice between the conflicting parties.[8] Is it proper that his wish to deter a certain kind of conduct become the ground for judgment against an equally deserving party?

At least the presumption of equal treatment puts the decision maker to the task of discovering and articulating reasons, whether of justice or policy, for imposing unequal treatment; if that responsibility is taken seriously, even a weak presumption of equality may have important consequences. It has not been wholly without fruit in our constitutional law, and signally so in the area of race discrimination. It has a potential application to the problems of compromise that could be equally dramatic and, over time, could be broadly influential in our systems of dispute resolution.

THINGS BEING EQUAL

So far, then, we have identified our subject as the authoritative resolution of civil conflict in which the process of decision employs an initial presumption of equal entitlement and in which the deciding authority is empowered to apportion. Given such a presumption, and other things being equal between the parties, justice lies in an equal apportionment. Now we wish to consider contrasting applications of this rule. Our first task will be to clarify what we mean by "other things being equal" in potential cases of apportionment. Thereafter we must inquire what follows in those cases where things are found to be unequal between the parties and, finally, in those cases where external concerns of policy are considered. Are apportionments other than 50-50 and winner take all possible? By what rationale would they be governed? What evidence is relevant?

What counts as relevant to be set against the presumption depends, as we have noted, upon the purposes of the decision-making system. There are reasons, good and bad, to resist apportioned outcomes. Some have to do with the parties themselves; there is no commutative basis for apportionment if one party's claim is based wholly upon perjury. Other concerns are external to the parties; the court may object to a 50-50 split in cases of disputed ownership if the outcome will be an incentive to theft. For the moment we will continue to assume that our sole purpose is to define justice between two parties in conflict, eliminating temporarily and artificially all external concerns of policy in order that we may concentrate upon the commutative relation.

Let us suppose that justice between the parties turns upon an issue of fact. A and B each claims to own a particular pig. At the trial the evidence leaves the issue in equilibrium. The decider has two ways of looking at such a factual standoff. If the important consideration is that one of these parties is a "real owner," the two available forms of decision—winner take all and equal apportionment—present a dilemma between random selection and deliberate error. Either the judge must be 100 percent wrong half the time or half wrong all the time. But if we cease to ask the unanswerable question of who the "real owner" is and inquire, rather, given this evidence what is the just resolution by an authoritative decider, the dilemma disappears; for the presumption of equal treatment would entitle each to demand half the value of the animal. Of course, if the parties agree, a random selection of a sole winner would also be just. However, the imposition of a random choice against the will of either would be problematic, for a one-sided result would not express the factual equilibrium perceived by the decider; it would be unjust from the point of view of the *system of decision*.[9] This conclusion would hold even for that half of the cases in which the "real cases,' prevailed by chance.

The law is filled with "pig cases."[10] There is no experience more common to judges and juries than the factual standoff; most easy cases do not get litigated. If justice between the parties were the only object of our legal system, the historic dominance of winner-take-all outcomes would appear to constitute systematic unfairness. But in addition to justice there are many considerations of policy. One general fear is that the practice of apportionment would tend to corrupt potential litigants and deciders alike. Human affairs would be planned in the light of the apportionment system, and once in conflict, litigants would conduct settlement negotiations with an eye to the possibility of an imposed compromise. Whether this would increase litigation or stimulate dubious claims is doubtful but would at least be a legitimate concern of the system. Likewise, finders of fact might be tempted to lean toward an equilibrium in order to avoid the duty of imposing the harsher outcome of winner take all even where it represented the just solution between the parties. No doubt there are also cultural and psychological explanations for winner-take-all.[11]

Consider, now, a second form of equilibrium or standoff. In this example my brother Fred borrows my car, removes the hi-fi, and sells it to you representing himself to be the owner. Fred is insolvent; you or I—or you and I—must suffer. The facts are clear; what we face here is not a balance of proof but an equilibrium of values at two levels. First, as between the parties there is no reason to prefer one to the other. Each is innocent; each was as careless or careful as the other. Justice seems to require an even split. Second, at the level of policy, there is an equilibrium of conflicting concerns—the security of ownership versus the security of transfers. (If the reader disagrees about the balance as the case is put, let him alter the facts to produce his own view of equilibrium.)

The law has found such cases difficult, and properly so. It is a pity that it has not seen fit to apportion the loss equally. Someday it may move in that direction. Note that in the hi-fi example the just result is not impeded by systemic needs for deterrence. Neither party would be tempted deliberately to create the conflict, since each stands to lose. Further, from the point of view of the system an apportionment is preferable, because it permits *both* of the conflicting policy values to be recongized in the outcome.

Thus, where the crucial issues of fact are in equilibrium, or where the facts are determinate but conflicting policies are in equilibrium, the basic presumption of equality of treatment would favor an even split. For convenience this may be summarized as the principle of insufficient reason; lacking adequate grounds to depart from the origginal equilibrium position, an even split represents both justice and wise policy.

THINGS UNEQUAL

Justice Brandeis is said to have remarked once that "To be effective in this world you have to decide which side is probably right; and, once you decide, you must act as if it were one hundred per cent right."[12] Brandeis (who may have been speaking only of politics) thus identified one of the two principled solutions that are possible for cases in which the decision maker finds the parties not in equilibrium; one is an uneven apportionment, and the other is winner-take-all. It is, of course, the latter approach that has generally been preferred by the law.

The competing solution of an uneven apportionment would be based upon either of two rationales, depending upon the particular facts. Either it would express the probabilities of a factual unknown or the relative weights assigned by society to conflicting values. In the pig case, for example, if the factual question of ownership came out as a 60-40 probability in the mind of the finder of fact, the value of the pig would be so apportioned. By contrast in cases of value conflict such as the hi-fi example, if the policy of security of buyers weighed 60-40 in importance relative to that of security of owners, the value would be so apportioned.

Before we reject these quantified outcomes as an exaggerated nicety of judgment, we should note that a number of our states do just this in automobile accident cases involving mutual fault. This is the solution of "comparative negligence."[13] As a tool of judicial administration it seems to be no worse than the alternative doctrines. I concede that the quantification of factual probability and of the relative weight of policy values is artificial; the question remains: Artificial compared with what? If one party has established but a bare preponderance in the decider's mind, which is the more factitious outcome—a 60-40 apportionment or winner-take-all? The difficulty of being precise cannot by itself justify abandonment of whatever precision is possible. Justification must come, if at all, in terms of extrinsic considerations such as deterrence and similar policies unrelated to the particular parties—in other words, through considerations other than commutative justice.

The rationale for uneven apportionments should be seen as a principle of sufficient reason. Once a decision system accepts the presumption of equal treatment, departures from a 50-50 apportionment require justification for each increment of departure. To infer directly from a nonequilibrium of fact or value that one party should be the exclusive victor is a non sequitur.

A NONEGALITERIAN APPROACH

How would this system of apportionments be affected by a conclusion that human beings are unequal in their characters, hence in desert? For example, suppose that relative desert of parties to a conflict were initially quantified by age, children being worth, say, 60 and a middle-aged man 40. In principle the form of analysis just given would still apply but with different effect. An equilibrium of proof, other things being equal, would result in a 60-40 judgment favoring the child.

Seeing this emphasizes that the equality presumption is but one of many that could lend themselves to apportioned outcomes. It is, however, the only one that can be given a plausible intellectual base. It is also the only starting position consistent with modern political theory. Nevertheless, it would be intelligible if one were to label all systems of apportionment "compromise," even those proceeding from a premise of inequality. The necessary feature is not the parties' equality but their being assigned relative desert of whatever weight. Any judgment between them other than winner-take-all would represent an apportionment — hence a compromise — under the analysis here.

CONCLUSION

Perhaps in this finite area of civil disputes we have moved somewhat closer to a definition of compromise. For these cases it seems fair and useful to describe compromise as conflict resolution based upon some original presumption of relative entitlement of the parties (preferably equality); other things being equal, that presumption re-

202 JOHN E. COONS

quires the proportional division of a disputed good. Any departures from the original proportionality of entitlement would be grounded either in relevant facts peculiar to the parties' relation or in the impact of relevant conflicting policies.

Where no public policy affects the outcome, compromise in this sense of precise apportionment becomes indistinguishable from commutative justice. Apportionment seeks recognition as the *normal* solution to private conflict, the beginning point for social intervention. The claim, in short, is not trivial. It implies that our present system of civil jurisprudence with its commitment to winner-take-all begins at the wrong end. Perhaps the existing mode of decision could be justified in the mass of cases by a demonstration of policy objectives inconsistent with apportioment. That justification has never been seriously attempted, perhaps because winner-take-all has never been challenged. It would be a worthy employment of jurisprudes and law reformers to criticize the rationale for polarized outcomes in particular cases and, where the challenge is unmet, to develop rules for a more precise commutative justice.

NOTES

1. A splendid step in that direction is Melvin Eisenberg, "Private Ordering Through Negotiation: Dispute-Settlement and Rulemaking," *Harvard Law Rev.*, 89(1976), 637; see also John E. Coons, "Approaches to Court Imposed Compromise—The Uses of Doubt and Reason." *Northwestern Univ. Law Rev.*, 58 (1964), 750. Aside from these efforts the idea of compromise has been largely neglected by Anglo-American jurisprudence.

2. Karl Jaspers, *Der philosophische Glaube*, (Munich: R. Piper, 1948), pp. 56ff., as translated in Spiegelberg, "Equality in Existentialism," *Nomos IX* (New York: Atherton Press, 1967), pp. 193-213, at 194.

3. John Rawls, *A Theory of Justice* (Cambridge: Harvard University Press, 1972), pp. 19, 505ff.

4. Rawls's work is principally concerned with fairness in the manner in which the world's goods and powers are to be shared—what is traditionally called distributive justice. Here we are concerned with justice between two parties in conflict. An equality of capacity is more effective to Rawls's purpose than ours and in any case was dictated by his form of analysis. Once the strategy of an "original position" is adopted, there is no choice but to rely upon potentiality; since by hypothesis no one has

yet acted, no one has yet acquired desert except by his postulated qualities. Once we come to issues of individual conflict, however, it would be an unwarranted leap to pass from sheer power to desert without an intervening choice having been exercised by the individual.

5. Private manuscript, "Sentencing Through the Looking Glass," on file with the Center for Law and Society, University of California, Berkeley. For other examples of official character analysis see *Repouille* v. *U.S.*, 165 F.2d 152 (1947) (as a basis for naturalization, applicant "must have been a person of 'good moral character' for the five years which preceded"); *Currin* v. *Currin*, 25 Cal. App. 2d 644, 271 P.2d 61 (1954) (immoral character inferred from adultery bars child custody; *Orlando Daily Newspapers Inc.*, 11 F.C.C. 760, 3 R.R. 624 (1946) (broadcast license application denied for vituperation, vilification, and intemperance in expression). The *Repouille* case exemplifies the external or "objective" character of the judgment. Repouille had committed a "mercy killing" under pitiable circumstances and from tenderest motives. Otherwise he had led a blameless life. The one act was taken as proxy for his character, barring his naturalization.

6. "Perhaps the equal impossibility of certain knowledge in all these cases is one of the best reasons for the equal treatment of those whose inequality cannot be accurately assessed." Spiegelberg, "Equality in Existentialism," p. 209.

7. For an entry to the vast literature on the constitutional significance of "rationality" see Paul Brest, "Foreword: In Defense of the Antidiscrimination Principle," *Harvard Law Rev.*, 90 (1976), 1.

8. The interplay of the rationality test and the importance of the substantive matter at stake in the dispute is well considered in the dissent of Justice Marshall in *Rodriguez* v. *San Antonio Independent School District*, 411 U.S. 1, 70 (1973).

9. On the other hand, if one stresses the process rather than the substantive outcome, the 50-50 chance seems perfect justice; my own sense of justice drives me to emphasize the outcome, but this feeling is purely intuitive and not very strong. The recent article by H. Greeley, "The Equality of Allocation by Lot," *Harvard Civil Rights—Civil Liberties Law Rev.*, 12 (1977), 113, though interesting, does not make much progress toward ordering this difficult relation between chance and justice.

10. Here is a set of them from my earlier article, *Northwestern Univ. Law Rev.*, 58 (1958), 750, 753-54. Some are examples of factual, some of policy, equilibrium:

1. *A* and *B* are unsecured creditors of *X* whose assets are insufficient to satisfy both *A* and *B*.
2. An Act of God destroys part of the grain stored in Jones' grain elevator by *A*, *B*, *C*, and Jones.

3. The good ship Marylyn survives a tempest by throwing overboard cargo belonging to A. Cargo of B and C is thereby saved.

4. A and B collide at an intersection with resulting damage and injuries. Both were negligent, but B was more negligent.

5. A check, of which A is the holder, bears what is apparently B's signature. B denies signing such a check. Handwriting experts disagree with each other. There is no other evidence.

6. A swears he is the owner of an unbranded cow in B's possession. B swears the cow is his. There is no other evidence.

7. A and B both enjoyed the favors of C, a young lady, on a given evening. C has in due course and at the appropriate time given birth to a child. A, B, and the child have similar blood types.

8. A purchases a hi-fi set at a reputable store. The set was sold to the store by X who had borrowed it from B. B demands its return. The store is insolvent. X is gone.

9. T leaves an ambiguous will. It is impossible to tell whether he intended X or Y as his devisee of Blackacre.

11. Ibid., pp. 787-93.

12. As remembered by Professor Nathaniel Nathanson having received it (probably) from Thomas ("The Cork") Corcoran. Cardozo is essentially in agreement: "[S]ince a controversy has arisen and must be determined somehow, there is nothing to do, in default of a rule already made, but to constitute some authority which will make it after the event. Someone must be the loser; it is part of the game of life." Cardozo, *The Nature of the Judicial Process* (New Haven: Yale University Press, 1965), p. 143.

   Obviously, it would be a serious logical lapse to apply the Brandeis approach separately to multiple issues in a single case. That is, where the relevant rule of law requires a party to prove each of two facts and each is found to be 51 percent probable, it would be incorrect to infer a probability that both were true. No doubt what Brandeis meant (as applied to our problem) is that, viewing each dispute as a whole, reaching a decisive conclusion has positive systematic values. His conception of a decisive conclusion was total victory by one party.

13. See John Fleming, "Foreword, Comparative Negligence at Last—By Judicial Choice," *California Law Rev.*, 64 (1976), 239.

INDEX

Action, 124-26; collective, 126, 133
Adequacy, 179, 181
Adjudication, 20-21, 25
Agyrrhius, 80
Alienation, 114, 116
Altruism, 12-13
Appointment rules, 78
Apportionment, 197-201, 202
Apter, David, 126
Arbitration, 4; vs. litigation, 165, 167; vs. negotiation, 52-55; solution, 15, 17, 22
Arbitrator, 14, 164, 165, 192, 195
Aristocracy, 77-78
Aristotle, viii, 69-85
Aspiration level, 128-29
Authority, 9; compromise between permissiveness and, 145-47; "public," 98, 100; in third-party dispute settlement, 19, 20-21, 22
Avineri, Shlomo, 118

Bargaining, 14, 15, 16, 17, 18, 22, 26-27, 29, 40, 92; collective, 3, 11; offensive or "pure," 15-16, 28; and Original Position, 59-60; power, 131, 172, 174; spirit, 133
Barker, Sir Ernest, 135, 148-149
Bauer, Bruno, 113

Beccaria, Cesare, 152
Begriff, 93
Begriffsjurisprudenz, 186
Benditt, Theodore, viii, 26-37
Bentham, Jeremy, 152, 153
Berlinguer, Enrico, 106, 109, 110
Bildung, 98
Bodenheimer, Edgar, 142-59
Brandeis, Justice Louis, 200
Brecht, Bertolt, 104
Burke, Edmund, 7, 123-24, 148

Carens, Joseph, ix, 123-41
Carillo, Santiago, 109, 110
Causation, 180-81, 182, 183
Civil War in France, The (Marx), 117
Class, and political justice, in Aristotle, 70-71, 73, 74, 75-76, 77, 78, 80-81
Class Struggles in France, The (Marx), 116-17
Coercion, 164, 166
Cohen, Carl, 132, 135
"Commitment to union," 136
Communication, 14, 16, 90
Communism, 105, 106-107, 108, 119. *See also* Eurocommunism
Communist Party of the Soviet Union (CPSU), 108; Twentieth Congress, 106

205